INTERNATIONAL POLITICAL ECONOMY SERIES

General Editor: Timothy M. Shaw, Professor of Political Science and International Development Studies, and Director of the Centre for Foreign Policy Studies, Dalhousie University, Halifax, Nova Scotia

Recent titles include:

Pradeep Agrawal, Subir V. Gokarn, Veena Mishra, Kirit S. Parikh and Kunal Sen
ECONOMIC RESTRUCTURING IN EAST ASIA AND INDIA: Perspectives on Policy Reform

Deborah Bräutigam
CHINESE AID AND AFRICAN DEVELOPMENT: Exporting Green Revolution

Steve Chan, Cal Clark and Danny Lam (*editors*)
BEYOND THE DEVELOPMENTAL STATE: East Asia's Political Economies Reconsidered

Jennifer Clapp
ADJUSTMENT AND AGRICULTURE IN AFRICA: Farmers, the State and the World Bank in Guinea

Robert W. Cox (*editor*)
THE NEW REALISM: Perspectives on Multilateralism and World Order

Ann Denholm Crosby
DILEMMAS IN DEFENCE DECISION-MAKING: Constructing Canada's Role in NORAD, 1958–96

Diane Ethier
ECONOMIC ADJUSTMENT IN NEW DEMOCRACIES: Lessons from Southern Europe

Stephen Gill (*editor*)
GLOBALIZATION, DEMOCRATIZATION AND MULTILATERALISM

Jeffrey Henderson (*editor*), assisted by Karoly Balaton and Gyorgy Lengyel
INDUSTRIAL TRANSFORMATION IN EASTERN EUROPE IN THE LIGHT OF THE EAST ASIAN EXPERIENCE

Jacques Hersh and Johannes Dragsbaek Schmidt (*editors*)
THE AFTERMATH OF 'REAL EXISTING SOCIALISM' IN EASTERN EUROPE, Volume 1: Between Western Europe and East Asia

David Hulme and Michael Edwards (*editors*)
NGOs, STATES AND DONORS: Too Close for Comfort?

Staffan Lindberg and Árni Sverrisson (*editors*)
SOCIAL MOVEMENTS IN DEVELOPMENT: The Challenge of Globalization and Democratization

Anne Lorentzen and Marianne Rostgaard (*editors*)
THE AFTERMATH OF 'REAL EXISTING SOCIALISM' IN EASTERN
EUROPE, Volume 2: People and Technology in the Process of Transition

Stephen D. McDowell
GLOBALIZATION, LIBERALIZATION AND POLICY CHANGE: A Political
Economy of India's Communications Sector

Juan Antonio Morales and Gary McMahon (*editors*)
ECONOMIC POLICY AND THE TRANSITION TO DEMOCRACY: The Latin
American Experience

Ted Schrecker (*editor*)
SURVIVING GLOBALISM: The Social and Environmental Challenges

Ann Seidman, Robert B. Seidman and Janice Payne (*editors*)
LEGISLATIVE DRAFTING FOR MARKET REFORM: Some Lessons from
China

Caroline Thomas and Peter Wilkin (*editors*)
GLOBALIZATION AND THE SOUTH

Kenneth P. Thomas
CAPITAL BEYOND BORDERS: States and Firms in the Auto Industry,
1960–94

Geoffrey R. D. Underhill (*editor*)
THE NEW WORLD ORDER IN INTERNATIONAL FINANCE

Henry Veltmeyer, James Petras and Steve Vieux
NEOLIBERALISM AND CLASS CONFLICT IN LATIN AMERICA: A
Comparative Perspective on the Political Economy of Structural Adjustment

Robert Wolfe
FARM WARS: The Political Economy of Agriculture and the International Trade
Regime

International Political Economy Series
Series Standing Order ISBN 0–333–71110–6
(*outside North America only*)

You can receive future titles in this series as they are published by placing a standing order.
Please contact your bookseller or, in case of difficulty, write to us at the address below with
your name and address, the title of the series and the ISBN quoted above.

Customer Services Department, Macmillan Distribution Ltd
Houndmills, Basingstoke, Hampshire RG21 6XS, England

Industrial Crisis and the Open Economy

Politics, Global Trade and the Textile Industry in the Advanced Economies

Geoffrey R. D. Underhill
Professor of International Governance
University of Amsterdam
and
Lecturer in International Political Economy
University of Warwick

338.47677
U55i

First published in Great Britain 1998 by
MACMILLAN PRESS LTD
Houndmills, Basingstoke, Hampshire RG21 6XS and London
Companies and representatives throughout the world

A catalogue record for this book is available from the British Library.

ISBN 0–333–57849–X

First published in the United States of America 1998 by
ST. MARTIN'S PRESS, INC.,
Scholarly and Reference Division,
175 Fifth Avenue, New York, N.Y. 10010

ISBN 0–312–21594–0

Library of Congress Cataloging-in-Publication Data
Underhill, Geoffrey R. D.
Industrial crisis and the open economy : politics, global trade,
and the textile industry in the advanced economies / Geoffrey R.D.
Underhill.
p.   cm. — (International political economy series)
Includes bibliographical references and index.
ISBN 0–312–21594–0 (cloth)
1. Textile industry.   2. International trade.   I. Title.
II. Series.
HD9850.5.U53   1998
338.4'7677—DC21   98–17294
                                                 CIP

This book is printed on paper suitable for recycling and made from fully managed and
sustained forest sources.

10   9   8   7   6   5   4   3   2   1
07   06   05   04   03   02   01   00   99   98

Printed and bound in Great Britain by
Antony Rowe Ltd, Chippenham, Wiltshire

To Magdalena

Contents

List of Tables

Preface and Acknowledgements

The research project which lies behind this book was extensive, and as a result the book itself has undergone a number of metamorphoses. The project began in the early 1980s as a study of industrial adjustment in France and Europe. The question I was posing in the research was an important one in those early stages of the globalisation process: what do states do, indeed what *can* states do, as their industrial structures become transnationalised? It seemed that states had lost to global markets a number of traditional instruments of policy at a time when, politically, they needed them more than ever. The last half of the 1970s had been years of acute industrial crisis, and the early 1980s proved worse. Firms became more multinational, trade patterns changed rapidly as a result of liberalisation policies, and company failures and job losses mounted. A world which had been relatively certain and had produced the most miraculous economic growth in history was clearly at an end.

It seemed that states were faced with an economy which increasingly cut across traditional national borders, and yet the domestic political ramifications of industrial crisis were undiminished for state officials in search of policy responses to deal with the problems of unemployment, apparently perpetual industrial adjustment, and popular unrest at declining income growth. The way in which states came to terms with these immense problems, which unseated many governments, from the Labour Party in the UK (1979) through the coalition of the Right in France (1981) and the Social Democrats in Germany (1982) to the Liberal Party in Canada (1984), not to mention President Carter's attempted Democratic revival in Washington (1976–80), is now history, but is worth repeating briefly. States began to choose radical market-oriented solutions, deliberately divesting themselves of both policy instruments and the day-to-day management of distributional conflict in their societies. Labour had to adjust to the new climate with less sympathy from governing coalitions, firms had to learn to survive without the institutionalised programmes of assistance which had been their crutches in the post-war period, and economic structures began to change rapidly in what was eventually labelled globalisation.

xi

Market-led adjustment allowed governments to indulge in the fantasy that distributional questions could effectively be depoliticised and were properly the responsibilities of 'markets,' as if the market were some supreme being to whom sacrifice was long overdue. The strategy worked for a while for most, and the result was a considerable acceleration of the process of global economic integration.

When I began this research, based on the French and European textile and clothing sector, it took on the flavour of a study in comparative political economy. While I had been schooled in various dimensions of international relations, including the economic aspects, I have never regretted the time it took me to understand the specificities of particular advanced political economies. Nonetheless, it made rather less sense to maintain such a gulf between comparative and international political economy. It is interesting by way of example that at the time one tended to treat the then European Economic Community as a sort of occasional constraint on national policies, but not something which was integral to decision-making. The same could be said of international regimes such as the GATT. But it became increasingly clear that as market structures were breaching the boundaries of national economic development strategies, the institutional structures of governance in the global economy were changing as well. With the advent of the Single Market Programme in Europe and the prospect of the Uruguay Round, transnationalisation and the new market-led policy environment forced welcome changes in the discipline of political economy as well. It was no longer possible to make a meaningful distinction between *comparative* and *international* political economy.

Comparative political economy had once been about the characteristics of individual states, and most scholars were single-country specialists with some comparative expertise. The differences among domestic political economies continued to be relevant, but the spotlight turned more on the linkages, the interdependencies, among them. These linkages had always been there, but one supposes it was a matter of degree. If state and market had always been one for the political economist, the distinction between domestic and international was dissolving too. If all politics are ultimately local (and I have not scanned my dictionary of quotations to find out to whom the aphorism should be attributed), then globalisation too could only be understood in terms of the changing patterns of economic structure and distributional conflict of individual political economies. In Europe, the institutional framework of the EU became more and more central as a set of transnational political processes, and these were reflected in the often contrasting institutional and structural settings of the individual member states. Europe was merely the most advanced of a number of emerging transnational policy processes, as the Canada–US Free Trade Agreement, which became the basis of NAFTA, soon demonstrated. Though the climate in the discipline of international relations was far from conducive at the time, it was time to bring the idea of transnational relations and interdependence back into the picture. Some had never lost sight of this, but it was a considerable struggle within the discipline to see these ideas prevail over the sterility of state-centric realism.

Soon the boundaries of this research project began to change as the 1980s came to a close and the 1990s began. It became a study of the ways in which the political economies of international trade and domestic industrial adjustment, which had once been treated in a scrupulously separate manner, were one and the same. The artificial barriers erected by our intellects for the supposed sake of clarity, but which had become ends in themselves as gurus and their disciples in University doctoral programmes aggressively manned their temples, slowly gave way. The discipline of international political economy became central to understanding international relations, especially once the bean counters of Cold War security studies were put out of business. How anyone had ever thought that one could meaningfully separate out economic from political phenomena I do not know. As I have said many times to my students, if politics is not about what goes into people's pockets, it cannot be about anything at all. Distributional conflict, whether looked at locally, nationally, or globally, is where it's at; distributional issues are what people fight about, though they might use anything from religion to ethnicity to opposing political philosophies as a ideological underpinnings for their struggles. What needed development was the conceptual framework with which to consider the global state–market complex in new ways, breaking the intellectual shackles of the past, and I hope this book is a contribution to the discipline in this way.

So what had been a study in comparative political economy became an EU-scale project, and moved steadily towards the global. What finally emerged in this book was a case study of international trade and industrial adjustment spanning twenty years of contemporary globalisation. Studies of manufacturing industry had meanwhile gone out of fashion somewhat as many (including myself) turned towards monetary and financial questions. However, as either Smith or

Ricardo or indeed Marx might have pointed out, someone had to produce the value, through industrial processes based on labour, which those financial markets later played with as derivative monetary instruments. Interdependent with global financial markets were rapidly changing production structures corresponding to changes in the practices of firms, in labour markets, and in international trade patterns. This was the daily practice of globalisation, and despite fashion I helped to foster, one could not ignore manufacturing industry in the global political economy. Despite the best efforts of neo-liberal governments, jobs, income levels, and social instability continued to be relevant to the politics of the advanced economies.

Of course the difficulty with the ways in which this research project changed over time is that it grew dramatically in scope. There was always something new to know and one never seemed to get to the end. In addition, globalisation hit the British university system, increasing the pressure on us to generate revenue by developing new teaching programmes, to increase contact hours, to administer what we had created, and to do so with fewer resources. The detailed, old-fashioned research on which this project was based did not fit well in the new climate. Nonetheless, when the Uruguay Round finally finished with an agreement (and I won a number of bets with my students, rather sceptical as they were of the viability of international cooperative efforts), it provided a natural punctuation mark for the project. By 1996 I had finished the research itself and began writing the book in a year of research leave, the first I had ever had since beginning my career. The writing process, particularly the last chapter, hung on into the 1996–7 academic session, my leave over, and the work saw completion in the early autumn of 1997.

Of course no research project by a single scholar could cover all aspects of international trade in the textile and clothing sector. Even though everything is indeed related to everything else, as the apostles of chaos theory might rightly have it, the study was always about the advanced economies as opposed to the LDCs as parties to the MFA. Even so, I could not possibly have gone into detail about the industrial adjustment processes in all the developed countries involved in the MFA, and I do not pretend to have produced a detailed history in this regard. I have tried to focus on what was most important, and on the expanatory factors as I saw them. So many, particularly specialists in the political economies of specific countries, may feel I have left things out or got them wrong relative to their specialised knowledge. In the end I had to come up with a manuscript, word limit and all, which someone might take the time to read. I have had to make use of key examples to illustrate more general points. The whole project in fact relied on the idea that one sector could serve as a basis for important generalisations about the broader political economy of trade liberalisation, with all the epistemological difficulties that implies. I have turned over a vast amount of primary research material in the course of the study, and I hope it shows in the product.

It might also be possible to claim that I have not developed exhaustively the theoretical points made in the course of the analysis. I certainly have not been exhaustive in my citation of the theoretical literature in international political economy, and this is deliberate. I believe the case study speaks well for itself, and those familiar with contemporary debates in the discipline will have no difficulty fitting the analysis into the larger conceptual picture. Meanwhile, the absence of exhaustive theoretical discussion may have made the book more readable for policy-makers and analysts outside the narrow confines of scholarly debates.

It is time to acknowledge the many people who helped me bring this work to fruition, and to indulge in cliché, I cannot really begin to do so as fully as I might wish; there are too many. May I begin by thanking all those patient employees of libraries and documentary collections who helped me over the years. Without them I could not have located the vast array of official sources and private studies, only a small number of which are actually cited in the book, which are the foundation of any major research project. Secondly, I would like to thank the many people who volunteered to submit to my often overly extensive interview questions. Without the dozens of hours of their time which they donated to this research, I could never have carried it off. The interviews greatly enhanced the understanding which I gained from the documentary record, and allowed me inside knowledge which made sense of much which otherwise might have remained obscure.

I would also like to thank the many colleagues with whom I have interacted over the years. Some were directly instrumental in helping me with the research project and manuscript of the book, others were influential or supportive in other, either practical or intellectual ways. I owe a debt to all of them. The full list would be very long and I do apologise if I leave some out. In alphabetical order, thanks to all of you: Michael Atkinson, Benoît Boussemart, Peter Burnham, Barry Buzan, Phil Cerny, Bill Coleman, Robert Cox, Jacques de Bandt, Kevin Featherstone, Stephen Gill, Eric Helleiner, Richard Higgott,

Joseph McCahery, Partrick Messerlin, Helen Milner, Lynn Mytelka, Kim Nossal, Chris Pierson, Jeremy Richardson, Susan Strange, Richard Stubbs, Vincent Wright, and Mark Zacher. I would not want to forget either the ideas generated through interaction with my many students over the years. In particular, however, may I take a moment to thank Tim Shaw, editor of the International Political Economy Series, whose constant encouragement helped bring this book to press. However long it seemed to take, his enthusiasm for receiving the manuscript never seemed to diminish.

Finally, may I thank my family, who went on supporting me even when my frequent exhaustion and bad temper had taken over. While completing this project, I have had all too little time in which to watch the birth and growth of whom I regard as the most wonderful children in the world, and to support a spouse who has always been under the pressure of her own demanding career. I have dedicated the book to her.

University of Warwick GEOFFREY R.D. UNDERHILL

List of Abbreviations

AAMA	American Apparel Manufacturers Association
AEIH	Association Européenne des Industries de l'Habillement (see also ECLA)
AFTAC	American Fiber, Textile, and Apparel Coalition
ATC	Agreement on Textiles and Clothing (Uruguay Round)
ATMI	American Textile Manufacturers Institute
CBI	Caribbean Basin Initiative (US)
CFDT	Confédération Française et Démocratique du Travail
CGT	Confédération Générale du Travail
CIRFS	Comité International de la Rayonne et des Fibres Synthétiques
CIRIT	Comité Interministériel de Rénovation des Structures Industrielles et Commerciales de l'Industrie Textile
CITA	Committee for the Implementation of Textile Agreements (US)
COMITEXTIL	Comité pour la Co-ordination des Industries Textile de la Communauté Européenne
CTCOE	Centre Textile de Conjoncture et d'Observation Economique
DMC	Dolfus-Mieg and Company
ECLA	European Clothing Association (English version of AEIH above)
ELTAC	European Largest Textile and Clothing Companies
EU (EC)	European Union (formerly European Community)
EURATEX	European Apparel and Textile Association (successor of merger between COMITEXTIL, ELTAC, and AEIH)
FDES	Fonds de Développement Economique et Social (France)
FDI	foreign direct investment
GATT	General Agreement on Tariffs and Trade
ICI	Imperial Chemical Industries
ITCB	International Textile and Clothing Bureau

LDC	less-developed countries
LTA	Long Term Arrangement on Cotton Trade
MFA	Multi-Fibre Arrangement
NAFTA	North American Free Trade Agreement
NIC	newly industrialising countries
OECD	Organisation for Economic Co-operation and Development
OETH	Observatoire Européen du Textile et de l'Habillement
OPT	outward processing traffic
PECO	Pays de l'Europe Centrale et Orientale (in English, Central and East European Countries)
RPR	Rassemblement pour la République
SGICF	Syndicat Général de l'Industrie Cotonière Française
STA	Short Term Arrangement on Cotton Trade
TRIMs	Trade Related Investment Measures (Uruguay Round)
TRIPs	Trade Related Intellectual Property (measures)
UIH/UFIH	Union des Industries de l'Habillement, later Union Française des Industries de l'Habillement
UIT	Union des Industries Textiles
USTR	United States Trade Representative (Office of the)
VER	Voluntary Export Restraint
WTO	World Trade Organisation

Introduction

This is a book about international trade from the 'bottom up'. Through sectoral case-study material covering some twenty years, it seeks to analyse the socio-economic roots of the global trade regime, and to look at the complex interplay between what Rosenau has referred to as the micro and macro levels.[1] In broad terms, this work will demonstrate that *it is the intricate relationships between micro-level economic practices of firms, the politics of industrial adjustment in particular states, and the bargaining among them on a multilateral and bilateral basis, which accounts for the ways in which the politics of the trade regime unravel over time.* The case illustrates that there was a systematic and mutually constitutive relationship between the changing structure of production and trade in the sector, and the changing politics of the trade regime over time. Firms employed their institutionalised political resources to structure global production and exchange, especially where they were unwilling or unable to adapt their strategies at the micro level. State and market were not opposing principles or dynamics; the state and the market together functioned as integrated ensembles of governance for the management of distributional conflict across levels of analysis.

In this sense, this is also a book about *conceptualising the transnational market economy across political and jurisdictional boundaries.* Changing patterns of international trade involve the expansion of market and often production structures across these familiar boundaries. The study seeks to link the economic behaviour of agents, each with their peculiar strengths and weaknesses in the political economy, to their socio-political and institutional setting and to interstate bargaining processes as sources of structural market change. In turn, structural change implies a challenge to the perceived self-interest of agents and their strategies as they interact in the sectoral political economy. This book will seek to employ the case material to illustrate the ways in which market structure is constantly the subject of political conflict – the extent to which the characteristics of the market are inherently and constantly contestable.

The market is therefore to be seen as a socio-political institution extending across state boundaries but integrated into the politics of states and relations among them in the global system. The intimate connections between organised market actors (including, but not

1

limited to, producer firms and their associations) and political authorities at various levels of analysis in the global system will be a principal
preoccupation of the study. The global political economy is therefore
portrayed not as an anarchy segmented by national sovereignties,[2] but
as more of a seamless web of institutional and economic interdependencies. This is not to presuppose a cooperative order, but the lines of
cooperation and conflict are far from contiguous with, and are certainly not reducible to, the borders of nation states.

FOCUS OF THE STUDY

This work will seek to answer two principal questions: first, why did
the MFA emerge as a counterpoint to the general trend towards the
liberalisation of trade in manufactured goods in the post-war period?
Why did the agreement become more protectionist over time despite
clear evidence of its inefficacy in dealing with competitive pressures in
the global economy? Second, and perhaps intuitively more difficult to
respond to, why did the same states which sponsored and strengthened
this protectionist accord agree to dismantle it in the context of the
Uruguay Round of trade negotiations?

The importance and complexity of the politics of international trade
has been highlighted by the conflicts of the Uruguay Round negotiations. The link between the trade regime and distibutional conflicts in
domestic societies became clear: domestic actors competed in the
various institutional layers of state policy processes so as to structure
the costs and benefits of adaptation to the new forms of competition
the Round negotiations threatened to introduce. Industrial adjustment
processes under global constraints and domestic competition for specific trade policies were as one integrated game to control the terms of
trade and competition. The distinction between the politics of trade at
multilateral and domestic levels proved specious. Nevertheless, our
understanding of the politics of international trade has been somewhat
limited by traditional approaches to the discipline of international
political economy and a relative scarcity of systematic case-study
analyses.[3] Furthermore, neo-classical economic liberalism has tended
to focus almost exclusively on the economic dynamics of international
trade, separating market phenomena out from their socio-political
context. Neo-classical perspectives tend to argue the futility of state
intervention on the basis of misleading underlying assumptions about
the nature of markets.[4] Liberal internationalist currents have in turn

focused to a fault on the framework of international institutions and regimes within which trade bargaining takes place while not necessarily overcoming the weaknesses of state-centric realism.[5]

This book aims to make a contribution to this debate.[6] It develops our understanding of the political economy of post-war liberalisation, which has been accompanied by apparently permanent protectionist reflexes in particular economic sectors. It focuses specifically on international trade in the textile and clothing sector and on the rise and eventual demise of the multilateral system of voluntary export restraint agreements known collectively as the Multi-Fibres Arrangement (MFA).[7] The MFA was the culmination of many years of voluntary export restraint agreements (VERs) in the textile and clothing sector. These had begun with the Short-term Arrangement (1960–61) and Long-term Arrangement (LTA 1962–73) for cotton textiles. The MFA, signed in 1973, first implemented in 1974, and renewed regularly since then, effectively extended the terms of the LTA beyond cotton textiles to a much wider range of textile and clothing production. Renewals in the 1970s and 1980s extended VER quotas to an ever wider range of product categories. These developments in the international trade regime came on a background of profound and deepening industrial crisis in the sector in a wide range of advanced industrial economies. This crisis in the sector was characterised by accelerating job losses, low profitability among firms, a precipitous decline in investment levels, a loss of domestic market share to imports, and rising capital and technology costs. The industrial crisis in the sector combined with structural adjustment problems of an equally severe nature in a number of other older industries in Europe and North America, specifically steel,[8] shipbuilding,[9] footwear, and in some cases even automobiles, consumer electricals, and bulk chemicals production.

By the time of the Ministerial Declaration commencing the Uruguay Round trade negotiation,[10] the MFA had become one of the principal targets of the newly industrialising (NICs) and less-developed countries (LDCs) against which it systematically discriminated. One of the gains they might enjoy as a result of full participation in the Round was the dissolution of the accord.

Unlike most VER arrangements, the MFA was neither bilateral nor was it extra-legal in terms of international trade law. The MFA was under the umbrella of the GATT despite its openly discriminatory characteristics which clearly violated the rules and norms of the trade regime. In this sense *the MFA was and remains the most spectacular and comprehensive protectionist agreement in existence and became accepted practice within the trade regime.* The MFA remained in force despite the successful completion of the Tokyo Round negotiations and the commitment of the advanced industrial countries to a 'rollback' of protectionist measures against the developing countries in the context of the Uruguay Round ministerial declaration. One task of this book is therefore to explain the rise of this exceptional and multilateral protectionist agreement in the context of the global trade regime.

Nonetheless, one of the substantial accomplishments of the successful Uruguay Round Final Act of 15 December 1993[11] was the Agreement on Textiles and Clothing (ATC), an accord to dismantle the MFA over a period of ten years.[12] The second and perhaps more difficult task of the book is therefore to explain the sources of liberalisation in a sector which has enjoyed entrenched protection across a wide variety of advanced industrial economies in Europe, Japan, and North America.[13] There is of course considerable room for scepticism on the part of seasoned observers as to whether the agreement will ever be implemented. Nonetheless, the Uruguay Round ATC accord represents a significant victory for advocates of liberalisation in a sector where protectionist reflexes appeared most entrenched.

As the analysis in this book cuts across domestic, regional, and global levels of analysis, the empirical focus will be fairly broad. In the period from the LTA to the first MFA, which took effect in 1974, the United States appears as the most important state-level actor in galvanising the participants in the trade regime to accept what was widely recognised as a fairly 'liberal', in the sense of tolerant, form of protectionism. The first MFA, while certainly covering a wider range of products than the LTA, was much more limited than successive renewals of the accord. By the early 1970s, the European Union (at that time the European Community or EC) and particularly France as a member state became increasingly central to the mounting protectionism in the sector.[14] As liberalisation *within* the EU was accomplished parallel to the implementation of the tariff liberalisation which resulted from the Kennedy Round of GATT talks, the French industry, supported by the British and others in the EU, began systematically to press for control of the EU's trade policy agenda in the sector. This was successfully captured in time for the first renewal agreement, reached in 1977. The French government was instrumental in seeing that the agenda was controlled by protectionist forces, and this 'capture' was maintained into the late 1980s. The United States was not dissatisfied with this tightening of the MFA but no longer took the leading role as will be demonstrated. By the mid 1980s, however, the United States was once again pressing hard for intensified protectionism even as the Uruguay Round, theoretically to liberalise the MFA, was beginning.

Much of the empirical analysis, then, will focus on the role of France and the EU in building transnational alliances to support a policy of VERs in textile and clothing trade, and on the United States. Interestingly, Japan was never a party to the MFA although the Japanese industry eventually found itself competing with difficulty with producers in low-wage countries, and Japan therefore features little in this study.[15] The French sector was particularly vulnerable to the liberalisation process of the Common Market and GATT for a number of reasons. While the pressures of the international market led the French government to press industrialists towards a strategy of adaptation and adjustment, favouring the larger internationally active firms, the particularities of state–industry relations and the political resources of the industrialists permitted them to capture the trade policy agenda and press for protection in clear defeat of a state-led strategy in a country renowned for its robust state institutions. The French government then successfully built alliances with supportive and reluctant EU partners alike, playing on their respective domestic interest associations and enhancing the political influence of their economic liabilities along the way. From a position of relative weakness in international bargaining, France was able to mobilise what became a sustainable transnational coalition in favour of a GATT-approved and highly discriminatory trade regime for the bulk of textile and clothing trade between the western market economies and the LDCs and NICs based on tight 'voluntary' export quotas. The initially reluctant US government found it easy to find common cause with beleaguered segments of its own domestic sector and support the move. Textile and clothing interests were powerful in the Congress and could muster a clear majority for protection of the sector at any time. Presidential vetoes were scarcely able to contain this constant threat to the general thrust of American trade policy.

Because the political economy of the MFA crosses domestic, regional (EU), and global (GATT) levels of analysis, this study will frequently explore the domestic policy processes of key states and the political actors involved. Owing to the central role played by France in organising the EU's trade policy agenda, France will receive considerable attention and, in addition, will serve as a detailed illustration of the role of domestic processes in the international trade regime. This is not to argue that the domestic processes of other states were necessarily less important, but the scope of this book is already broad. However, where protectionist forces linked across borders at the EU level, as they frequently did, attention will be drawn to this. The internal processes particular to the United States will also receive attention where this contributes, as it will, to a more substantial understanding of the dynamics of global bargaining within the GATT and the opposition of developing to the advanced industrial countries.

In short, as an empirical study this book will cover the broad range of political processes which lay at the source of the increasingly protectionist and exceptional trade regime known as the MFA. This does not mean that the book is specifically about the domestic politics of textile adjustment and trade policy formation. The point of the analysis, as will be discussed below, is that *a comprehensive understanding of the political economy of international trade requires the integration of levels of analysis.*

THE ARGUMENTS: THE POLITICAL ECONOMY OF TRADE LIBERALISATION

Although the two questions posed (why protectionism? why eventual liberalisation?) are answered separately, the arguments adopted in fact imply a simultaneous answer to both. On the rise of protectionism,[16] at the most general level, the book argues that the sources of protectionist reflexes in the advanced industrial countries are inherent in the nature of the open economy itself. International trade bargaining, regional dynamics, production and market structures, and domestic adjustment problems are all part of the same integrated equation. Even in a situation of highly institutionalised cooperative rules and norms, such as under the post-war GATT system, cooperation and conflict coexist simultaneously as two sides of the same coin.[17] While states may on the one hand attempt to provide public goods to underpin cooperation through international bargaining, this process coexists with the political and inherently conflictual management of the distributional politics of the adjustment process at domestic, in some cases regional (e.g. EU), and global levels.[18] In an era of transnational capital, productive processes, and trade, this distributional politics is greatly complicated and the state develops 'schizoid' characteristics in the face of the contrasting imperatives of globalisation and domestic political legitimacy. The state[19] attempts to manage largely domestic economic constituencies and interests upon which it depends for its legitimacy and the effectiveness of policy, while trans-nationalisation of trade and production has reduced the economic space controlled by the state and the effectiveness of domestic policy instruments in the first place. The state remains the political focus for the distributional politics of economic adjustment and change but has lost power to the agents of market forces in the global economy when it comes to resolving these dilemmas.[20]

To put this more specifically, it is argued that there is a dynamic interaction between the structural market changes which took place in global textile and clothing markets on the one hand, and the politics of domestic industrial adjustment on the other, and that trade policy and the trade regime are an inherent part of industrial adjustment policies. The process began with the political decisions to liberalise trade in manufacturing industry. Trade liberalisation and the relative liberal-isation of long-term capital flows led to a rapid internationalisation of trade and production in the sector as firm strategies responded to the new legal framework. The generalised move towards liberalisation took place as a result of economic recovery in Europe and Japan, and the relative compatibility of domestic manufacturing sectors.[21] The distribution of costs and benefits across domestic societies and among states in the system would be acceptable to the principal protagonists in the bargaining.

Liberalisation in international trade happened on two fronts. In the first place, the Kennedy Round broke the long-standing logjam which had been in place since the failure of the United States to ratify the Havana Charter incorporating the International Trade Organisation.[22] This logjam had been periodically addressed but was if anything reinforced in the 1950s with the US decision to exempt agriculture from the GATT,[23] and the European and Japanese determination to put post-war recovery and national economic development strategies before liberalisation.[24]

In the second place, and in a more regional context, the EU's internal customs union (completed in 1968) began to intensify competi-tion on European markets at roughly the same time as the Kennedy Round was coming to a conclusion. These changes in the nature of the trade regime, toward a more liberal regime at least as far as manu-factured goods were concerned, must also be placed on a background of systematic attempts by less-developed countries to industrialise and export towards the lucrative markets of the advanced economies. The textile and clothing sector was one of the key sectors in this process.

It should be made clear that the more liberal trade strategies of the advanced countries often went hand in hand with what are typically thought of as 'mercantilistic' national development strategies. The case of France under de Gaulle, long associated with protectionism, illustrates the point amply. While the French government can hardly be accused of a liberal market strategy and developed an indicative planning process centred on state intervention to foster growth and competitiveness, liberalisation within GATT and the EU was nonetheless seen as a market stick to the state interventionist carrot. Despite speculation that de Gaulle would, on coming to power in 1958, scupper the Treaty of Rome establishing the then EC, he opted to remain part of the Community and the customs union portion of the Treaty was implemented a full eighteen months in advance. Most countries employed a similar mix of policy instruments to accomplish the goals of national economic development strategies, and none embraced wholesale liberalisation, and certainly not the United States with its ever-wary Congress.

Liberalisation, a fact of EU and GATT membership simultaneously, yielded new strategies among enterprises in developed and developing economies alike, accelerating foreign direct investment and altering traditional patterns of imports and exports. Competition was greatly intensified among European and US firms (at home and on third country markets), most of which had largely relied on their domestic markets in the past. The industry began to internationalise rapidly, a process of structural change which produced its share of winners and losers and touched off a new round of distributional conflict within the sector.

Furthermore, changing social structures led to important shifts in final consumer demand for textile products: Engel's law effects[25] reduced the growth rate of the market for finished textile products, which began to stagnate so as to induce a serious battle for market share. Less formal social relations, and changing occupational patterns in western societies from the 1960s led to new fashions and growing demand for new products not produced by traditional manufacturers, and slower and more volatile growth in the market. This was exacerbated in the 1970s by external shocks such as the oil crisis and growing monetary instability. This led to the emergence of generalised economic crisis in the form of the stagnation of growth and investment, coupled with intense inflationary pressures, as producers, participants in the labour market, and consumers bid for the diminishing distributional spoils of the period.

The transnationalisation of economic structure emanating from the liberalisation process therefore altered the strategic options of those firms which were placed well enough to adapt one way or another. A sizeable number of firms began to respond to the new situation by transnationalising their production strategies. This, combined with the imports linked to liberalisation, created a 'feedback effect' into domestic systems and the politics of the domestic state in the international political economy in the form of intensified competition on domestic markets. This 'feedback effect' is inherent in the political economy of liberalisation: international cooperation to establish liberal norms through the trade regime sparks restructuring and a dynamic new politics of domestic industrial adjustment, with some firms adjusting either internally or through transnationalisation, and others facing a grim future with little prospect of further independent development, even possible closure.

The motivations for the new protectionism in textiles should therefore come as no surprise: the dynamics of intensified competition set in train by liberalisation (in context of both EU and GATT) would result in the need for a strategic response from firms. Some firms, aggregated into national sectors, were of course better placed than others. Some adjusted easily through altered company strategies, often taking advantage of the opportunities offered by the more liberal regime in trade and production in order to transnationalise their strategies through foreign sourcing/reimportation, overseas investments in lower cost production, increased exports, or some combination of these. Others were less successful and came to represent growing economic liabilities to their national economies. As the 1970s proceeded and the economic difficulties of the advanced economies deepened and broadened, the political salience of plant closures and restructuring began to rise. The greatest pressure would fall on 'traditional' firms with inadequate capital resources, little technological know-how, weak managerial skills, and poor knowledge of volatile market conditions. As it turns out, these firms had fashioned regulatory and political structures which permeated the state, capable of appropriating political and financial resources to avoid exposure to competitive pressures.

This leads to emphasis on a second explanatory factor: the institutionalised political resources of associational groups embodied in a particular economic structure and pattern of interest intermediation.[26] This will tend to be different for the respective sectors, depending on their strategic position in the national macroeconomy. Textile and clothing interests, however, have demonstrated a consistent ability to command political resources in the policy process across a number of industrialised countries.

The textile sector, initially in the United States and then in key European countries, especially France, represented an ongoing liability to their respective national economies. In the case of both the US and Europe in the 1970s, however, their institutionalised political resources, the product of a long history of implantation in these societies, permitted industrialists to resist the option of change and adjustment to new competitive pressures. While not successful at attracting the level of subsidy and official aid of the steel or shipbuilding sectors (textiles was in a structurally less important position in the respective national economies), associational patterns and their political articulation within the body of the state permitted them to set the sectoral trade policy agenda.

The so-called new protectionism[27] of the MFA became the principal policy tool for the avoidance of economic adjustment, a process which would have effaced many firms and traditional industry practices in a whirlwind of bankruptcies, mergers/takeovers and capital-intensive investment programmes. Powerful domestic interests representing economic liabilities were able to command sufficient political resources so as to constitute a political blockage to the process of economic change, preserving domestic industrial structures beyond their sell-by dates.

The answer to the second question is more difficult to provide.[28] The argument so far has highlighted the reciprocal effects of structural economic change, in this case liberalisation, on political processes with respect to industrial adjustment and international trade. In order to understand the eventual achievement of an accord to liberalise the MFA, it is necessary to focus on the effects which transnationalisation and intensified competition had on the economic structure of domestic sectors, particularly in key countries such as France.

In the first place, a number of dynamic firms demonstrated that adjustment to competition was more than possible and resented feather-bedding of their less innovative brethren. They did not need protection. This book will present powerful evidence that economic adjustment *was* a viable option for the firms in advanced economies, despite the wage cost differentials, particularly in the textile as opposed to clothing sector. A large number of firms found enhanced export opportunities in the more open trade regime of the EU and GATT, particularly in Italy; market access became a key policy concern for them. Successful domestic and, in particular transnational, firms in advanced countries were therefore worried by the ever tightening protectionism of the MFA.

In addition, it was not in the self-interest of all firms in Europe and the US to support the MFA and other forms of protection. Crucially, the profitability and survival of a growing number of dynamic firms came to depend upon the intra-firm/intra-industry trade related to transnational production strategies. Particularly in Germany and Holland, though later in France and Italy as well as the United States, clothing firms and integrated textile concerns developed strategies of foreign sourcing to cope with wage cost differentials, and this strategy required imports as much as exports.

Strategies involving foreign sourcing, based mainly on so-called 'outward processing traffic' or OPT,[29] involved the export of manu-factured (and usually designed and cut) fabrics for labour-intensive clothing assembly activities in low-wage countries. In Europe this took place in contiguous regions such as the Mediterranean countries or East and Central Europe. In the US, foreign sourcing took place in Asia but especially in Mexico, Central America, and the Carribean. There came a point where this intra-industry trade developed to such an extent that special legal devices were developed and constantly enhanced to allow reimportation of OPT and articles on favourable terms. These firms only tolerated the protection of the MFA by ensuring that they would have first call on the strict import quotas for their own use, or that they could circumvent MFA quotas in the process: the regime was open for them as firms operating across bor-ders, but closed to traditional inter-firm exports from new producer countries. As transnationalisation of the industrial structure proceeded apace, the MFA became as much an obstacle as a rampart.

The protectionist policy at best bought time and at worst exacerbated the crisis for western textile sectors. It pushed LDC and NIC producers upmarket, confronting the competitive advantage of western firms head-on, and did nothing to abate the ongoing pressures of trade liberalisation among the high-wage countries of the OECD. Slowly it became clear that economic adjustment was the only remaining option other than an end to liberal trade among high-wage producers themselves, but also a viable option for domestic industries in many segments of textile and clothing production. The considerable success of the Italian industry, including firms like Benetton involved in the labour-intensive clothing assembly process, was a case in point. LDC/NIC exports were hardly the root cause of the problem anyway, as will be demonstrated. This situation made it possible to contemplate the dismantling the MFA as part of the agenda of the Uruguay Round GATT talks, and an accord was eventually reached. Few textile and clothing lobbies broke ranks with protectionist sentiment and openly campaigned for liberalisation, but the transnational protectionist coalitions slowly dissipated and lost their momentum.

If the MFA was one consequence of the 'feedback effect' of trade liberalisation, it did not and was never intended to halt the process of adaptation, despite constant attempts to broaden its scope and strengthen its conditions. The MFA did not apply to advanced OECD countries, and in the case of the EU it excluded Mediterranean and others with preferential trading links to Europe. Not all product categories were covered, and nor by any means were all the sources of intensified competition. Restructuring would have continued if for no other reason than that competitive pressures in the sector were largely generated by the industries of the high-wage economies anyway. Given that economic restructuring is a dynamic, not a static process, representing the aggregate response firms to the changing market and trade regime, it implies changes in the competitive positions of firms. Over time adjustment either takes place or unsuccessful firms withdraw from the market, unless protectionism can provide overwhelming barriers to competition, which the MFA did not.

One might therefore highlight three developments which contributed to providing fertile ground for the acceptance of a more liberal trade regime in textile and clothing products. First, competition across product ranges continued among OECD country markets and with lower-wage producers with preferential trading arrangements through the EU's association agreements with, for example, the Mediterranean countries. Second, the production structure continued to transnationalise. Companies coped with competition through overseas foreign direct investment (often in NICs, LDCs, or in the then East Bloc countries) and increasing use of foreign sourcing strategies. In this way they in turn intensified the pressure on their less innovative and adaptable competitors in their home market. In other words, much of the competition was the fact of western firms adopting integrated transnational production strategies in the first place. Third, many hopeless companies went to the wall or were taken over by their more successful competitors. As NIC/LDC-based producers and the more innovative advanced country firms multiplied their advantages, the MFA was of declining utility and governments seldom demonstrated a willingness to extend indefinitely financial subsidy programmes to the sector. The pressure on traditionally organised firms with few capital resources (and even less knowledge as to what to do with those they did have) eventually proved too great in most cases.

One should perhaps add to these three factors the general set of tradeoffs involved in the inter-state bargaining of the Uruguay Round. The US strategy in initiating the Round had been to load it with so many issues that all participants, including the developing countries, would see significant advantages to its successful conclusion. Clearly one of the biggest prizes for the developing and newly industrialising countries was dismantlement of the MFA. As the cost of dismantling it had steadily reduced for the high-wage economies, it became increasingly possible for an agreement to be reached.

As firms adjusted or went to the wall, there was a slow shift in the policy preferences of the sector. In particular the transnationalisation of many firms' strategies implied a certain aversion to continuing or at least to increasing protectionism. As firm strategies began to rely on export markets, retaliation became a worry. More importantly, firms which relied either on the importation of intermediary goods, or on foreign sourcing/OPT for certain production operations and eventual reimportation, began to see import quotas as a barrier to their competitive advantage in the market. These policy changes were in fact underway in the mid 1980s, even as the MFA appeared at its most unassailable. However, as the adjustment process in the sector worked its way on the industrial base, the pattern of material interests perceived by producers began to change. This paved the way for a Uruguay Round in which the MFA was conceivably dispensable and in the end was, in fact, dispensed with, though not without some cumbersome conditions and escape clauses. *The rise of intra-firm and intra-industry trade, associated with more integrated transnational production strategies, lies at the bottom of the eventual abandonment of multilateral protectionism in the textile and clothing sector.*

Once again a crucial variable remains to be distinguished: the associational structure of the sector and the pattern of state–industry relations. If one is to argue that political processes and market structures are reciprocally related, then it is important to insist that policy preferences must in fact be articulated successfully within the body of the state.[30] The capture of key bureaucracies by protectionist forces may curtail the chances of a counter-protectionist coalition, even if protectionist coalitions become economically of little significance; by the same token a weak associational system and correspondingly low

political salience of an industry's difficulties may preclude protectionism as a reaction to intensified competition in the first place.

This book also puts forward a number of subsidiary arguments. The
first concerns our understanding of the international division of
labour. Traditional trade theory is based on Ricardo's notion of
comparative advantage and the arguments building on his work which
are associated with Heckscher and Olin. The theory of comparative
advantage (and many industrial policies based on it) generally predicts
that relatively labour-intensive, 'old industry' sectors like the textile
and clothing sector are fated to become the preserve of countries with
low wage costs, shifting the international division of labour in the
sector inexorably in favour of developing and newly industrialising
countries. This view when applied to the textile and clothing sector is
mistaken. The analysis of sectoral cost structures which is undertaken
in this study reveals that the decline of the industry in the advanced
economies is in no way an inevitable development, and that in textiles
(as opposed to clothing production) the cost advantages remain
heavily tilted towards the advanced high-wage economies. Firms in
industrialised countries, given of course sufficient capital resources,
were capable of achieving cost structures with substantial advantages
in competition with low-wage producers. This did not apply equally
to all segments of the sector, and the clothing assembly process was
the most vulnerable to low-wage competition. Even here, however,
proximity to volatile fashion markets proved for many a significant
competitive advantage if combined with a sufficiently flexible production process to adapt to the ever-changing market. Where more
capital-and technology-intensive production processes were concerned, the advantages for firms in advanced country economies were
significant on the whole. This applied to most upstream production
processes[31] associated with intermediary inputs to the clothing
industry and other final users of textile products. In sum, determinist
arguments about the shifting structure of the international division of
labour are misplaced and misunderstand the dynamics of the contemporary global economy. This also implies that free-market versions
of the development prospects of LDCs are grossly optimistic, but that
is another matter.

This in turn has implications for our understanding of the international division of labour, traditionally based on the concept of comparative advantage in international trade. Theories in this Ricardian
tradition focus on national endowments of factors of production and

the relative costs of each in the respective trading countries. The expectation is that these countries will specialise in the sectors where they have a relative advantage in terms of factor costs.

This view poses two important problems. First, there is an underlying and abstract assumption of free trade which underpins the adjustment process.[32] This assumption is seldom a reality, even in a situation of a liberal trade regime such as that of the contemporary WTO, the EU, or NAFTA. There is a multiplicity of variables in addition to factor costs in production which are parallel to production costs in the international division of labour: socio-cultural variables such as the skill levels and flexibility of the labour force, social attitudes to technological change, the nature of a country's financial system and sources of finance capital, organisational attributes of firms, and 'the weight of the past can be very heavy.'[33] This point is echoed in the new trade theory:

> In arguing that trade is driven to an important extent by increasing returns rather than comparative advantage, the new trade theorists also inevitably introduced some arbitrariness into the pattern of specialisation and trade: in the new view, at least within limits, who produces what is the result of history, accident, and ... past government policies rather than underlying differences in national resources or aptitude.[34]

Second, the focus of theories of comparative advantage on production costs separates production from the markets it must serve. International trade is as much about consumption and demand as about factor costs. As this study will demonstrate, many of the problems of the textile and clothing sector and its crisis in individual countries were not the result of high cost structures, but of inappropriate products for rapidly changing markets. As society changed, so did tastes, and yet these continued to differ from country to country to a greater or lesser degree. An attempt must be made to associate production costs with the complexity of the markets on which products are sold. This greatly complicates the notion of 'advantage' in international trade and the terms on which competition takes place. The division of labour is linked to the division of markets, and the field of competition is vast, changing and expanding continuously where product and production innovation and technological advance are developed. Comparative advantage is therefore neither monolithic nor immutable, but instead has multiple perameters where 'the stability of demand elasticity coefficients and scales of comparative costs are constantly threatened by international conjuncture, the diffusion of technical progress, and the results of economic policies'.[35] The pattern of international specialisation is more complex and dynamic than traditional trade theory allows.

In this light, any analysis which focuses on a structural account of the division of labour across an entire sector is bound to be misleading. Instead what is needed is an approach which focuses on the firm (and in some cases state policy-makers) as 'bearer' of structure in international competition[36] and the freedom and autonomy disposed of by firms as actors in the larger structural setting.[37] Discussion of the international division of labour by sector can prove inappropriate, tending to consign industries to the past in industrialised countries. Adopting the firm, albeit in its larger structural setting to which it contributes, as the locus of the competitive equation avoids the pitfalls of structural analysis and permits a more meaningful understanding of the emergence of policy preferences over time.

The distinction between *comparative* advantage versus *competitive* advantage is useful here.[38] While *comparative* advantage refers to the Ricardian concept of factor endowments among sectors in a national economy, *competitive* advantage 'refers to the relative export strength of the *firms* of one country compared to the firms in *other* countries selling in the same sectors in international markets'.[39] The competitive advantage of one country's industrialists may well result from a comparative or indeed absolute advantage in that sector. However, the notion of competitive advantage permits the introduction of sociocultural, historical, or political variables 'that help or hinder the international performance of different firms'.[40] In this sense, firms in a particular sector may have gained a competitive advantage where the national economy is judged, according to factor endowments, to be at a comparative *dis*advantage: 'The firm cannot be reduced to a totally determined subsystem with a neutral effect on the functioning of the industrial system.'[41]

These arguments imply that *advantage in international trade is eminently complex and manipulable in the inevitable absence of perfect competition*, as recent developments in the new international trade theory demonstrate.[42] The new trade theory changed two crucial assumptions of the old Ricardian framework: countries (properly, firms in countries) specialise not only because of the differing factor endowments encountered there, but also because trade permits increasing returns and economies of scale to firms, 'which makes specialisation advantageous *per se*'.[43] This permitted a focus on intra-industry patterns of specialisation, which remained nonethelsss fully compatible with the traditional models of inter-industry specialisation across sectors. In addition, the new trade theory introduced the assumption of imperfect competition as the norm, permitting a focus on the specific practices of firms, states, and policy processes. Thus the new trade theory leaves considerable scope for state polices as well as the institutionalisation of private networks of cooperation in the market.[44] This in turn tells a lot about the nature of markets as social institutions and the political processes which surround them, a point which will be taken up below in the discussion of theoretical concerns.

An important point here is that the production process for any finished good is typically highly segmented into distinct stages and operations, each involving different combinations of factors of production.[45] This is very much the case in the complex production stream of the textile and clothing sector. A pattern of *intra-sectoral* specialisation can emerge across national borders,[46] led by the strategic choices of firms in the industry. Intricate networks of firms and patterns of intra-industry trade are the result, in which the competitive advantages of firms can be based on a wide array of production and marketing strategies in a context of historical and policy variables. Industrial adjustment processes do not just happen across entire industrial sectors, but *within* them as well.[47] It is more meaningful to interpret the process of specialisation based on the concept of 'international division of productive processes'[48] involving the specialised intra-industry competitive advantages of firms, than to use the broad brush strokes of traditional theories of comparative advantage.

A third subsidiary argument in this study is relevant to trade policy-makers. The study implies a cautionary tale when it comes to liberalisation policies. Co-operative agreements aimed at trade liberalisation are not necessarily stable. Because trade and industrial adjustment policies are part of the same equation viewed from different ends, it implies that for successful liberalisation policies, adopted to take advantage of the benefits of trade, must be based on solid socio-economic foundations the same as any regime of political economy. If the costs of adjustment to trade competition prove excessive for socio-economic coalitions with substantial political resources to their name, international agreements will prove unstable not because of a lack of benefits in any aggregate sense, but because of the *distribution* of costs and benefits across a complex socio-economic whole. Co-operative liberalisation implies ongoing distributional conflict as the costs of adjustment are measured up by socio-political actors in the global system. In this sense the pace of liberalisation cannot be forced and policy-makers must be careful to avoid imposing abstract economic models on the real world of political economy. Gains from liberalisation are always possible for some, but the collective underpinnings must be secure first. Furthermore, 'there is a dirty little secret in international trade analysis. The measurable costs of protectionist policies – the reductions in real income which can be attributed to tariffs and import quotas – are not all that large.'[49] Protectionist trade policies such as the MFA may not be efficient in the purely economic sense, but they are certainly efficient policies when it comes to managing the distributional tensions forced by liberalisation, and their real economic costs remain limited.

This situation implies a number of dilemmas for the political legitimacy of states in an era of increasingly international capital. It has been argued that domestic politics is integral to outcomes in international trade. Trade and foreign investment policies result in the growth of markets across borders, with significant adjustment costs in a number of sectors of the economy. This creates pressures on state economic managers as it simultaneously reduces their capacity to deal with them. Enhanced levels of economic interdependence in turn increase the costs imposed on other countries if states do intervene to manage the situation, and the stability of the cooperative agreements is thus endangered. The benefits of liberalisation are thus only achievable at a cost to the political legitimacy of national governments and state apparatus. States may be called upon to manage economic liabilities at precisely the moment that trade agreements prevent them from doing so, enhancing their schizoid condition in a situation of globalisation. The risk of serious trade conflict heightens the need for international cooperative agreements to be based on sound socio-economic foundations as the necessary underpinnings of workable international market institutions. If the foundations of trade policy are not properly understood, the possibilities for a breakdown of the international trade regime will consistently remain for developing and developed countries alike.

IMPLICATIONS FOR THEORY

These complex arguments are in sharp contrast to a number of traditional theoretical explanations of protectionism and trade policy outcomes in international relations. They do not focus on systemic power variables, seeking to explain regime development as a function of declining US hegemony.[50] Systematic attention is drawn to the two-way relationship between domestic and international factors, building on work by Milner and Friman on the empirical level,[51] and theoretical work by Gourevitch and Underhill.[52] In bringing in domestic factors, however, the book does not limit itself to typologies of domestic state institutions or to different patterns of state–industry relations.[53] This work places changing market structures and corresponding patterns of distributional conflict among agents at the centre of the analysis. In doing so it highlights the reciprocal linkages between the system of competitive states and changing market structures in the politics of trade. The peculiarities of market structures in specific sectors affect the political interplay of interested actors across levels of analysis. In this way the book will explain why, despite the ongoing widening and deepening of the liberal international trade regime on a global (GATT/WTO) and regional (EU/NAFTA) level, there is a persistence of pro-tectionism in important sectors of the economy, and why that can be overcome under certain (transnational) market conditions. There is a clear two-way relationship between political decision-making and structural economic change. Political interaction and conflict gen-erates a transformation of market structure, while changes in structure simultaneously alter the competitive constraints upon agents in the political economy. The political conflicts which are the central feature of this process of structural transformation are mediated by the institutions of the state and cooperative international regimes in the global political economy. The state is still the focal point of the politics of international trade, but state policies have become internationalised through the trade regime and economic structures transnationalised through the changing patterns of the market.[54] The state has to man-age domestic economic liabilities endowed with the institutionalised political resources to resist the costs of an adjustment agenda.

The arguments, then, imply a number of conceptual points which can be developed more systematically to enhance our theoretical understanding of international trade in particular and the international system and international political economy. These theoretical points can be summarised as follows: (i) *the nature of the state in the inter-national political economy and the relationship of states to markets*; (ii) *the question of interdependence and the nature of the international system*; (iii) *the issue of actors in the international system and the agent–structure debate*; and (iv) *the issue of levels of analysis*. All of these issues were implicitly, and sometimes explicitly, referred to in the arguments above.

In the first place the study establishes a clear and systematic link between the politics of micro (firm), national, regional, and international levels of analysis.[55] Although the institutional setting differed at these various levels, the issues around which patterns of cooperation and conflict revolved in this case of global trade remained remarkably constant. These issues were largely driven not by concerns for state power or for welfare maximisation relevant to realist and economic liberal models respectively, but by distributional conflict among the relevant socio-economic groups involved in networks of interdependence through their respective markets and political institutions. The perceived self-interest of the agents or actors involved in these institutionalised interdependencies were integral to the responses of states as social institutions and, hence, the international trade regime, to a profound industrial crisis in the textile and clothing sector of the older industrialised economies. The different responses of national textile entrepreneurs, mediated through their respective patterns of state–industry relationships and bureaucracies, strongly affected the patterns and outcome of bargaining at the regional (EU) and international (GATT) level. The complex patterns of discord and cooperation on the issue of trade and production in the textile and clothing sector became institutionalised in the MFA and the GATT. The importance of different patterns (and politics) of interest intermediation at national and regional levels is difficult to underestimate.

Second, this case highlights the conceptual relationship between the political and economic domain, or states and markets as it has been put elsewhere.[56] The political decisions concerning the trade regime, combined with the strategies of firms in their associational context (local, national, regional, sometimes international) were aimed at affecting the distribution of advantages and disadvantages in the transnational market for textile and clothing products. In this sense, policy decisions interacted with firm strategies to produce structural market change. In turn, the aggregate responses of the firms shaped the constraints on the market actors involved and formed new, constantly changing structural parameters which affected the self-interest of the actors. Firms were integrated into the processes of policy formation through the political strategies of their representative associations.

This case is therefore a clear demonstration of the two-way relationship between markets and politics, of the ways in which market institutions and political institutions are in fact inseparable ensembles of governance. The construction of markets is mediated by the politics of the state and other layers of institutionalised authority in the global political economy. Following a formula developed elsewhere,[57] the perceived self-interest of actors in the context of a given market structure provides the dynamic of change through institutionalised political action. Self-interest expressed as both policy preferences and competitive practices link politics and markets as the core of contemporary global order. As the structure of economic relationships become increasingly transnational in a sector, patterns of self-interest and corresponding policy preferences shift, in this case first to protectionism and later towards a grudging acceptance of phased liberalisation.

The structure of the market is central to our understanding of economic and political change, but structure is not in itself a causal variable as is implied by so many analyses of political economy. It remains a static concept, a set of constraints on actors which can be mapped or assessed at any particular point in time: 'Structure *does* inform one of the terms under which the political interactions of particular agents or groups occur at a particular time in history.'[58] This demonstrates that the market is inherently contestable and that political decision-making lies at the heart of market structure and the pattern of distributional gains and losses which changing market structures imply. The industrial adjustment process, integral to the intergovernmental negotiations in the GATT, involved political conflict concerning the legal and institutional framework of the market across and within state boundaries, within which individual firms and their associations would interact. The MFA sought to structure the market so as to stifle particular forms of competition, to the advantage of firms in the advanced economies. In such a model there is no presumption of equilibrium in the liberal economic sense – but rather a view of the market as embedded in socio-political institutions[59] (some of which are global in nature), which are the site of political conflict over who will get what, where, and how.

In this sense, the underlying social change in advanced economies which was a major achievement of the post-war era was an important variable in the political economy of trade in the textile and clothing sector. The relative fulfilment of material needs and changing social customs leading to less formal patterns of social interaction meant that declining proportions of consumers' disposable income were spend on clothing by consumers, the main end-use for textile products (Engel's law). This affected the growth of aggregate demand in the market, but less formal social relations affected some producers more than others: there was a precipitous decline in demand for the products of traditional producers in the sector, sparking the emergence of a new, more volatile, and more widespread fashion market based on the new, more casual patterns of social interaction and the greater amounts of leisure available to all members of society.

This brings the discussion to the agent–structure debate and the question of actors in the international political economy. An understanding of the structure of markets and production in a particular sector is clearly an important starting point for any analysis in political economy. It reveals the potential patterns of perceived self-interest which are likely to come into play in the political process. However, structure means little without the concept of agency.[60] This study emphasises the importance of process versus structural variables,[61] and the importance of understanding the respective roles of different sorts of interdependent actors in their market and institutional context. Furthermore, it is clear from this study that the political economy of global trade involves a wide range of actors which are integrated into a complex series of institutions of governance in the global economy. State, market, and the global trade regime, conceptualised as an integrated ensemble of governance, are engaged in a process of market structuration which is inherently conflictual in nature. The nature of the global trade regime depends on the outcome of this political interaction. Firms, associations, international institutions, and state bureaucracies are all central to trade policy, and vital to the determination of 'national' interests and the dynamics of inter-state bargaining. The whole question is just *whose* national interest and what processes lead to the social construction of the national interest. This is an open question the answer to which involves analysis of the institutional setting of policy processes and the political conflict among agents. In this sense, when it comes to national trade policy there never is a national interest as such – it is a construct or discourse which is developed to dominate and to legitimate particularistic coalitions of interest.

As has already been emphasised, particularly important in this case-study was the *associational structure of the textile and clothing sector and the nature of state–industry relations in the different countries involved.* Where socio-economic coalitions representing economic liabilities were endowed with substantial and institutionalised political resources, sometimes involving the capture of important state bureaucracies, then the policy preferences of these groups were likely to prevail.[62] Depending on the position of these actors relative to the patterns of competition in the market, they articulated their policy preferences within the body of the state and related international organisations and regimes. Once the trade policy agenda had been successfully commandeered by protectionist forces across the European Union and the United States, forging an effective transnational coalition for protection, it was difficult to prise these entrenched interests away from dominance of the sectoral policy agenda despite clear state policy commitments to a market-oriented policy of adjustment in the sector. However, what the policy process could not accomplish, the process of market interaction did: the open economy had set in train a long-run ferment of restructuring which eventually reshaped the interests of the actors in the political game so as to yield a hesitant liberalisation of the trade regime. Liberalisation could not occur until the protectionist interests were sufficiently dissipated and fragmented to free the state from its capture by this particular set of particularistic interests.

The multiplicity of actors involved in the emergence of the global trade regime also raises the question of the nature of the international system itself and how we conceptualise 'levels of analysis'. The global system has often been portrayed as caught between the anarchy of the system of competitive states and the patterns of interdependence of the market. Such accounts usually imply in addition a clear division between the order of the domestic domain, and the anarchy of the international. This work supports the view that these are false dichotomies.[63] The anarchy of competing states and the interdependence of the market system are fully compatible characteristics of global politics when one concedes that state and market are integrated, not separate, forms of socio-economic governance. The evidence from this study clearly demonstrates that it is just as difficult to divide the global system neatly into levels – global, regional, national, local – as it is to separate the political from the economic domain. The interdependence of the actors in the politics of the international trade regime cuts across these levels of analysis. The continuity of contentious issues and political processes across levels of analysis was far more striking than the contrast in dynamics to be found on each. The dynamics of internal (domestic) industrial adjustment were fully integrated with the political economy of trade policy, which is why this book is a simultaneous contribution to both domestic and international political economy.

It is certainly true that the system of states constitutes an 'anarchy' with no overarching political institutions to *impose* outcomes. Once defined, states pursued their national interests through the inter-governmental regime of which GATT was the institutional core. However, the bargaining among states was more than a projection of national specificity into the global domain; the conflicts of domestic and intergovernmental politics were revealed as part of an integrated whole. In addition, domestic associations and firms developed relationships across borders with corresponding interests in other states, operating through the institutions of the market and with commensurate effects on state policies and the trade regime itself. These ties of interdependence which operate through both market and political association fed back, as has been argued, into the political conflicts of state and other political authorities. 'Levels of analysis' emerges as an abstract category dear to the realist school, through which is manufactured a world of competition among unitary, rational state actors which this study reveals to be a misleading image. 'Levels of analysis' refers in the end to little more than the complex layers of institutions of governance and regulation which are relevant in particular circumstances. The interdependencies among states and their societies at a time of industrial crisis was by far the more relevant characteristic of the international system where this study is concerned.

This is not to say that states themselves were irrelevant – far from it. States were throughout demonstrably the repositories of legal and regulatory decision-making prerogatives with respect to the international trade regime. The most important political processes took place within the institutional structures of the state. However, the state increasingly supported a series of transnational market institutions which eroded its own capacity to manage the tensions of distributional conflict. The problems of domestic economic management intensified at precisely the historical moment that state capacities began to dissipate to the institutions of the global market. Herein lies, as was argued above, one of the formidable dilemmas of contemporary democratic legitimacy: the essential incompatibility of transnational markets with nationally based decision-making processes, and in turn the relative underdevelopment of transnational policy processes, even in the contemporary European Union.

All this has implications for the way in which we conceptualise the state in the international political economy. The inadequacy of the unitary rational actor model has been alluded to. The state revealed itself as an institution permeated by the material interests of the market. In that these were transnational, the state was not limited to its exclusive territorial jurisdiction. The organisational characteristics of the different states involved in the politics of the textile trade regime proved equally important in shaping the ways in which state policy processes became projected into the international arena. The decision-making processes of the state and of interstate bargaining, embedded in the distributional conflicts structured by the market, remained the political focus for socio-economic conflict concerning the mode and distributional outcome of governance in the global system.

The state, then, lies at the heart of the global system of production and trade in a complex of simultaneous cooperation and conflict about the nature, extent, and costs of socio-economic interdependence. State and market constitute an integrated set of regulatory institutions despite multiple sovereignties, just as much as the politics of federal states such as Canada or Germany imply a parcellisation of functional and territorial jurisdictions.[64] The trade regime in the textile and clothing sector has oscillated over the past twenty years from moderate protection towards a tighter system of quotas, and now towards a step-by-step liberalisation under the Uruguay Round agreement. Nonetheless, if the aguments of this book are correct, even the success at liberalisation does not indicate an end to conflict over trade or industrial adjustment policies in the sector. Once a liberal regime is negotiated, conflict is more likely to focus on the implementation process than on changing the agreement itself. It is well known that implementation is often where the war is lost, the battle having been won by those in favour of reform or change. Given its complex market structures, the textile and clothing sector is likely to act as a bellwether for the GATT, now the World Trade Organisation (WTO), as a whole. This reveals the *potentially unstable basis of trade agreements and the ongoing nature of distributional conflict in a context of fragmented state institutions in symbiotic flux with the structures of the transnational market economy.*

STRUCTURE OF THE BOOK

Chapter 1 will seek to explain the nature and causes of the crisis in the textile and clothing sectors of high-wage countries. Chapter 2 will focus on the entrepreneurial practices of French and other European textile industrialists in an attempt to situate them in relation to the international market economy. These two chapters will therefore develop an image of the economic structure of the sector at national, regional, and international levels of analysis, in keeping with the

argument outlined above that understanding the incentives and
constraints of economic structure is a prerequisite to understanding
the interplay of organised interests in their respective institutional
contexts.

Chapter 3 will examine the patterns of interest intermediation in the
EU, particularly France, and how they facilitated avoidance of adaptation to changing economic structure, making comparisons with the
US. The aim is to outline how associational groups and their member
firms responded to changing economic structures, and what
institutionalised political resources they possessed within the system of
states.

Chapters 4 and 5 will explain how textile and clothing interests
successfully articulated their policy preferences within the domestic,
EU, and global bargaining contexts across the United States and
Europe – how they captured the global trade regime. Chapter 4 will
deal with the period of strengthening protectionism, roughly from
1974 to 1986, when the MFA was developed and successfully
reinforced in the renewal process. Chapter 5 will examine the parallel
processes of structural change in production and the market alongside
the preparation and negotiation of the Uruguay Round, including the
final outcome. The Conclusion will summarise the various strands of
argument developed throughout the book and further develop the
theoretical implications of the work for understanding the process of
economic change and the relationship of domestic and international
domains where politics and markets are concerned. Finally, the
Appendix contains the text of the agreement reached in the Round
(ATC).

Notes

1. See by James N. Rosenau: 'Before Co-operation: Hegemons, Regimes,
   and Habit-Driven Actors', in *International Organization*, vol. 40/4,
   Autumn 1986, pp. 849–94; ——, *Turbulence in World Politics: A Theory
   of Change and Continuity* (Princeton University Press, 1990); and ——,
   'Governance, Order, and Change in World Politics', in Rosenau and
   Ernst-Otto Czempiel, *Governance Without Government: Order and Change
   in World Politics* (Cambridge University Press, 1992), pp. 1–29.
2. As is argued by theorists of the realist and, in particular, neo-realist
   traditions; see for example Robert Gilpin, *The Political Economy of*

International Relations (Princeton University Press, 1986); Stephen Krasner, 'International Political Economy: Abiding Discord', in *Review of International Political Economy*, vol. 1/1, pp. 13–20. For a critique of the realist position, see Helen V. Milner, 'The Assumption of Anarchy in International Relations Theory: A Critique', in *Review of International Studies*, vol. 17/1, January 1991, pp. 67–85.

3.   In particular, the recent dominance of realism and of Hegemonic Stability Theory (HST) in international political economy, which focus almost exclusively on states as actors at the international systemic level of bargaining, has failed to grasp the complexity of linkages between the domestic and international levels of analysis, of linkages between structural economic change and patterns of political conflict, and the importance of non-state actors in the political economy of trade. See for example by Stephen Krasner, 'State Power and the Structure of International Trade', in *World Politics*, vol. 28/3, April 1976, pp. 317–43; and 'The Tokyo Round: Particularistic Interests and Prospects for Stability in the Global Trading System', in *International Studies Quarterly*, vol. 23/4, December 1979, pp. 491–531. A specialised study of international textile trade employing the systemic level of analysis and neo-realist explanatory framework and which yielded a particularly misleading explanation was by Vinod K. Aggarwal; for a critique of Aggarwal and of neo-realist approaches to understanding international trade in general see Geoffrey R.D. Underhill, 'Industrial Crisis and International Regimes: France, the EEC, and International Trade in Textiles 1974–1984', in *Millennium: Journal of International Studies*, vol. 19/2, Summer 1990, pp. 185–206.

4.   For a discussion and critique of the assumptions of neo-classical trade theory, see Michael Kitson and Jonathan Michie, 'Conflict, Co-operation, and Change: The Political Economy of Trade and Trade Policy', in *Review of International Political Economy*, vol. 2/4, Autumn 1995, pp. 632–57.

5.   On what has come to be called 'neo-liberal institutionalism', see Robert O. Keohane, *International Institutions and State Power* (Boulder: Westview Press, 1989).

6.   The book builds on research undertaken over a number of years, developed in articles published since the late 1980s: see Geoffrey R.D. Under-hill, 'Industrial Crisis and International Regimes', op. cit.; —— 'Neo-Corporatist Theory and the Politics of Industrial Decline: The Case of the French Textile and Clothing Industry 1974–1984', in *European Journal of Political Research*, October 1988, pp. 489–511; —— 'When Technology Doesn't Mean Change: Industrial Adjustment and Textile Production in France', in Michael Talalay, Chris Farrands and Roger Tooze (eds), *Technology, Competitiveness, and Culture in the Global Political Economy* (London: Routledge, 1997), pp. 139–50.

7.   The full name of the accord is 'Arrangement Regarding International Trade in Textiles', originally published by the GATT in 1974 and subsequently with protocols of renewal as negotiated.

8.   See Yves Mény and Vincent Wright (eds), *The Politics of Steel: Western Europe and the Steel Industry in the Crisis Years 1974–1984* (Berlin:Walter de Gruyter, 1987).

9.   See work by Brian W. Hogwood, *Government and Shipbuilding: The Politics of Industrial Change* (Farnborough: Saxon House, 1979).

10.   See the text of the Punta del Este GATT Ministerial Declaration on the Uruguay Round, 20 September 1986, as reprinted from GATT, in Hugo Paemen and Alexandra Bensch, *From the GATT to the WTO: The European Community in the Uruguay Round* (Leuven: Leuven University Press, 1995), pp. 271–80.

11.   General Agreement on Tariffs and Trade, Trade Negotiating Committee, *Final Act Embodying the Results of the Uruguay Round of Multilateral Trade Negotiations* (Geneva: MTN/FA, UR-93-0246, GATT Secretariat, 15 December 1993).

12.   See GATT, Uruguay Round, *Final Act*, II, annex 1A-5, pp. 1–32 in Appendix.

13.   Though textile and clothing industries remain among the largest sectors of manufacturing industry in the advanced economies, there has been relatively little scholarship on trade in the sector. Besides the misleading study by Aggarwal mentioned above, see an excellent study focusing on Japan, the US, and Germany by H. Richard Friman, *Patchwork Protectionism: Textile Trade Policy in the United States, Japan, and West Germany* (Ithaca: Cornell University Press, 1990); William R. Cline, *The Future of World Trade in Textiles and Apparel*, rev. edn (Washington, DC: Institute for International Economics, 1990).

14.   A conclusion shared by Cline, *The Future of World Trade*, op. cit., pp. 150–1.

15.   This is partly because Japan was the original target of American VERs in the textile and clothing sector in the 1950s. The Japanese were not however averse to protectionism in the sector: see Friman, *Patchwork Protectionism*, op. cit.

16.   By trade protectionism in this context is meant a series of either unilateral or multilateral official policies, both tariff and non-tariff, which impede the flow of goods and services across political boundaries. This book is not dealing with non-government protectionist measures such as business practices, cartels, cultural differences, and the like.

17.   My thanks to Marisa Diaz-Henderson for drawing my attention to this point; see M. Diaz-Henderson, *Understanding International Co-operation and Conflict: Agriculture in the Uruguay Round Negotiations and the CAP-92 Reform Process*, unpublished PhD thesis, University of Warwick, 1998.

18.   See discussion in Paolo Guerrieri and Pier Carlo Padoan, 'Neomercantilism and International Economic Stability', in *International Organization*, vol. 40/1, Winter 1986, esp. pp. 35–40.

19.   The state is here conceived of as a series of fragmented and often competing sets of institutions, permeated by particularistic interests representing social forces in the political economy. Different coalitions may dominate particular institutions of state depending on historical patterns and the issue at hand.

20.   See Philip G. Cerny, *The Changing Architecture of Politics: Structure, Agency, and the Future of the State* (London: Sage, 1990); Susan Strange, *The Retreat of the State* (Cambridge University Press, 1996).

21. Andrew Shonfield, C. and V. Curzon, T.K. Warley and George Ray *Politics and Trade*, vol. I of Shonfield (ed.), *International Economic Relations of the Western World 1959–1971* (Oxford University Press, 1976), p. 35.

22. Richard Gardner, *Sterling–Dollar Diplomacy in Current Perspective* (New York: Columbia University Press, 1981), ch. xvii.

23. See Shonfield *et al.*, *Politics and Trade*, op. cit., pp. 10–52, 168–203.

24. See Alan S. Milward, *The Reconstruction of Western Europe 1945–1951* (London: Methuen 1984); Peter Burnham, *The Political Economy of Post-War Reconstruction* (London: Macmillan, 1990).

25. Engel's law asserts that as incomes rise in the economy, basic necessities such as food and clothing will be satisfied and occupy a diminishing proportion of household expenditure and these goods become identified as 'inferior'. See Organisation for Economic Co-operation and Development, *Textile and Clothing Industries: Structural Problems and Policies in OECD Countries* (Paris, 1983), p. 29; hereafter referred to as 'OECD Report'. This asserts that income elasticities for clothing products appeared to be well below one.

26. See Geoffrey R.D. Underhill, 'Neo-Corporatist Theory and the Politics of Industrial Decline: The Case of the French Textile and Clothing Industry 1974–1984', in *European Journal of Political Research*, vol. 16, 1988, pp. 489–511.

27. The protectionism of the 1970s is referred to as the 'new protectionism' largely because it came after the major push for liberalisation in the Kennedy Round, but there was nothing particularly 'new' about the quantitative restrictions and other non-tariff barriers which made up the policies of the time.

28. The discussion here will draw on a number of works concerning antiprotectionist forces, e.g. Helen V. Milner, *Resisting Protectionism: Global Industries and the Politics of International Trade* (Princeton: Princeton University Press, 1988); I.M. Destler and John Odell, *Anti-Protection: Changing Forces in United States Trade Politics* (Washington, DC: Institute for International Economics, 1987); and on new theories of international trade developed from the 1980s onwards, e.g. Alain Bienaymé, *Stratégies de l'entreprise compétitive* (Paris: Masson, 1980); Paul Krugman, 'Does the New Trade Theory Require a New Trade Policy?' in *The World Economy*, vol. 15, 1992, pp. 423–33.

29. Foreign sourcing is the generic term which will be employed in this book to denote the various forms of transnational production strategies employed in the global textile and clothing industry. Foreign sourcing strategies include a number of specific practices involving intra-firm and intra-industry trade: the use of overseas production subsidiaries involving FDI; the use of imported intermediary inputs in domestic production; and strategies involving subcontracting to overseas firms. The practice of overseas subcontracting is most common, especially in the clothing industry: domestically produced fabric from high-wage countries is exported for labour-intensive assembly into finished clothing products by low-wage producers, and reimported by the firm which initiated the process (sometimes for re-export as domestic products).

Much of this type of foreign sourcing takes place under special trade policy regulations designed to facilitate the process, usually known as 'outward processing' regulations, and a substantial proportion of foreign sourcing in the industry is thus referred to as OPT. The role of foreign sourcing in the industry is particularly significant for Chapter 5 in explaining the dismantling of the MFA.

30. Underhill, 'Industrial Crisis and International Regimes', op. cit.; Milner, *Resisting Protectionism*, op. cit.

31. 'Upstream' production processes begin with raw fibre preparation (or manufacture in the case of synthetics), followed by spinning and weaving, dyeing and printing processes. The 'downstream' production processes are therefore those closer to final consumption, such as clothing assembly and finishing operations. What should be clear is that products in upstream processes serve as inputs for downstream production, and there is therefore an intricate set of interdependencies as upstream textile producers seek market outlets in downstream manufacturing activities.

32. See Bienaymé, *Stratégies de l'entreprise*, op. cit., p. 67.

33. N. Thiéry, 'Preface', in Bienaymé, *Stratégies de l'entreprise*, op. cit., pp. 4–5.

34. Paul Krugman, 'Does the New Trade Theory Require a New Trade Policy?' in *The World Economy*, vol. 15, 1992, p. 425.

35. Bienaymé, *Stratégies de l'entreprise*, op. cit., pp. 90, 67.

36. Ibid., p. 78.

37. Benoît Boussemart, *Industrie de main d'oeuvre et division internationale du travail: l'avenir de l'industrie textile de la région Nord-pas-de-Calais*, 3 vols, unpublished thesis, Doctorat ès en Sciences Economiques, Université de Paris X (Nanterre), December 1984, p. 311.

38. See discussion in John Zysman, *Governments, Markets, and Growth* (Oxford: Martin Robertson, 1983), pp. 37–41.

39. First emphasis added; Zysman, *Governments, Markets, and Growth* op. cit., p. 39.

40. Ibid.

41. 'Preface' by Jacques de Bandt in Benoît Boussemart and Jean-Claude Rabier, *Le Dossier Agache-Willot: un capitalisme à contre-courant* (Paris: Presses de la Fondation Nationale des Sciences Politiques, 1983), p. 13. The literature on international political economy has recently begun to focus increasingly on firms as actors in the international system. A pioneering work is by John Stopford and Susan Strange, *Rival States, Rival Firms* (Cambridge: Cambridge University Press, 1991). All in all, the role of firms and their associations is under-researched in the international relations literature: see Geoffrey R.D. Underhill, 'Organised Business and International Relations Theory', in Justin Greenwood and Henry Jacek (eds), *Organised Business and the New Global Order* (London: Macmillan, 1998).

42. See Krugman, 'Does the New Trade Theory?' op. cit., pp. 424–8.

43. Ibid., p. 425.

44. Richard Stubbs draws attention to the importance of private networks of capital associated with success of the Asia-Pacific region in interna-

tional trade: 'Asia-Pacific Regionalization and the Global Economy: A Third Form of Capitalism', in *Asian Survey*, vol. xxxv/9, September 1995, pp. 785–97. Research on Italian industrial districts also explains much of Italy's export success in certain sectors such as textiles and clothing: F. Pyke, G. Becattini, and W. Sengenberger, *Industrial District and Inter-Firm Co-operation in Italy* (Geneva: International Institute for Labour Studies, 1990). All of this research is a long way from the abstract models of perfect competition which are a feature of traditional international trade theory.

45.   Bernard Lassudrie-Duchêne, 'Décomposition internationale des processus productifs et autonomie nationale', in Henri Bourginat (ed.), *Internationalisation et autonomie de décision* (Paris: Economica, 1982), p. 45.

46.   Ibid., p. 46.

47.   Patrick Messerlin, 'Présentation: Les conditions actuelles des spécialisations internationales', in Bourginat, *Internationalisation et autonomie*, op. cit., p. 20.

48.   Henri Bourginat, 'Introduction', in Bourginat *Internationalisation et autonomie*, op. cit., p. 12.

49.   Paul Krugman, 'Dutch Tulips and Emerging Markets', in *Foreign Affairs*, vol. 74/4, July–August 1995, p. 31.

50.   See in particular the account by Vinod K. Aggarwal, *Liberal Protectionism: The International Politics of Organised Textile Trade* (Berkeley: University of California Press, 1985).

51.   Milner, *Resisting Protectionism*, op. cit.; Friman, *Patchwork Protectionism*, op. cit.

52.   See by Peter Gourevitch: 'The Second Image Reversed: The International Sources of Domestic Politics', in *International Organization*, vol. 32/4, Autumn 1978; *Politics in Hard Times: Comparative Responses to International Economic Crises* (Ithaca: Cornell University Press, 1986). See also by Geoffrey R.D. Underhill, 'Conceptualising the Changing Global Order', in Richard Stubbs and Geoffrey Underhill (eds), *Political Economy and the Changing Global Order* (London: Macmillan, 1994); and 'Industrial Crisis and International Regimes', op. cit.

53.   Peter J. Katzenstein, *Small States in World Markets* (Ithaca: Cornell University Press, 1985).

54.   There are various theoretical accounts of the 'internationalisation' of the state which can be referred to: see for example Robert W. Cox, *Production, Power, and World Order* (New York: Columbia University Press, 1987), esp. pp. 253–65; Cerny, in *The Changing Architecture of Politics*, op. cit., develops an alternative formula, based on the notion of the 'competition state', which engages in a process of re-regulation of the economy to promote international competitiveness of national economic actors and seeks to integrate domestic market structures into the international domain. In doing so, it paradoxically undermines many of its own policy tools through which it was able to manage economic policy prior to the emergence of the open economy.

55.   See note 1.

56.   Susan Strange, *States and Markets*, 2nd edn (London: Pinter, 1994).

57. See Underhill, 'Conceptualising the Changing Global Order', op. cit., esp. pp. 34–8.
58. Ibid., p. 35.
59. On the relationship between markets and political institutions, see Karl Polanyi, *The Great Transformation* (Boston: Beacon Press 1944); also John Lie, 'Embedding Polanyi's Market Society', in *Sociological Perspectives*, vol. 34/2, 1991, pp. 219–35.
60. On the importance of structuration in international theory, see Cerny, *The Changing Architecture of Politics*, op. cit.; also Alexander Wendt, 'The Agent–Structure Problem in International Relations Theory', in *International Organization*, vol. 41/3, Summer 1987, pp. 335–70.
61. See Gourevitch, op. cit., p. 904.
62. A number of studies have emphasised that policy preferences must be translated into successful political strategies if they are to be realised. See Underhill, 'Industrial Crisis and International Regimes', op. cit.; Milner, *Resisting Protectionism*, op. cit., esp. ch. 7; J. Schott and J.W. Buurman, *The Uruguay Round: An Assessment* (Washington, DC: Institute for International Economics, 1994).
63. This point is admirably made in Milner, 'The Assumption of Anarchy', op. cit.
64. Mike Smith employed this argument in relation to the foreign economic policies of the European Union; see M. Smith, 'The European Community: Testing the Boundaries of Foreign Economic Policy', in Stubbs and Underhill (eds), *Political Economy*, op. cit., pp. 453–68.

1 Material Underpinnings: Economic Structure and Industrial Crisis, 1974–84

The purpose of this chapter is to begin developing a comprehensive picture of the material underpinnings of the trade policy process which led to the emergence of protectionism in the textile and clothing sector. In accordance with the arguments presented in the introduction, it is important to draw systematic linkages between (a) the dynamics of economic structure at the level of domestic economies and international production and markets; (b) the policy preferences of the various actors involved; and (c) the actual unfolding of the political conflicts over the nature and distributive impact of the market which occurred over time across levels of analysis and institutions of the international system.

The limited aim of this chapter is to outline the changing economic structure of the textile and clothing sectors in some of the key industrialised economies. This will demonstrate the sector's ongoing importance to the advanced economies and provide some objective reasons why the industry remains salient to the distributional politics of these societies. The chapter will then go on to illustrate the extent of decline and adjustment in the textile and clothing industries of key market economies, focusing on the period from 1974 to approximately 1984 and the lead-up to the launch of the Uruguay Round of GATT trade negotiations in 1986. Comparisons across countries and other economic sectors in difficulty will place the sector's problems in perspective. The analysis will also place the sectoral industrial crisis in its wider context of generalised economic difficulties in the 1970s and 1980s.

Finally, the chapter will go on to argue that, despite the clear signs of sectoral decline in a number of advanced economies, there was nothing inevitable about the shift in the international division of labour in the sector towards low-wage economies. The 'competitive equation' in the sector remained complex and the industry, with the possible exception of the downstream clothing sector, was far from the caricature of labour-intensive manufacturing facing inevitable eclipse at the hands of less advanced and lower wage societies. A wide variety of factor mixes could yield competitive cost structures for firms trading in the global economy. An equally wide variety of firm strategies could be observed in advanced industrial economies. Lower wages were not necessarily the route to successful global competition in a sector in the throes of rapid transnationalisation, as the numerous success stories in Western Europe, the United States, and Japan demonstrate. The analysis begun here in this chapter will then be extended in subsequent chapters to examine the sources of the crisis in the industry, the failure of firms to adapt to competition, the associational groups which articulated the policy preferences of firms, and the nature of the relationship between state institutions and these private associational groups in the policy processes which led to a definition of the public interest and, in turn, the international trade regime for the sector.

ECONOMIC DIMENSIONS OF THE SECTOR: COMPLEXITY AND FRAGMENTATION

The textile and clothing sector revealed itself to be diverse, complex, and fragmented.[1] As this study will attempt to make clear, even from a purely economic point of view (assuming such exists) textile and clothing industries were far from the caricature of traditional labour-intensive sectors dismissed by champions of the 'new technology' or 'sunrise' industries. In fact, the most striking feature of the textile industry was the great diversity of competitive combinations of factor mixes which were possible. If clothing is treated separately, new production technologies in textiles placed the industry among the highly capital-intensive sectors which could readily compete with low-wage economies, assuming that adjustment and modernisation were carried out.[2] The situation requires more than the generalisations often made about 'traditional' industries and the need for redeployment.

There is no one unified textile manufacturing process, and the sector produces many products for a range of markets in industry and households. However, the diverse production techniques and processes are linked in a complex web of relationships from the processing of raw fibres to the assembly of clothing and other finished products. There is a continuous stream of value added – a transformation of raw materials and intermediary goods into finished products. This flow of value added lends unity to a series of otherwise heterogeneous transformatory processes.

In the production stream, the preparation of raw materials and the production of artificial and synthetic fibres serve as basic inputs. The intermediary stages are spinning, weaving, the dyeing and printing sector, and the knitting industry producing both knitted fabrics in some cases finished garments directly. The clothing industry traditionally provided the market for the majority of textile products, but other uses in household and industrial textiles have become increasingly important (see Tables 1.1 and 1.2). These different activities are also classified by the type of fibre used, such as the woollen industry, the cotton industry, linen, or jute, but the introduction of man-made fibres and mixed-fibre fabrics has rendered this traditional mode of classification obsolete.

Table 1.1   Consumption of textile products in industrialised countries by final use, 1978 (%)

Product group	6 EEC + UK	USA	Japan	Industrialised countries
1. Apparel	51	45	40	47
2. Habitat	34	34	28	37
3. Technical/industrial	15	21	32	16

Source: *France, Assemblée Nationale, Rapport fait au nom de la commission d'enquête parlementaire chargée d'examiner les problèmes de de l'industrie textile et les moyens à mettre en oeuvre pour les resoudre*, 6ᵉ législature, no. 2254, 18 March 1981, (elsewhere 'National Assembly Report'), vol. ɪ, p. 31.

Table 1.2   Evolution of textiles consumption in Western Europe by final use, 1970–9 (%)

Period	Apparel	Home furnishings textiles*a*	Carpets	Technical/ industrial	Total
1970–3	53.5	19.5	11.5	15.5	100
1974–9	51.0	21.8	12.0	15.5	100

a Including household linen.

Source: Pierre Hoffmeister, 'Le Textile européen: secteur en crise', *Revue d'économie politique*, 6, 1980, p. 931.

Despite the variety of production processes, each with distinct technologies and possible factor mixes, each stage of the production process is essentially interdependent with the others.[3] Of the value of the average finished product, only about 15 per cent comes from outside the sector as inputs. The sector is therefore fairly self-contained for all its diversity, but each segment of the production stream may be produced in a separate locale, and the products of the different stages of the production process can be produced either within an integrated company structure or they can be traded individually as intra-industry trade across either domestic or international markets. The industry can notionally be located across a wide range of local economies so as to benefit from different combinations of factors of production. However, the dependence of upstream activities on downstream production for market outlets means that the dislocation process, once begun, can be difficult to control. If the downstream markets of domestic producers are removed and a long-established set of interdependencies in the market disturbed, this can 'put into question the operation of the whole system'[4] and lead to the collapse of segments of the domestic industry.

(a) Contribution to Domestic Economies

The contribution of the textile and clothing sector to the national economies of advanced industrial societies remains considerable and is usually underestimated by most observers. There is a tendency to see steel, chemicals, or automobile manufacture as major industries, but not textiles and clothing. However, to cite the case of France at the height of the crisis in the sector, household expenditure on textiles and clothing products in 1982 was about 122 billion francs, more than the combined expenditure on autos, electrical equipment, radio and television.[5] Although the weight of textile and clothing products in household budgets has tended to decline across the OECD, in most advanced economies it remained between 7 and 10 per cent of total private consumption at constant prices.[6]

To make comparisons to the overall manufacturing sector, in 1977 (well into the crisis period) the textile and apparel sector still represented some 4.9 per cent of value added in German manufacturing, 6.3 per cent in the United States, 6.9 per cent in Japan, and 6.7 per cent in the United Kingdom.[7] Turnover in the French textile and apparel sector in 1982 was over 6.4 per cent of total manufacturing turnover,[8] double that of steel and almost at the level of the automobile sector. In most countries the industry was even more important in terms of employment. Using 1977 figures once again, in Italy it employed 15 per cent of the manufacturing workforce, 13.3 per cent in Japan, 12.1 per cent in the US, 11.2 per cent in France, 11.1 per cent in the UK, although only 8.2 per cent in Germany,[9] in some of these cases more than the automobile sector. One estimate in the early 1980s linked some 800 000 French jobs to activities dependent on textile and clothing manufacture, including textile machinery, marketing, services, and the production of basic inputs.[10] The sector's contribution to the economy was steadily declining relative to other activities and continued to do so, but it still had to be counted among the major industries in western market economies.[11]

(b) Regional Distribution in National Economies

Particularly in Europe, but also in the United States, textile and clothing industries were an important feature of the older industrial regions.[12] As the industrial revolution owed much to textile and clothing industries this is not surprising, but it did mean that the economic prosperity of key regional constituencies in a number of the advanced economies were intimately linked to the textile and/or clothing industry's fortunes. This meant that any precipitous decline in the sector would have a disproportionate impact concentrated in particular regions where alternate economic activities would, initially at least, be difficult to develop.

France and Britain will serve to make the point here. In the UK, textile and clothing industries were significant employers in Lancashire and the greater Manchester region as far as the cotton industry was concerned. The cotton industry was in persistent difficulty, with major job losses in an already poor region from the early 1960s onwards.[13] The woollen industry was typically associated with West Yorkshire and parts of central Scotland. Other textile and clothing regions included Northern Ireland, and specialised centres such as lace production around Nottingham or the clothing industry in inner cities.[14] All of these regions experienced severe and generalised economic difficulties from the mid 1970s onwards.

The French case was not dissimilar and will serve as a more detailed example. Pockets of the textile and clothing industry were dispersed across the national territory, particularly in the case of the clothing sector,[15] but patterns of considerable regional concentration could be discerned. There was a considerable concentration of the clothing industry in the Paris region (about 20 per cent of total sectoral employment in 1979), doubtless due to the role of the fashion industry as a magnet for clothing manufacturers, and the Nord and the Pays-de-Loire boasted a concentration of national employment in the sector of 10.9 per cent and 10.2 per cent respectively, and the Rhône-Alpes had 8.3 per cent.

In the case of textiles proper, certain regions again figured prominently. In 1979 nearly 27 per cent of employment in the sector was in the Nord-Pas-de-Calais, and just under 20 per cent was concentrated in the Rhône-Alpes. The Nord was the most important and diversified textile and clothing region, claiming almost all activities in the sector, but the woollen industry was particularly important.[16] The cotton industry, perhaps most affected among textile activities by low-wage competition, was associated historically with the Vosges valleys of the Lorraine and parts of Alsace. Finally, it should be mentioned that as in the British case textile and clothing industries were important in several regions seriously affected by the decline of manufacturing across a range of industries. These were the older industrial areas of France, chief among them the Nord-Pas-de-Calais and the Lorraine, where the decline of the coal and steel industries was a major trauma for local economies for over a decade. Alsace and the Pays-de-Loire (heavy machinery) also suffered from industrial decline after the world economic slowdown in 1974–5.

(c) Corporate Structure

A final general feature of the sector is its dualistic corporate structure in most advanced economies. There was in the first place a clear division between the mass of small and medium firms which made up the majority of firms in the industry, even more so in clothing than in textiles, and the relatively limited number of very large firms or conglomerates. These larger firms and conglomerates were on a variety of patterns. They might be specialised in one activity, or vertically integrated, horizontally integrated across a particular segment of the industry, or they might lack rationalisation altogether, depending on the situation. In the United States, artificial fibres production was dominated by huge multinational chemical companies such as Dupont, a situation not dissimilar from other countries. Overall the US had in the mid 1980s (which followed a long period of restructuring and concentration) some 6000 textile mills and 15 000 clothing firms organised in 21 000 plants.[17] The essential dualism of the sector can be illustrated by the fact that while the two largest US textile firms accounted for some 86 000 workers alone, the average size was only 110 workers per mill. In the clothing industry small size was particularly marked as a feature.

The larger firms have been capable of large-scale investments leading to considerable productivity growth. The textile sector in fact outperformed the manufacturing industry average in terms of labour productivity growth rates in the period 1973–85, and this despite wage growth. In the clothing industry, where technological progress has been much less pronounced, productivity growth tended to lag behind the manufacturing average but it was far from absent altogether.

The UK sector also exhibited a contrast between large, integrated concerns and the small and medium sized producers. Nonetheless, in the post-war period, British synthetic fibres producers such as Courtaulds and ICI became significant integrating and restructuring forces in the industry.[18] The UK in fact had the most concentrated industry overall, with the five largest firms accounting for half or more of employment and sales respectively by 1976, with the other half of the sector made up of small and medium producers which survived as best they could.[19] However, concentration (despite considerable efforts at modernisation[20]) did not necessarily yield good results and performance of the sector was far from remarkable.

In France yet another pattern of dualism emerged, but once again with the clear division between a few large firms and a mass of smaller concerns. The conglomerates which emerged were usually horizontally integrated and had in some cases adopted an internationalised production strategy.[21] However, the extent of concentration in the sector is often exaggerated. Large firms *did* emerge (Table 1.3), but if there was a general move toward concentration, it was limited to the period 1968–73.[22] The trend somewhat reversed itself in the 1970s, especially in clothing. In 1981, the small and medium firms[23] comprised nearly 95 per cent of enterprises and continued to account for over half of total turnover in the sector.[24]

Using the French case again as an example, there was no clear correlation between size and performance. Although productivity and export performance do appear to have been higher on average in the larger firms,[25] a number of small firms have done very well (among the most dynamic and fast-growing in French industry[26]), and most large firms were not renowned for their spectacular profits or great dynamism.[27] Size was clearly not the only factor affecting performance. In Italy and Germany, small and medium firms were particularly dynamic. They developed considerable flexibility in adapting to changing market conditions and intensifying competition.

The clearest dichotomy was between the successful manufacturers, large or small, and the many traditional and often marginal

Table 1.3   Top ten textile or clothing firms in the EU, 1980 (thousands of French francs)

Rank	Firm	Country	Turnover	Employees (no.)	Net profit
1	Courtaulds	UK	16 791 218	88 000	−68 740
2	SNIA-Viscosa	Italy	7 708 218	32 000	
3	Coats-Patons	UK	6 770 133	60 000	325 768
4	Prouvost SA	France	4 986 313	19 893	18 274
5	Groupe Dollfus-Mieg	France	4 731 336	21 318	−74 071
6	Boussac-St Frères (Agache-Willot)	France	4 120 675	26 419	
7	ABZ Zentral-esankaufagentur	Germany	3 947 850		
—	Texunion (DMC)	France	3 540 233	13 384	−45 502
8	Tootal	UK	3 310 184	43 954	71 214
9	Rhône-Poulenc Textile	France	2 548 082	8 522	−1 851 627
10	Triumph International Group	Germany	2 327 325		

Source: *Le Nouvel Économiste*, Spécial 5000, December 1981.

family-owned firms which consistently refused to face up to the consequences of the internationalisation of trade and production in the sector.[28] The stagnation and immobilism of these firms was one of the principal difficulties of the sector, a problem repeated across the advanced industrial economies to a greater or lesser extent.

DECLINE AND ADJUSTMENT IN THE TEXTILE AND CLOTHING SECTOR

The mid 1970s ushered in a period of considerable crisis for the textile and clothing sectors of a number of the larger industrialised economies. The crisis differed in intensity and effect from country to country and therefore the analysis which follows will necessarily rely to an extent on generalisation. However it is hoped that a portrait of the sector's difficulties can be developed, using some national case data as an illustration of the sorts of adjustment problems to be found across the sector in the high-wage economies of Europe and the US. Given that the textile and clothing industry's crisis came in combination with prolonged restructuring problems in other industrial sectors as well, it is not difficult to argue that the industry's problem's had considerable political salience for the governments involved.

Most national textile and clothing industries were declining relative to other industrial sectors throughout the post-war period, particularly in terms of employment levels. This tended to accelerate with the onset of generalised economic crisis associated with the oil shock of 1973–4. Some were more successful at adjusting than others and each showed a unique pattern of development or lack thereof. It is worth noting that there were usually marked differences between textile production on the one hand, and clothing assembly on the other, with the textile industry resisting competitive pressures better on the whole.

Germany, the US, and Italy are three national cases of relatively successful adjustment, but each followed a divergent pattern, emphasising the point that a variety of strategies could yield a competitive and export-oriented industry even in high-wage countries. Germany's industry adapted to competitive pressures earlier than most. It is often seen as an example of market-led adjustment, although it has been pointed out that protection was an element of the German strategy: various import quotas were used in the 1960s and early 1970s,[29] before the MFA came into force, along with other forms of public assistance.[30] That said, the German industry had in retrospect a two-prong strategy. On the one hand it divested itself of the more labour-intensive downstream production activities, particularly in clothing assembly, through foreign sourcing. Much of this was to the then German Democratic Republic and other East Bloc countries.[31] On the other hand it invested heavily in productivity improvements and capital-intensive technologies in the production of high-value and high-quality products, including finished clothing.[32] The majority of firms were small-to-medium sized, and this appears to have contributed to the flexibility and specialisation of the industry in its constant quest for adaptation to the EU and larger global market. Despite high wage and social security costs, the German industry was exporting nearly half of its production by 1983.[33] This did not stop a substantial decline in employment levels, but these were largely due to productivity improvements in both textile and clothing activities as opposed to import pressures.[34] The rising value of the Deutsche Mark and the renewed economic recession at the end of the 1970s was a particular difficulty, and if one measures output growth from 1970 to 1978, it remained relatively stagnant.[35] Nonetheless, firms remained on the whole healthy and the German industry became the second largest exporter after Italy.

The US industry was in general more successful than that of most of its European counterparts. The decline of the dollar throughout the 1970s certainly helped produce this result, and in fact the sector encountered renewed difficulties in the period from 1983 to 1985 as the dollar rose to record levels. The most dramatic sign of decline was the fall in employment levels. Employment levels in the clothing industry hit a peak in 1973. It had fallen by 7 per cent by 1980, and by 19 per cent by 1986. In the textile industry, the peak was again in 1973 at 980 000 workers, but declined by an annual average rate of 2.9 per cent from 1972–3 to 1985–6, leaving only 68 per cent of the peak level or 669 000 workers.

Other aspects of the industry's evolution present a more positive picture in the US. Production levels in textiles peaked in 1979, with an average annual growth rate of 0.45 per cent from 1972–3 to 1985–6, considerably better than the OECD average. While profitability was affected by the successive recessions, it compared favourably to the US manufacturing average, with the clothing production sector faring generally worse than textiles.[36] On the whole the US textile sector remained robustly competitive, but the clothing industry less so. The textile industry had a relatively consistent trade surplus from 1973 onwards,[37] which reached a sizeable $1.07 billion in 1979[38] before declining under the combined impact of the rising dollar and global recession. Even by the mid 1980s, however, a time of great difficulty for the industry, textile imports measured by value only accounted for 9.5 per cent of domestic consumption, 31 per cent in the case of clothing production, which yielded an average of 22 per cent for the sector as a whole.[39]

The Italian case is remarkable for the success of both the textile and clothing industries. A few figures will illustrate this. First and fore-most, Italy is by far the largest net exporter of textile and clothing products in the world, maintaining a healthy surplus in both the textile and the clothing segments of the sector. Italy's export *surplus* in textile and clothing trade grew proportionately more in the 1970s than that of Korea or Hong Kong, and was of course much larger,[40] and the 1979 Italian export surplus in textiles and clothing combined was, at $5.7 billion, nearly equal to the combined surplus of all the developing countries with the industrial areas.[41] Although employment levels declined in line with productivity gains,[42] from 1972–3 to 1983, textiles output grew by an average annual rate of 2.4 per cent and 1.9 per cent for clothing output. Compare this with the UK's annual average *decline* of 4.8 per cent for the same period![43]

Despite this aggregated success, there were Italian firms in trouble. Here the dualism in the industry's structure asserted itself once again. The largest Italian firms were confirmed loss-makers, usually as part of state-owned industrial holding companies. They often received substantial state subsidies in order to survive, limited in theory by EU guidelines and competition policy.[44] The small and medium firms demonstrated a much better grasp of changing patterns of demand and were sufficiently flexible to respond to intensified competition in particularly innovative ways. The Italian sector underwent a process of so-called 'deverticalisation', or the reversal of the vertical integration process, and substituted forms of co-operatively managed sharing of market, production, and design information which replaced many larger firms with networks of leaner, more successful ones.[45]

However, the crisis in some national textile and clothing sectors was rather more serious, good examples being the UK and France. Not only was there a clear decline, in terms of production and employment levels, relative to other sectors of the economy. There was also an absolute decline in the production levels of most branches of the industry and a serious and ongoing *loss of the domestic market share* held by national producers, a loss which was far from being fully compensated by corresponding growth in exports.

An analysis of the industry in France in the 1970s and early 1980s will serve as an example of a national sector which suffered a severe crisis. The 1974 oil shock had a sizeable impact on the fortunes of the French industry, which though inefficient and uncompetitive, had at least benefited from a steadily expanding market and so had not been forced to contemplate an absolute decline in production levels.

(a) Demand and Foreign Trade

Consumption of textile products is functionally divided between industrial/technical uses, household textiles (linen, furnishings, etc.), and clothing. Throughout the 1970s, demand for industrial textiles and household products increased. Consumption of clothing and accessories on the other hand decreased. While apparel end-use remained important, the actual share of final demand for textiles held by clothing declined, with the proportion of final demand for other uses rising correspondingly (see Tables 1.2 and 1.4).

Considering household expenditure on textile products on its own, overall consumption stagnated in the mid 1970s and then declined, despite a brief rebound in 1981–2.[46] The crisis appears to have radically

Table 1.4   Domestic textile and clothing consumption by end-use in France, 1980 (%)

Product group	Household consumption	Intermediary consumption		
		Textile and clothing sector	Other industrial sectors	Total
1. Spun yarns	10	87	3	100
2. Woven fabrics	41	31	28	100
3. Knitted fabrics and apparel	88	9	3	100
4. Clothing	95	—	3	100

Source: Micheline Vincent, 'Vingt Ans du textile-habillement', *Economie et statistique*, no. 138, November 1981, p. 25, after Compatibilité Nationale.

altered household demand for textile products – it had grown steadily up to 1973, even outstripping growth in overall private consumption for a time in the 1960s.[47] The crisis led to a drop in the growth rate of disposable income and private consumption, and clothing consumption actually dropped as a proportion of household budgets.[48] This trend in demand for the industry's products was a function of changing social behaviour and lifestyles.[49]

Against this background of stagnant and even declining demand for the industry's products, coupled with the emergence of new producer countries, trade competition on world markets intensified.[50] The French sector proved particularly weak in competition with other industrialised countries where there was no inherent labour-cost disadvantage. This was especially the case in the more capital-intensive textile activities where new technologies and opportunities for modernisation were abundant and where there was little, if any, cost advantage for the low-wage economies. Labour-intensive clothing activities suffered less in France, but were considerably affected by low-wage competition. The domestic industry seemed largely incapable of competing on either front, and any growth in the French market was usually absorbed by foreign producers to the detriment of the domestic firms. This was despite considerable growth in the exports of many French firms. Inexorably, the trade balance moved from surplus to yawning deficit: textiles proper were the first to go into the red in 1976; textiles and clothing together were in deficit by the end of the decade; and, by 1981, the clothing industry itself, a traditional French strength, followed the others into the red.

(b) Production and Employment

The combined dynamics of changing demand functions and foreign trade competition had a profound impact on production and employment levels in the textile and clothing sector. These two dynamics led to a staged collapse in production levels and to massive job losses in particular. Growth in textile and clothing production was constantly outpaced by other industrial sectors, falling from an index level of 100 in 1973 (peak) to 90 in 1979 and below 80 by mid 1980.[51] Even in 1981–2, when there was a relatively strong surge in demand, production levels continued to fall sharply in the face of intensified international competition.

This drop in production came in surges.[52] 1975 proved a bleak year as the impact of the oil shock was felt. In 1977, production levels recovered somewhat, only to begin their fall once again with the second oil shock in 1979. The average annual growth rate from 1973 to 1979 was −1.5 per cent.[53]

In many ways, the employment situation during the crisis was even worse.[54] Limited rationalisation and productivity growth added to the declining production levels to create enormous annual job losses by the end of the 1970s. In fact, employment losses were the most telling indication of the sector's precipitous decline. Employment losses had been almost continuous after the war (once the recovery period was over) but until the crisis these were mostly due to productivity growth and restructuring in the industry. However, they accelerated sharply in 1973 and again in 1979 with the impact of general economic slow-down. In 1980, there were some 26 000 jobs lost in the industry, and this number approached 29 000 in 1981, though a government programme slowed the flood to a trickle for the next two years or so. This was not without political significance.

(c) Other Features of the Crisis in French Textiles and Clothing

The crisis affected other aspects of the industry's performance. The traditional low profitability in the sector worsened in the crisis period, despite some recovery in 1977–8, with firms closing continuously. Some of the more spectacular bankruptcies became major political issues at the time. Rather ominously for the long-term prospects of the industry, investment fell continuously among surviving firms, dipping well below levels sufficient to replace antiquated equipment, let alone support a major modernisation effort. From an index level of 100 in

1973, it sank to 55.2 in 1980, well below corresponding figures for the EU as a whole.[55] This drop was greater than for any other manufacturing sector.[56] Furthermore, the drop in investment was greater than the corresponding drop in production – declining steadily as a proportion of both turnover and value added. It was also well below levels in other national textile and clothing industries.[57]

Steady decline must, therefore, be seen as one of the salient features of the sector's development in France after 1974, manifest in almost all indicators of industry performance. Some activities, however, fared better than others, just as demand for some product groups increased during the period, providing opportunities for those firms which were quick to seize the initiative. What is striking is the ability of foreign producers (and, by logical extension, French importers) to adapt faster than national firms to changes in the French textile and clothing market, which may be an interesting comment on the behaviour of traditional French entrepreneurs.[58] Proximity to local markets should have been an important advantage. Some French firms prospered greatly, but the majority sank into a defensive stupor.

The only national sector of a major country to fare worse than the French industry was in the United Kingdom. The UK was the one country in which Cline was able to identify significant textile job losses directly attributable to import competition between 1970 and 1980: the share of imports in domestic consumption more than doubled.[59] Performance in the clothing industry, although heavily in deficit, did not deteriorate as dramatically,[60] but the net trade balance (exports minus imports as a per cent of apparent consumption) deteriorated sharply for both textile and clothing activities.[61] By 1979 the value of exports only represented 79 per cent of imports in textiles and 63 per cent in clothing, or 72 per cent for the two combined.[62] Production in UK textile activities fell by some 37 per cent between 1973 and 1983, by 12 per cent in the clothing industry, and employment levels fell by over 50 per cent and by 37 per cent respectively from 1973 to 1982.[63]

Overall, it seems clear that a number of crucial trading countries involved in textile production suffered considerable job losses and frequently declining production levels as well. National industries differed as to the speed and starting point of the restructuring of the 1970s and early 1980s, but of the major producers only Italy can be said to have come through the period of industrial crisis virtually unscathed, although with fewer jobs to show for it nonetheless. The political salience of these industrial difficulties across the advanced economies differed according to a number of political, economic, and institutional variables, but few governments escaped the campaigns of textile producers and unions throughout the decade from 1974 to 1984; for some the pressure had been ongoing since the 1950s.[64] The next section, however, demonstrates that while decline and adjustment was characteristic of many of the OECD textile industries, it was far from inevitable.

GLOBAL COMPETITION AND PRODUCTION COSTS: THE 'COMPETITIVE EQUATION' IN TEXTILE AND CLOTHING INDUSTRIES

This section will argue systematically that there was no inevitable shift in the international division of labour for textiles from developed to developing countries, and that the wage cost advantage for the LDCs as far as clothing production was concerned was moderated by other factors. The available combinations of factor mixes which could yield competitive cost structures for firms involved in textile production were numerous, taking advantage of considerable advances in technology, and a number of successful firms with competitive strategies could be discerned even in those domestic industries which fared badly in aggregate terms, such as the UK and France. The success stories of the Italian industry (especially in clothing production) and to a lesser extent the US sector demonstrate that firms could indeed prove themselves in international competition.

Traditional explanations of the decline of the textile and clothing industries of the industrialised countries tend to point to differences in factor costs, particularly labour, and the logic of comparative advantage (see discussion of trade theory in Introduction above). The international division of labour was taken as a structure of comparative advantage to which the textile and clothing sector must inevitably bow. Whether one considers the relatively low prices of imports, the level of labour costs, or strategies of internationalisation of production, a common and often assumed premise was that comparative advantage in the industry, particularly clothing, had shifted to some considerable degree towards the developing countries.

This is precisely what must be determined, if for no other reason than that the industry in a number of countries had frequently used the argument to justify a policy of protection and subsidy with a view to preserving employment levels and, of course, firm profitability. The simple fact that the majority of textile *and* clothing exports were still generated by the industrialised economies, to say nothing of the bulk of world production, undermines this assumption.[65] An examination of the nature of production cost structures in the late 1970s and early 1980s, and, subsequently, the sources of international trade competition in the sector, reveals that this fatalistic point of view was not justified.

(a) Changing Technologies and Costs

Firms must adapt to changing markets through product innovation and choice, but they respond to competition through costs. It is therefore important to be aware of the evolution of technologies and corresponding cost structures which were to be found in the textile and clothing sector at the time. Technological development presented both opportunities as well as challenges to the industry, and an ongoing case for adaptation as opposed to fatalism.

Technological developments in textiles in particular greatly altered potential patterns of factor mixes and the resulting structure of production costs. These made possible not only substantial gains in productivity of labour, but also altered the balance of capital and labour in the structure of production costs. The corollary of course, in the absence of a major expansion in capacity, was job losses in the sector, but not the loss of the industry itself. What follows is a brief account of the principal technological developments in the post-war textile and clothing industry, the most important of which dated from the 1970s.

Synthetic fibres production was the first major development. It resulted in a highly capital-intensive industry which provided some 50 per cent of world consumption of textile fibres by 1978 (see Table 1.5), usually higher in industrialised countries.[66] The development of low-cost synthetic yarns was a major factor in encouraging other technical innovations in the industry. New techniques resulted in products which traditional machinery could not process, spurring the development of faster, automated production units, eventually backed up by computer technology to streamline input inventories, coordinate diverse production processes, and directly link marketing to production.[67]

The most important individual developments were in spinning and weaving, and as such they can be used as examples.[68] In spinning, the development of turbine or 'open-end' processes by Czech engineers in 1973 eliminated several stages in yarn production and increased speeds over traditional spindles by about four times. In 1980, a system of

Table 1.5   Evolution of world consumption of textile fibre types, 1958–78 (in thousands of tonnes and %)

Year	Wool	Cotton	Artificial[a] and synthetic fibre and yarn	Total
1958	1 384	9 741	2 730	13 855
1968	1 621	11 952	7 411	20 984
1973	1 432	13 713	11 492	26 737
1978	1 458	13 006	13 673	28 137
1973/1958	+ 3.5%	+ 40.8%	+ 321.0%	+ 93.0%
1978/1973	+ 1.8%	−5.0%	+ 19.0%	+ 5.2%
1978/1958	+ 5.3%	+ 33.5%	400.8%	+ 103.6%

[a] In this category, there is considerable variation between the various elements of the subsector artificial fibres and yarns, synthetic fibres and yarns. The former grows enormously from 1958 to 1973, but declines from 1973 to 1978. The latter grows slowly from 1958 to 73, very rapidly from 1973 to 78.

Source: *France, Assemblée Nationale, Rapport fait au nom de la commission d'enquête parlementaire chargée d'examiner les problèmes de de l'industrie textile et les moyens à mettre en oeuvre pour les resoudre*, 6e législature, no. 2254, 18 March 1981, (elsewhere 'National Assembly Report'), vol. iii, annexes, p. 66, after CIRFS (Comité International de la Rayonne et des Fibres Synthétiques).

rings spinning on an air-cushion began to replace classic bobbins to complete the system. In weaving, classic looms gave way to shuttleless looms. Classic looms could produce some 250 to 300 metres of fabric per minute, but the new air-jet and water-jet systems produced from 900 to 1 300 metres per minute. Improvements were also made in knitting processes. Fabric production rates became far faster than traditional weaving, reducing labour per unit of output by from four to thirty times. Knitting technologies could also combine the fabric production and finished garment stages and machines were far more flexible, capable of use in small decentralised production units.[69]

The major catch to these developments was cost. A turbine spinner cost fifteen times more than ordinary spindles, and projectile looms cost more than double traditional shuttle looms. These new techniques radically increased the cost of investment per work post[70] to a level 'well above the average for manufacturing industry.'[71] The greater expense was often only justified if the machinery could be operated continuously, so labour practices which avoided excessive down-time had to be developed. Nonetheless, not all improvements were prohibitively expensive, especially as micro-computers made information and coordination technology available to small and large firms alike.

Though costly, these technological advances had a considerable effect on the potential factor mixes in the textile industry and, by implication, the range and nature of competitive advantages available to firms. The traditional view of textiles as a labour-intensive industry, with labour costs in value added generally above the manufacturing average, turns out to be quite inaccurate. 'To begin with, the industry offers scope for exceptionally large variations in the combination of labour and capital.'[72] Technological innovation was therefore a powerful weapon in the strategies of firms, but with all the risks inherent in an uncertain market.

Where standard technologies were concerned, the differences in labour productivity among different producers remained small. In such a case, labour costs would be crucial to deciding overall production costs, and thus competitive advantage. However, in textiles, 'technological progress has provided manufacturers in high labour cost locations with the possibility of resisting competition by changing factor proportions.'[73] By increasing capital intensity in line with technological developments, firms could diminish the importance of labour in their costs to levels well below the average for manufacturing industry.

There is a problem, however – as soon as the new technologies become diffused, the same competitive pressures might reappear. Yet there were and remain obstacles to the use of highly capital-intensive technologies in most low-wage developing countries. Skilled technicians and workers may be unavailable or prohibitively expensive. More importantly, capital costs are most often significantly higher, particularly if capital rationing is in force, in which case capital may be simply unavailable.[74]

Labour costs were therefore the low-wage countries' only real advantage. Altering factor proportions in high-wage countries could more than compensate. As technology progressed, labour became relatively less important as a factor, and most LDCs had little interest in moving up the technology ladder, thereby wasting their only natural advantage by duplicating industrialised-country processes. Some newly industrialising countries (NICs) did nonetheless manage this, displaying a determination to challenge the advanced nations on their own terms and developing a more highly paid and skilled workforce in the process. This was usually accomplished under the cover of a protected domestic market. The case of South Korea comes immediately to mind.[75]

Ultimately, competitiveness depended on the total costs which were a function of the variety of factor mixes employed in the strategies of firms, not comparative advantage. The OECD calculated that actual labour costs in textiles averaged some 38 to 47 per cent of total manufacturing costs[76] (lower with the most advanced technology). In comparing West German and US produced cotton yarn and woven fabric with South Korean imports, higher Korean capital costs, transport costs, and import duty made the landed price of the Korean products significantly *more expensive* than the German or US products.[77] Brazilian goods cost about the same as the German, with India 5 to 10 per cent cheaper than both (see Tables 1.6 and 1.7). In international competition non-production costs (tariffs, transport) must also be included, wherein cheap labour is only one of many possible advantages. For industrialised countries,

Table 1.6   Manufacturing costs, spinning, 1978 (US$ per kg of yarn)

Cost element	Brazil	Germany	India	Korea	USA
Waste costs	0.1474	0.1474	0.1474	0.1474	0.1474
Wage costs	0.1067	0.4728	0.0594	0.0591	0.2901
Energy costs	0.0642	0.1419	0.0709	0.0708	0.0471
Auxiliary material costs	0.0427	0.0396	0.0329	0.0323	0.0372
Capital costs	0.5478	0.4275	0.5300	0.6396	0.4496
Total manufacturing costs	0.9088	1.2292	0.8406	0.9492	0.9714
(Germany = 100)	(73.9)	(100)	(68.4)	(77.2)	(79.0)
Raw material costs (cotton) per kg Yarn	1.6493	1.7971	1.5254	1.7737	1.6635
Freight/insurance costs per kg yarn to Germany	0.2482	—	0.3325	0.3879	0.4271
Sub-total	2.8063	3.0263	2.6985	3.1108	3.0620
EEC duty per kg yarn	0.1964	—	0.1882	0.2178	0.2143
Total CIF (Germany) duty paid costs per kg yarn	3.0027	3.0263	2.8867	3.3286	3.2763
(Germany = 100)	(99.2)	(100)	(95.4)	(110.0)	(108.3)

Source: Organisation for Economic Cooperation and Development, *Textile and Clothing Industries: Structural Problems and Policies in OECD Countries* (Paris, 1983; elsewhere 'OECD Report'), p. 154.

Table 1.7   Manufacturing costs, weaving, 1978 (US$ per yard of fabric)

Cost element	Brazil	Germany	India	Korea	USA
Wage costs	0.0470	0.1966	0.0244	0.0252	0.1049
Energy costs	0.0278	0.0450	0.0293	0.0306	0.0199
Auxiliary material costs	0.0443	0.0362	0.0563	0.0526	0.0364
Capital costs	0.1777	0.1430	0.1789	0.2287	0.1442
Total manufacturing costs	0.2968	0.4208	0.2889	0.3371	0.3054
(Germany = 100)	(70.5)	(100)	(68.7)	(80.1)	(72.6)
Raw material costs (cotton) per yard of fabric	0.3070	0.3345	0.2840	0.3302	0.3097
Yarn costs per yard of fabric (derived from yarn mfg cost comparison)	0.1693	0.2290	0.1566	0.1768	0.1810
Freight/insurance costs per kg yarn to Germany	0.0630	—	0.0378	0.0454	0.0497
Sub-total	0.8361	0.9843	0.7673	0.8895	0.8458
EEC duty per yard of fabric	0.1338	—	0.1228	0.1423	0.1353
Total CIF (Germany) duty paid costs per yard of fabric	0.9699	0.9843	0.8901	1.0318	0.9811
(Germany = 100)	(98.5)	(100)	(90.4)	(104.8)	(99.7)

Source: Organisation for Economic Cooperation and Development, *Textile and Clothing Industries: Structural Problems and Policies in OECD Countries* (Paris, 1983; elsewhere 'OECD Report'), p. 155.

direct contact with the centres of technological progress (as well as the availability of highly-skilled engineering personnel) tends to provide ... a head start, and hence a permanent competitive edge, in the introduction of new labour-saving technologies as well as innovations that save energy and raw materials or improve the quality of standardised products.[78]

One estimate claimed that for low-wage countries to get a substantial competitive price difference of about 20 per cent in industrialised country markets, they would need production costs at least 50 per cent below western costs, with cheap labour the only means of doing so.[79] To summarise, the introduction of the new technologies could 'reverse competitive advantage to the benefit of older industrialised countries, and this all the more as they most closely incarnate the most optimal conditions for the use of these machines.'[80]

The clothing industry, however, remained a more labour-intensive activity throughout the world, with a few exceptions in large production runs in highly industrialised countries.[81] This was compounded by the fact that technological innovation in clothing assembly had been limited, though it did nonetheless progress. The patterning and cutting of fabric for sewing assembly were potentially highly automated and computer-controlled processes,[82] with substantial savings also made by minimising waste (production typically used only about 70 per cent of the total fabric actually required).[83] There was also considerable progress on the speed of sewing machines (but at a certain loss of flexibility in the process), and some automation of other standard processes and new assembly-line organisation techniques substituted machinery for labour.

However, the principal difficulty was the manipulation of fabrics, their positioning for operations, and down-time between operations, not the speed of the machinery or of individual tasks. Faster but more expensive machinery could, furthermore, somewhat sacrifice the convertibility and flexibility of the production unit which is needed to confront rapidly changing markets.[84] The cost of new machinery was prohibitive where production series were short and equipment not used continuously. These difficulties constituted a major obstacle to cost reduction.

This central difficulty of the clothing industry meant that it has tended to remain labour-intensive. How did this reflect on the competitive advantages of the firms in high-wage economies? Several factors partially attenuated the problem. Comparative labour costs 'matter essentially when it comes to exactly the same items.'[85] A process of specialisation and product differentiation could be undertaken, not as a defensive abandonment of labour-intensive product ranges, but in the sense of a positive use of new fabrics, higher quality inputs, and innovative fashion designs than was possible in most low-wage producer countries. Moreover, the low capital-intensity of clothing manufacture was much less relevant whenever it was possible, technically and economically, to break up the process of production,[86] often through transnationalisation and intra-industry trade. This was the justification of a positive use of foreign sourcing or overseas subsidiaries to maintain competitive national clothing production. Finally, adaptation to local markets and design functions were crucial advantages; a lack of knowledge of rapidly changing market conditions could constitute considerable costs to overseas producers. New products in volatile fashion markets could be out in a few days, well before the low-cost countries could make shipments. Rationalisation and innovation in the realm of product choice was important and proved crucial to the Italian success story.

Two different types of firm strategies emerged to confront the two apparently opposing imperatives of sufficient economies of scale to amortise the cost of modernisation on the one hand, and small, flexible production units to respond to rapid changes in fashion markets on the other.[87] However, the use of the most modern production management techniques, foreign sourcing, improving quality, and using adapted marketing strategies (such as the promotion of brand-names as in the Lacoste, Benetton, Levis, and other examples) could have married these two objectives in many cases. Such possibilities prompted Maurice Bidermann, then a leading French men's clothing manufacturer, to state that even the most standard items – T-shirts and blue jeans – could be produced in France. 'Any clothing article manufactured in under thirty minutes can be repatriated [from overseas production],' he said in 1982.[88]

Though in clothing the problem of labour-intensity remained, it should by now be clear that the firms in the high-wage OECD countries in fact had considerable room for manoeuvre to adapt to the challenge of globalisation in the textile and clothing sector. If a national industry declined precipitously, it was not due to some mystical, predatory force, which is the way the international division of labour and the pattern of comparative advantage was often portrayed by the industry and its supporters. The strategies of the firms involved in the sector were crucial variables in the success of the sector, and it was more than possible to achieve a competitive advantage in terms of cost. As was discussed in the Introduction in relation to the new international trade theorists, the pattern of specialisation in global trade is as much the result of state policies and historical practices than differences in national factor endowments.

(b) Competition in Developed Country Markets

This point is further strengthened by an analysis of the evolving pattern of global trade in textile and clothing products throughout the crisis period of the 1970s and 1980s. While the growth of imports from low-wage producers to the advanced industrial economies was dramatic, a closer analysis reveals that these imports were limited in terms of the product ranges involved and in absolute terms, and there were considerable variations according to the country involved.

Furthermore, it is crucial to place the rise of import levels in the light of improved export performance of most of the advanced economies and the emergence of transnational production strategies of many of the textile and clothing firms in the OECD area. The transnationalisation of production was in itself a source of imports from low-cost sources, although the impact of foreign direct investment is not as great as the practice of foreign sourcing.

To start with the global picture (see Tables 1.8 and 1.9),[89] in the textile sector taken on its own, imports from the LDCs to the advanced economies of Western Europe and North America constituted 15 per cent of the total in 1963. Ten years later they were only 13 per cent, rising to 15 per cent in 1976 and declining marginally to 14 per cent in 1978. Of far greater importance in terms of import competition were the imports which originated from within the group of advanced economies themselves. In 1963 in textiles this accounted for 73 per cent of the total, and this level had increased slightly to 75 per cent by 1978. By far the majority of trade competition in the sector took place *among the advanced economies.*

In keeping with the greater importance of labour cost advantages in the clothing industry, the growth of imports in this sector was more substantial. In 1963 imports from LDCs to the same group of industrialised countries was a moderate 19 per cent of total imports, but by 1973 this proportion had risen to 31 per cent, to 40 per cent in 1976, with a marginal decline to 38 per cent in 1978. Growth was, then, dramatic in the 1970s but tended to level off towards the end of the

Table 1.8 Real growth rates of clothing and textile imports to the industrialised countries of Western Europe and North America, 1963–78 (% per annum)

	Clothing			Textiles		
	1963–73	*1973–76*	*1976–78*	*1963–73*	*1973–76*	*1976–78*
LDCs	21.8	14.4	4.6	6.9	−0.4	2.5
Southern Europe	28.8	6.4	4.8	13.8	−0.8	5.8
Planned economies	30.5	7.9	7.1	12.5	0.1	1.6
Developed countries	11.7	−0.4	7.3	7.8	−4.5	4.4
World	15.3	5.6	6	8	−3.6	4.1

Source: Donald B. Keesing and Martin Wolf, 'Questions on International Trade in Textiles and Clothing', *The World Economy*, vol. 4/1, March 1981, p. 94.

Table 1.9   Changing shares held by competing suppliers of imports to
industrialised Western European and North American countries, 1963–78
(in %)

Supplier	Clothing				Textiles			
	1963	*1973*	*1976*	*1978*	*1963*	*1973*	*1976*	*1978*
LDCs	19	31	40	38	15	13	15	14
Southern Europe	3	8	8	8	3	5	5	5
Planned economies	1	5	5	5	2	3	4	3
Japan	9	3	2	1	7	3	3	3
Other developed	68	53	45	48	73	76	73	75
World	100	100	100	100	100	100	100	100

Source: Donald B. Keesing and Martin Wolf, 'Questions on International
Trade in Textiles and Clothing', *The World Economy*, vol. 4/1, March 1981,
p. 95.

decade. It must remembered, however, that 'imports' in many cases
had a high domestic content, the product of foreign sourcing strategies
of firms which often benefited from outward processing[90] customs
duty treatment by their governments.[91] The share of the advanced
economies in total clothing imports mirrored this movement, falling
from 68 per cent in 1963 to 48 per cent (49 per cent if one includes
Japan) in 1978.

There are some important qualifications to these broad trends.
Some countries, such as Finland and (most notably) Italy and were net
exporters of even clothing products. Furthermore, most LDCs
exported relatively simple products such as mass-market clothing or
unfinished cotton cloth, products with relatively low unit values.[92]
Although this changed over time as LDC production, particularly
from Asian 'tiger' producers grew in sophistication, nonetheless product differentiation and quick response to changing local market
conditions remained a successful strategy for firms in high-wage
economies. The fact is that much of high-wage production was not in
competition with products from LDC exporters, even in clothing
production where the wage advantage was most marked: 'labour costs
matter essentially when it comes to the production of exactly the *same*
items.'[93] Growing quality consciousness and the search for novelty
meant that many products are not produced abroad. Low-wage producers could only take advantage of their labour costs where mass-
market, standardised items of low unit value were concerned.

The argument that the impact of low-wage imports on the textile and clothing industries of advanced industrial countries is reinforced by the evidence presented by Cline that there have been very few job losses in Western Europe and North America which were attributable to import competition from whatever source. In the case of the United States, on which the most extensive discussion is developed,[94] Cline argues that textile imports had a positive impact on employment from 1972 to 1977, and even as the dollar rose to unprecedented heights in the 1980s the contribution of imports to employment decline in the sector was only one sixth that of productivity growth.

While in textiles import growth played a minor role in employment contraction, it was more marked in the US clothing industry. Still, it was not until the 1982–5 high dollar period that imports began to rival productivity growth as a source of employment reduction. With the exception of Great Britain, Cline argues that the situation was similar for Japan and Western Europe; for producers such as Italy, the impact of trade on employment has been heavily positive.[95] Even in Germany, where most of the clothing industry was transferred abroad through outward processing or overseas direct investment, it was estimated across the industry that for every job lost to imports from the LDCs, some fifty were lost through productivity gains, and that falling demand represented job losses twenty times those attributable to LDC imports for any single year of the 1970s.[96]

Another point to be made is that imports must be measured against the domestic market and against the export performance of the industrialised countries. A better picture of the impact of imports is therefore developed when penetration ratios (imports as a proportion of domestic consumption) and net trade ratios (exports minus imports as a proportion of domestic consumption) are employed (see Table 1.10). This shows respectively the segment of the market taken up by imports, and the value of imports not compensated for by exports. In the United States, imports in 1980 accounted for only 4.5 per cent of domestic textile consumption, or 16.7 per cent for the clothing industry.[97] In Italy, which one must be reminded had the largest textile and apparel trade surplus of *any* producer country, was more penetrated by imports at 18.3 per cent and 23.5 per cent respectively. However, net trade as a proportion of consumption was plus 10.5 per cent (textiles) and 112.6 per cent (clothing), reflecting strong overall performance, but only plus 2.1 per cent and minus 14 per cent for the United States. Germany had a high level of import penetration (34.7 per cent for textiles, 53.7 per cent for clothing), but very successful

Table 1.10   Trends in import penetration and net trade balance of major
industrial countries, 1970–80 (%)

	Textiles		Apparel	
	m/c	*(x−m)/c*	*m/c*	*(x−m)/c*
United States				
1970	4.5	−2.0	6.4	−5.3
1980	4.4	2.1	16.7	−14.0
Germany				
1973	27.2	3.0	32.1	−35.0
1980	34.7	−2.8	53.7	−20.6
France				
1980	26.0	−4.4	28.3	−3.5
Italy				
1973	15.2	10.4	12.5	73.0
1980	18.3	10.5	23.5	112.6
United Kingdom				
1970	14.1	7.1	13.5	−1.2
1980	32.9	−2.4	38.6	−14.1
Japan				
1970	4.0	14.9	4.4	18.5
1980	7.4	10.1	10.7	−7.2

m = imports; c = apparent consumption; x = exports.

Source: William R. Cline, *The Future of World Trade in Textiles and Apparel*, rev. edn (Washington, DC: Institute for International Economics, 1990), calculated from table 5.4. GATT, *Textiles and Clothing*, 1984, appx IV, p. 61; GATT, *International Trade 1982/83*, table A-7; and United Nations, *Yearbook of Industrial Statistics*, 1976.

export performance in textiles compensated for this to yield a net trade balance measured against consumption of only minus 2.8 per cent, and a deficit for clothing of 20.6 per cent which actually improved over the 1973 figure. The upshot of this discussion is that, if penetration ratios from *all* import sources, as given in the figures above, are seldom more than a quarter of domestic consumption, and if imports from LDC origins are a minority of total imports across the sector in most high-wage countries, then it is difficult to argue that the international division of labour was shifting inexorably in the favour of low-wage producers.

It would be useful to turn to France as a detailed example, especially as it is argued in this book that France was one of the key supporters of an increasingly protectionist MFA quota system. Here import growth was considerable but the case once again illustrates the extent to which imports as a factor in the industry's decline can be greatly exaggerated. The general picture is one of a significant deterioration of the French trade balance in textiles and in clothing, but the impact of import competition from the LDCs appears relatively limited. The French industry had more difficulty coping with imports from countries where there was no wage advantage, and in fact French specialisation in certain fashion products meant that the clothing industry remained in a situation of trade surplus longer than the textile balance.

In France, using a 1980 figure, imports only accounted for 26.3 per cent of the combined domestic market for textile and clothing products.[98] The *net* penetration ratio in value terms, namely

$$[(\text{Exports} - \text{Imports}) \div \text{Apparent domestic consumption} \times 100]$$

which measures the actual value of imports not compensated for by exports, for 1978 was only 9.7 per cent for clothing articles, where the LDCs have made their greatest inroads.[99] As each of these figures includes imports from *all* sources, of which the low-cost countries were only a minority part, it is clear that only a limited proportion of the market was actually displaced by the LDCs.[100]

At this juncture, it is worth rehearsing several important facts about French trade in textiles and clothing, which can be easily ascertained from trade figures.[101] First, imports from industrialised, 'high-cost' countries constituted the great majority on the French market. In fact, France imported more in relative terms from industrialised countries than she exported to them; twelve industrialised nations were the destination for 78 per cent of France's exports (1983) and the same twelve, with minor changes, were the source of *83 per cent* of imports.[102] Low-cost sources were in the minority, and the LDCs themselves only accounted for a portion of these (other low-cost suppliers were the Mediterranean countries and the then East Bloc). In most cases, particularly in textiles (where the French trade balance was weakest), LDC imports were simply not proportionately important enough to have caused the type of market disruption which is often attributed to them. Second, it can be established that France was *less* penetrated by extra-EU sources, the most of which were low-cost (excepting the United States, Canada, Japan and Australia–New Zealand), than her industrialised competitors. The EU as a whole received about 65 per cent of its clothing imports from LDC sources in 1980;[103] in the case of France this same proportion was only 25 per cent in 1979.[104] The bulk of market displacement was the result of *high-wage competition.* Ultimately, all that can be claimed is that LDC exports to France grew rapidly in absolute terms throughout the 1970s, particularly prior to the conclusion of the second MFA accord in 1977.[105]

The difference between textile as opposed to clothing import levels is also instructive. On the French market, LDC imports were usually of low unit value, consisting of cotton and/or synthetic/mixed-cotton-and-synthetic fabrics, sometimes in an unfinished state. These were products which depended little on tastes or fashion for their success.[106] This point is important – in keeping with the overall picture for advanced economies, but to a greater extent, LDC imports to France were limited not only in their absolute levels, but also in terms of the types of products concerned and their relevant unit values.

This is doubly significant when superimposed upon the overall structure of the French trade balance. Relative to the global pattern for most industrialised countries, the French balance in textile and clothing trade was weakest in the upstream textile activities, where industrialised-country competition was overwhelmingly predominant.[107] Conversely, the French industry was relatively resistant in the clothing sector, precisely where LDC competition is most intense. It is not insignificant that France managed to maintain the entire production stream from fibre and yarn production to finished clothing relatively intact, battered as it was in some places. The strong position in women's clothing trade for a long time prevented the overall sector going into deficit, and made the situation much more favourable than, for instance, in the UK, which lost most of its downstream activities to low-cost competition.[108] Germany, Japan, Holland, Switzerland and Austria, and to an extent the USA, also disengaged from their downstream textile activities.[109] The French industry *did* resist low-cost competition relatively well, even in downstream production where these producers were well-placed in terms of cost advantages.

It is perhaps most telling that industrialists, the main supporters of the low-wage import invasion thesis, were rather vulnerable when making such accusations. At the same time as professional associations clamoured for protection from the foreign clothing devil, many firms were busy fostering these imports to their own advantage, through reimports either from overseas production facilities or foreign sourcing, mainly outward processing. This was something that left-wing opinion seldom failed to point out.[110] There was considerable ambivalence in the position of the employers' Union des Industries Textile which demanded better insulation from imports while producing a white paper on how firms might profit from channelling imports from South-East Asia and the Maghreb.[111]

CONCLUSION

This chapter has established three main points by presenting some of the essential material underpinnings of the trade policy process in the textile and clothing sectors of advanced industrial countries. First, it has been demonstrated that the textile and clothing industries of the high-wage economies, while they have declined relative to a number of other sectors and some have undergone more dramatic downsizing, they still remain major employers and constitute sizeable proportions of manufacturing output in most economies. The second point was that the textile and clothing sectors of most advanced countries went through a period of persistent and often difficult adjustment throughout the 1970s and into the 1980s. This corresponded to a generalised downturn in most leading economic indicators and a situation of persistent industrial crisis across a number of the older manufacturing sectors (steel, leather goods, shipbuilding, autos) in Western Europe, North America, and to a lesser extent Japan.

If these two points are combined, there is a prima facie case for asserting that the adjustment problems of the textile and clothing industries of the advanced economies was a politically salient development in the ongoing economic policy processes of these countries. To add to this, the regional distribution of the textile and clothing industries in many countries accentuated this prima facie political salience: whole communities often depended on the fortunes of these sectors for their economic survival, and in some situations the crises of the older industrial sectors was cumulative. The American 'rust belt' or the French Nord-Pas-de-Calais regions suffered a simultaneous downturn in steel, auto, and textile and clothing sectors throughout the 1970s and 1980s. The sector was bound to be sensitive in the eyes of policy-makers. This period of course correlates to the persistent strengthening of the MFA system of textile and clothing import quotas in the international trade regime.

The third point is that there was no inevitability in the decline of those textile and clothing sectors which suffered the greatest contraction. Adjustment of firm strategies and the reduction of employment levels as investment in productivity improvements were implemented was indeed a necessary development if the production stream were to survive largely intact in high-wage economies. Nonetheless, the 'competitive equation' was sufficiently complex and admitted of a sufficient variety of factor combinations that sophisticated entrepreneurs could survive and prosper despite a levelling off of the growth rate of demand in the market, which was generalised across the industrialised countries.[112] The main thrust of intensifying competition came from the industrialised, high-wage economies anyway, although more in textiles than in the clothing industry. Many industrialised countries therefore improved their trade performance in the textile and clothing sector despite competition from low-wage producers. A wide variety of company strategies yielding success was possible, and absolute decline in production levels and a fall in domestic market share of home producers, while a frequent occurrence, was not the result of some inexorable shift in the international division of labour.

This last point links up with the discussion of comparative versus competitive advantage in the Introduction, and the point about firms as important actors in the global political economy and, specifically in this case, the trade regime. The firms and their entrepreneurial strategies act as 'bearers' of structure – the economic structure constituted by the changing international division of labour and the global market for textile and clothing products. This demonstrates that structure can only be properly understood in terms of the agents through which it is constituted. International trade cannot be thought of in economically deterministic terms, and is as much dependent on political and institutional variables than any 'pure' analysis of economic structures themselves, and this is increasingly accepted by economists theorising the new international economics. As this aspect of the argument is developed in further chapters, an image of the market as a complex social institution into which is integrated the political institutions of states in the international system will emerge.

Finally, the evidence presented in the chapter provides initial grounds for the assertion in the Introduction that policy-makers must be cautious in the implementation of trade liberalisation strategies as part of economic policy. Even though successful competitive strategies in the textile and clothing sector *were* possible, the fact that many firms clearly did not take advantage of the opportunities available meant that the material underpinnings of liberalisation in the sector were inherently unstable in the period under consideration. A sounder socio-economic base would be required in the sector if international cooperation to achieve trade liberalisation were to yield sufficiently

well-distributed benefits to enough of the interested coalitions involved
so as to succeed in the longer run.

Notes

1. For a more complete account of the economics of the sector in the 1970s
    and 1980s, see by way of example: T.G. Taylor, *The Role of the Textile
    Industry in a Developed Economy* (PhD thesis, University of Wales,
    Swansea, November 1981); OECD Report; Brian Toyne *et al.*, *The
    Global Textile Industry* (London: Allen & Unwin, 1984); and more
    recently, William R. Cline, *The Future of World Trade in Textiles and
    Apparel*, rev. edn (Washington, DC: Institute for International Eco-
    nomics, 1990).
2. Capital intensity in a modern textile firm is quite high among industrial
    activities; see Toyne *et. al.*, *The Global Textile Industry*, op. cit., espe-
    cially pt 1, pp. 19–20.
3. France, Assemblée Nationale, *Rapport fait au nom de la commission
    d'enquête parlementaire chargée d'examiner les problèmes de de l'industrie
    textile et les moyens à mettre en oeuvre pour les resoudre*, 6ᵉ législature,
    no. 2254, 18 March 1981, vol. ı, p. 122; hereafter referred to as 'National
    Assembly Report'.
4. Laurent Benzoni, 'Le Textile: industrie de l'avenir', in Bertrand Bellon
    and Jean-Marie Chevalier (eds), *L'Industrie en France* (Paris: Flam-
    marion 1983), p. 95.
5. Union des Industries Textiles, *L'Industrie textile française*, annual
    (Paris: UIT, 1982), p. 6.
6. OECD Report, p. 29.
7. Ibid., p. 15, following *UN Yearbook of Industrial Statistics* (annual), and
    OECD, *Textile Industry in OECD Countries* (annual).
8. Calculated from France, Institut National de la Statistique et des Etudes
    Economiques (INSEE), 'Entreprises non-finançières en termes de
    comptabilité d'entreprises', unpublished series (not adjusted for infla-
    tion), 1960; 1970–82 (hereafter referred to as 'INSEE unpublished
    series').
9. OECD Report, p. 15.
10. Laurent Benzoni, 'Le Textile', op. cit., p. 93.
11. Even in the late 1980s, the textile and clothing sector remained the single
    largest manufacturing employer in the United States; see Lane Steven
    Hurewitz, *Textiles*, a volume in the series by Terence P. Stewart (ed.),
    The GATT Uruguay Round 1986–1992: A Negotiating History (Dor-
    drecht: Kluwer Law and Taxation, 1993), p. 68, note 366.
12. In the US there had been a steady drift from the New England and
    north-eastern states to the southern states, such as the Carolinas and
    Georgia, in search of lower labour costs.

13.   Arthur Knight, *Private Enterprise and Public Intervention: The Courtaulds Experience* (London: Allen & Unwin, 1974), pp. 42–45.
14.   Robin Anson and Paul Simpson, *World Textile Trade and Production Trends*, Special Report no. 1108 (London: Economist Intelligence Unit, June 1988), p. 249.
15.   The following figures are taken from France, Conseil Economique et Social, 'Le Devenir des industries du textile et de l'habillement,' *Journal Officiel* (Avis et Rapports du Conseil Economique et Social), 25 February 1982; p. 221; hereafter referred to as 'CES Report'. See also Victor Prévot, *Géographie des textiles*, Paris: Masson 1979, and 'L'Industrie textile', *Economie-Géographie*, no. 192, February 1982.
16.   'L'Industrie textile,' *Economie-Géographie*, p. 2.
17.   These figures on the US are taken from William R. Cline, *The Future of World Trade in Textiles and Apparel* (Washington, DC: Institute for International Economics, 1990), pp. 83–92.
18.   Robert Jim Berrier, *The Politics of Industrial Survival: The French Textile Industry*, Unpublished PhD thesis, Massachussetts Institute of Technology, 1978, p. 40.
19.   OECD Report, p. 25.
20.   Berrier, *The Politics of Industrial Survival*, op. cit., pp. 40–64.
21.   See J-P. Gilly and François Morin, *Les Groupes industriels en France: la concentration de l'appareil productif depuis 1945* (Paris: Notes et Etudes Documentaires nos. 4605-6, La Documentation Française, 1981).
22.   Benoît Boussemart and Jean-Claude Rabier, *Le Dossier Agache-Willot – un capitalisme à contre-courant* (Paris: Presses de la Fondation Nationale des Sciences Politiques, 1983), p. 31.
23.   Defined by INSEE as those with under 500 employees, or, alternatively, with under FF100 million in turnover.
24.   Calculations from INSEE, unpublished series 1971–81, changing proportions of small, medium, and large firms in textile and clothing activities; proportion of the sector's turnover produced by small, medium, and large firms.
25.   CES Report, p. 219.
26.   See France, Ministère de l'Industrie (Centre d'Etudes et de Prévision), *Les Entreprises en très forte croissance* (Paris: La Documentation Française, 1981), p. 40.
27.   See the section on corporate structure and sectoral performance in Chapter 2.
28.   These are characterised by their family-owned structure, low investment levels, poor export performance, antiquated production processes, low profitability, and traditional management practices lacking in innovation and marketing strategies.
29.   H. Richard Friman, *Patchwork Protectionism: Textile Trade Policy in the United States, Japan, and West Germany* (Ithaca: Cornell University Press, 1990), ch. 6.
30.   See W.M. Corden and G. Fels (eds), *Public Assistance to Industry: Protection and Subsidies in Britain and Germany* (London: Macmillan, 1976), esp. ch. 6 by Neu.
31.   Cline, *The Future of World Trade*, op. cit., p. 135.

32. OECD Report, pp. 139–40.
33. Cline, *The Future of World Trade*, op. cit., p. 136.
34. Ibid., p. 125.
35. OECD Report, p. 140.
36. The above figures from Cline, *The Future of World Trade*, op. cit., pp. 25–9.
37. Donald B. Keesing and Martin Wolf, 'Questions on International Trade in Textiles and Clothing', *The World Economy*, vol. 4/1, March 1981, p. 92, after *UN Yearbook of International Trade Statistics*.
38. OECD Report, p. 52, after UN Commodity Trade Statistics and GATT.
39. Cline, *The Future of World Trade*, op. cit., p. 49.
40. Philippe Meunier, 'L'Evolution des échanges et de la pénétration étrangère dans le secteur du textile et de l'habillement', *Chroniques de l'Actualité de la SEDEIS*, vol. 24/12, 15 June 1981, p. 398.
41. OECD Report, p. 48.
42. A drop of only 13.2 per cent from 1973 to 1981, a period of more severe job losses in a number of countries; *UN Yearbook of Industrial Statistics*, 1981.
43. Cline, *The Future of World Trade*, op. cit., p. 128.
44. Ibid., p. 135.
45. OECD Report, pp. 27–8; see also Pierre Dubois and Giusto Barisi, *Le Défi technologique dans l'industrie de l'habillement: les stratégies des entrepreneurs français et italiens* (Paris: CNRS, Groupe Sociologie du Travail, 1982).
46. See figures from Union des Industries Textiles, *L'Industrie textile française* op. cit., p. 6, and from France, Sénat, *Rapport au nom de la commission d'enquête parlementaire chargée d'examiner les difficultés de l'industrie du textile et de l'habillement*, 2ᵉ session ordinaire de 1980–1981, no. 282, 6 June 1981, p. 212 (hereafter referred to as 'Senate Report'), after Centre Textile de Conjoncture et d'Observation Economique (Paris).
47. Senate Report, p. 212, p. 220; Micheline Vincent, 'Vingt Ans du textile-habillement', *Economie et statistique*, no. 138, November 1981, p. 26, based on figures from the Comptabilité Nationale.
48. Senate Report, p. 221; p. 223.
49. Including the operation of Engel's law (see Introduction, note 26). As aggregate levels of wealth increased, households spent proportionately more on goods such as culture and recreation, health, transport, and housing and less on basic necessities. Food and clothing fell considerably as a proportion of household expenditure (Senate Report, p. 221). Likewise, income elasticities for clothing products declined, making consumers more sensitive to price. There was also a noticeable shift in consumer preferences *within* the overall range of textile and clothing products (Pierre Hoffmeister, 'Le Textile européenne: secteur en crise', *Revue d'economie politique*, 6, 1980, p. 931, and National Assembly Report, vol. iii, p. 52; p. 55). Home furnishings were more in demand, and traditional wearing apparel such as suits, overcoats, women's fashion ensembles, and so on are increasingly replaced by lighter, more casual garments and sportswear products.

50. See tables on imports of textile and clothing products by geographic zone, in Union des Industries Textiles, *Statistique générale de l'industrie textile française*, (Paris: UIT, annual).

51. CES Report, p. 213. This compares unfavourably with the average for industry, which climbed from 100 in 1973 to 115 in 1979.

52. Taylor, *The Role of the Textile*, op. cit., pp. 440, 445–6, explains the economic mechanisms behind the decline of the textile sector in an industrialised economy.

53. National Assembly Report, vol. ɪ, p. 50 (figures adjusted for inflation).

54. This can be clearly seen from INSEE Unpublished Series on employment in the sector, from which growth rates can be calculated.

55. National Assembly Report, vol. ɪ, p. 59.

56. CES Report, p. 217.

57. France appears to have been the major exception to an OECD general rule: the OECD pointed out, referring to the textile and clothing industries of OECD nations, that 'The share of the textile industry in investment has been declining over time, but by no more than its share in production...the circumstantial evidence...does not suggest any *disproportionate* [original emphasis] reduction of investment activity in the textile industry' (OECD Report, p. 14).

58. This is the subject of extensive literature. See for example Suzanne Berger, 'The Traditional Sector in France and Italy', in Berger and Michael J. Piore, *Dualism and Discontinuity in Industrial Societies* (Cambridge University Press 1980); 'Comment' by D. Goldey on article by Suzanne Berger in H. Machin and V. Wright, *Economic Policy and Policy-Making under the Mitterrand Presidency 1981–1984* (London: Pinter, 1985). For a historical account, see Jean Lambert, *Le Patron* (Brussels: Bloud and Gay, 1969).

59. Cline, *The Future of World Trade*, op. cit., p. 123–5.

60. Keesing and Wolf, 'Questions on International Trade', op. cit., p. 92.

61. Cline, *The Future of World Trade*, op. cit., p. 124.

62. OECD Report, p. 49.

63. Cline, *The Future of World Trade*, op. cit., pp. 116–17, after *UN Yearbook of Industrial Statistics*.

64. See Friman on the US, Japan, and Germany; G.R.D. Underhill, *The Politics of Domestic Economic Management in an Era of International Capital*, unpublished DPhil thesis, University of Oxford, 1987, on France.

65. Keesing and Wolf, 'Questions on International Trade', op. cit., p. 99.

66. For example, 66 per cent of French fibre consumption in 1978; National Assembly Report, vol. ɪ, p. 52.

67. OECD Report, p. 18, p. 20. Also, Paul Wagner, 'Textile: la technique va tout changer', *L'Usine nouvelle*, no. 39, 27 September 1979, p. 106

68. For a more complete account of technological developments, see CES Report, pp. 245–250, also Wagner, 'Textile: la technique'; op. cit. and Anson and Simpson, *World Textile Trade*, op. cit. The following discussion draws largely on these accounts, except where noted otherwise.

69. OECD Report, p. 21.

70. See cost per workpost estimates in Communauté Economique Européenne, Commission, *Communication de la Commission au Conseil sur la situation et les perspectives de l'industrie du textile et de l'habillement*, COM(81) Final (Brussels, 27 July 1981; hereafter referred to as 'EC Report'), pp. 10–14.

71. Ibid., p. 11.

72. OECD Report, p. 84.

73. Ibid.

74. Ibid., p. 88; see also footnote 108, same page.

75. See Centre d'Etudes Prospectives et d'Informations Internationales (CEPII), *Les Economies industrialisées face à la concurrence du tiers-monde* (Paris: CEPII, August 1978; hereafter referred to as 'CEPII Report'), pp. 72–8, for the example of South Korea. In the late 1970s, imports of textile machinery into Korea were severely restricted in order to encourage the growth of a domestic textile machine tool industry. South Korea is now a growing exporter of such machinery, while rising wage costs are placing considerable pressure on the clothing industry.

76. OECD Report, p. 88.

77. Ibid.

78. Ibid.; this is particularly true of the introduction of computer-controlled processes, which require highly skilled maintenance and engineering staff and close cooperation between machine manufacturers and factory operators.

79. CEPII, op. cit., p. 65.

80. Benoît Boussemart and Jean-Claude Rabier, *Le Dossier Agache-Willot: un capitalisme à contre-courant* (Paris: Presses de la Fondation Nationale des Sciences Politiques, 1983), p. 26.

81. OECD Report, p. 83.

82. See David Bowen, 'Dream Factory', *Independent on Sunday*, 18 February 1996, p. B-1, feature article on the Italian clothing manufacturing firm Benetton.

83. CES Report, p. 248.

84. OECD Report, p. 23.

85. Ibid., p. 88.

86. Ibid., p. 85.

87. See Robert Weisz, 'Stratégies d'entreprises et modes de gestion dans l'industrie de l'habillement', *Revue française de gestion*, no. 39, January–February 1983, pp. 85–95, where there is good discussion of strategies and types of firms in clothing manufacture, and how they conflict and compete with each other. See also Dubois and Barisi, op. cit.

88. Hélène Pichenot, 'Habillement: Comment se retailler une place?; in *L'Usine nouvelle*, no. 26, 24 June 1982, p. 56.

89. The following figures are taken from Keesing and Wolf, 'Questions on International Trade', op. cit., p. 95.

90. Foreign sourcing must here be distinguished from outward processing. Foreign sourcing is the generic term for the practice of obtaining inputs from overseas. In the textile and clothing sector this usually meant exporting fabric and reimporting it as finished clothing, though imports of intermediary inputs also count as foreign sourcing. Outward

processing is essentially the same practice, but includes special state trade policy measures which permit the reimportation of finished clothing articles with customs duties applied only to the amount of value added performed overseas, a substantial advantage to domestic producers. This distinction will prove important in Chapter 5.

91. OECD Report, pp. 53, 58. This rise in clothing imports from LDCs must also be set against the dramatic *decline* of LDC fibre exports to advanced economies, a trend explained by rise of man-made fibres in textile and clothing production; see ibid., p. 46.

92. Keesing and Wolf, 'Questions on International Trade', op. cit., p. 86; Michel Texier, 'L'Industrie française de l'habillement', *Bulletin du Crédit National*, 2e trimestre, 1979, p. 46.

93. OECD Report, p. 88 (original emphasis).

94. Cline, *The Future of World Trade*, op. cit., pp. 92–7.

95. Ibid., p. 125.

96. From Sergio Spoerer, 'Industrie textile: où en sont les véritables concurrences?', in *Faim-Développement*, no. 82–3, March 1982, p. 9, citing figures from UNCTAD, *Fibres et textiles: dimensions du pouvoir des sociétés transnationales* (Geneva: UNCTAD, 1981).

97. The following figures are taken from Cline, *The Future of World Trade*, op. cit., p. 124.

98. Alain Bentejac, 'L'Industrie textile française à l'heure des négociations AMF: situation actuelle et perspectives d'avenir', *Revue du Marché Commun*, no. 460, October 1982, p. 478.

99. OECD Report, p. 56.

100. See Union des Industries Textile, *Statistique générale*, op. cit., years 1971–82, series on French Imports by Geographic Zone of origin (Paris: UIT, 1971–82); Evolution of French Imports of Textile and Clothing Products 1970–1979 by Supplier Zone, National Assembly Report, vol. III, p. 172; proportion of total imports and trade balance by supplier zone, National Assembly Report, vol. III, p. 169.

101. Calculations from annexe 3 of Benoît Boussemart, *Industrie de main d'oeuvre et division internationale du travail: l'avenir de l'industrie textile de la région Nord-Pas-de-Calais*, 3 vols, unpublished thesis, Doctorat ès en Sciences Economiques, Université de Paris X (Nanterre), December 1984, based on French Customs Statistics; also Union des Industries Textile, *Statistique générale de l'industrie textile française*, foreign trade figures (Paris: UIT, various years).

102. 'L'Industrie textile', *Economie-Géographie*, op. cit., p. 14.

103. EC Report, p. 20.

104. National Assembly Report, vol. III, p. 172.

105. See ibid., p. 172, and figures on the proportion of MFA signatory exporters in the textile and clothing imports of signatory developed countries 1973–9, National Assembly Report, vol. III, p. 238, after GATT sources.

106. Texier, 'L'Industrie française', op. cit., p. 46.

107. See Boussemart, *Industrie de main d'oeuvre*, op. cit., trade balance figures in annexe 3.

108. Taylor, *The Role of the Textile Industry*, op. cit., pp. 130–1.

109. CEPII Report, p. 44.
110. See for example *L'Humanité*, 21 May 1977, or Confédération Française et Démocratique du Travail (CFDT), Fédération Habillement-Cuir-Textile, *Livre Blanc pour le maintien et le développement des industries textiles, habillement, et cuirs en France* (CFDT, October 1978), p. 4.
111. 'Textile-Habillement: autant en emporte le redéploiement', *L'Economie en questions*, no. 16, April–June 1981, p. 20.
112. Texier, 'L'Industrie française', op. cit., p. 43.

2 International Competition, Domestic Industrial Crisis, and the Strategies of Firms

It has been argued that competitive firm strategies were indeed possible during the rise of the MFA accord, despite the competition from low-wage producers of textile and clothing products. This chapter will analyse the causes of the crisis in those advanced countries where the firms, despite the potential, failed to adapt. Thus the political economy of liberalisation began to work its way on the sector, the 'feedback effect' giving rise to defensive sectoral strategies aimed at adjusting the scope of international competition to the limits of the politically possible, rather than adjustment of the strategies of firms to the limits of the competitively successful. The state was permeated by particularistic interests which sought to structure the market in their own image.

It will be demonstrated that the failure to adapt was not rooted in any innate characteristics of international comparative advantage in the textile and clothing sector, but was allied to several developments to which firms in France and the UK in particular, as well as in other countries, declined to adapt. These changes consisted first of shifting patterns of consumer demand for the industry's products, which involved the elaboration of more sophisticated and flexible/sensitive marketing strategies for producers to be successful. Second, the technological developments described in the previous chapter demanded changes in investment behaviour, changes which often failed to materialise where traditional firms were concerned. Third, firms were able effectively to 'capture' state decision-making processes and to control the policy agenda in the increasingly sombre industrial climate. State policy instruments were used to limit competition and to block the process of adjustment which was both possible and necessary if the industry were to avoid a serious decline and loss of market share. Finally, these developments were of course linked to the dynamics of liberalisation itself, with the intensified competition on both domestic and third markets which resulted.

In the end, traditional textile and clothing firms found themselves caught between an adherence to traditional industrial cultures on the one hand, and intensifying pressures of shifting demand functions and growing transnationalisation of production and market structures, with the implication of intensified competition, on the other. In the case of the United States and in particular key countries in the European Union, coalitions of textile and clothing interests used their institutionalised political resources to block adjustment to the emerging realities of competition and change. This capture of the political agenda, sometimes through state subsidies but mostly through the protectionist trade policies of the evolving and strengthening MFA, was intended to reshape the market to preserve earlier advantages of firms which were unwilling to adapt. Liberalisation through GATT and the EU had exposed the weaker firms to considerable pressures already, and they responded by contesting the liberal nature of the market. However, they were only successful in attenuating the competition from low-wage producers. Liberalisation within the OECD area left weaker companies exposed to the full force of competition from those firms from advanced economies which had taken it upon themselves to maintain their competitive edge.

This chapter will largely draw on the French example to illustrate these points. It would be difficult in the space available to develop extended comparative examples. While the problems of the French industry have their particularities, they are effectively representative of the sorts of dilemmas which faced most national textile and clothing sectors. In aggregate, French firms confronted these challenges poorly, yet many firms proved the point that failure was far less than inevitable. As the competitive pressures of liberalisation grew, the political resources of the French and other European industries were employed to affect the terms of competition. A parallel process took place in the United States, though on a slightly different time-scale.

While similar stories could be told in segments of nearly any national textile and clothing industry of the advanced economies, the political strategy of the French industry proved central to the regular tightening of the restrictive import regime throughout the 1970s and 1980s. French interests (albeit with important allies) were successfully projected into the trade policies of the European Union as a whole. Producer coalitions sought to redistribute the costs of internationalisation in the face of their own incapacity or unwillingness to accept the sorts of changes which could have underpinned a successful competitive advantage in the sector. Trade policy became the surrogate for industrial strategy at either the firm or national level as interested parties mobilised to confront the results of prior political

decisions to induce a restructuring of the market through liberalisation.

INTERNATIONAL TRADE AND INDUSTRIAL ADJUSTMENT

The discussion in the previous chapter alerts the reader to the complexity of the competitive equation in the textile and clothing sector,
and to the multiplicity of factors involved in determining competitive
positions and patterns of specialisation. What is required at this stage
is a discussion of the factors linking the economic structural changes
borne of liberalisation to the crisis in the sector. This section will
therefore focus on linking on a conceptual as well as empirical level: (i)
the evolution of final demand in the sector, (ii) changing patterns of
international trade competition, and (iii) the strategies of firms in their
context of industrial culture and state policies. This builds on the
discussion in the Introduction to the book, where the concepts of
comparative advantage and competitive advantage were distinguished,
and the importance of new theories of international trade specialisation were highlighted.

The notion of 'competitive advantage' and the ideas of the new trade
theorists have permitted the inclusion of historical, socio-cultural,
institutional, and policy variables in an analysis of patterns of specialisation in international trade and production.[1] This notion of competitive advantage highlighted the role of the firm as the 'bearer' of
economic structure, and also highlighted the insertion of the firm in
the wider processes of the political economy, including the state and its
associated international institutions, demonstrating the limitations of
attempts to explain through structural economic factors alone. This
move away from classical theories of specialisation permits a genuine
political economy approach which conceives of state and market as an
integrated whole.

The analysis in Chapter 1 revealed that firms had to adjust to two
principle imperatives in the textile sector: rapidly changing patterns of
demand, and intensifying domestic and international competition. The
relationship between the two is important. Without markets and the
demand functions they imply, production makes little sense. Nonetheless, there is a tendency for many studies of international trade to
focus solely upon production factors and the resulting international
trade flows, a result of undue emphasis on national factor endowments
and aptitudes. The problems of industrial adjustment must take

account of these 'multiple parameters'[2] of international trade specialisation. What is important is *how* the key factors of demand (markets) and comparative costs operate in relation to each other in a particular sector.

Demand is dynamic and is rooted in the socio-economic fabric: consumers of different categories, with different needs, wants, tastes, habits, and income levels constitute 'demand', including industrialists who use intermediary goods. Demand is therefore in constant evolution, and there are many combinations of socio-economic factors and economic policies which influence demand structure. Demand becomes the arbiter of productive activity through the structure of the market. The pattern of international competition indicates the relative competitive positions of firms. If competition translates the competitive positions of firms, then it often renders a cruel judgement by eliminating some and promoting others.

However, successful competition on global markets implies a *simultaneous* response of firms to the dynamics of domestic and international demand functions (markets) on the one hand, and an ability to compete with other firms on the basis of cost, on the other. Having the best cost structures in terms of production is of little use if the products do not suit the market, and having the right products, or even quality, is of little use if costs are not competitive. Patterns of demand and of international competition thus form two important parametres of the industrial adjustment process. Furthermore, the dynamics of demand and of global competition are interrelated in the responses of firms. In attempting to respond to the challenges of shifting demand and patterns of competition, firms constantly restructure the market over time, manipulating sociological factors such as tastes or fashion through product innovation, and competitive factors such as technology, organisational strategies, labour skills, and other elements of production costs.

However, this picture should not be thought of in simple economic terms, of competition and the market. The strategies of firms includes their insertion in the policy processes of the state. It is the overall resources of firms as agents in the international political economy, including their political strategies, which are inseparable and yield the structure of the market and parallel production functions. What was important in the textile case were the *reciprocal* effects which the strategies of firms, national policies, and the international division of labour had on each other in structuring the competitive equation. *The textile and clothing case demonstrates the integrated nature of the global*

*political economy and the need to move away from structural economic
accounts of industrial change in an era of globalisation.*

However, sometimes it helps to focus on particular elements of the
story, the better to provide a picture of the whole later. Therefore, an
in-depth analysis changing markets and production functions constitutes an important starting point for our understanding. In order to
understand the difficulties of the textile and clothing sector in the
advanced economies and to explain its problems we will have to focus
on markets (including international trade), production cost structures,
and more ephemeral elements such as the institutional capacity of
firms to respond to the challenges they confront. Emphasis will be
placed on the nature of demand (revenue, price, and socio-cultural/
psychological influences) and the corresponding structures of production so as to identify the problems of the sector which are intrinsic
to the way firms have responded to these same markets and trade
competition. The way these features formed part of a larger global
political economy of trade will be the focus of later chapters. Let us
begin, then, by analysing the socio-economic foundations of the rise of
protectionism, using the French industry as a typical example of a
textile and clothing sector in difficulty.

THE TEXTILE PROBLEMATIC: THE FRENCH CASE

The difficulties of the textile and clothing sector in France were
cumulative. The interrelatedness of the factors discussed below is the
key to understanding the troubles of the sector. In brief, many firms
failed to adapt to changing market conditions spawned by the social
movements of the 1960s and 1970s. When demand growth stagnated
or declined these firms found themselves in a difficult position. To add
to their problems, import competition (particularly but not exclusively) from the advanced economies intensified as the trade regime
was liberalised. Many of these firms were immersed in traditional industrial cultures and associational patterns which rendered innovation
in terms of either product or production processes unlikely. These
firms came to rely on their political resources to ensure their survival.

(a) The Nature of Demand for Textiles and Clothing Products

The global level of consumption of textile products, and, in particular,
household consumption, fell in relative terms from the mid 1970s and

even in absolute terms at the end of the decade.[3] Second, there were also major shifts in consumer preference *among* textile products in addition to the trend. Industrial textiles were a growing market, as were knitted goods and certain categories of casual/leisure garments. Traditional 'heavy' and more formal outerwear (coats, men's suits, tailored outfits for women) were in retreat.

The shifts in demand seem to have been caused by two related developments, beginning with the evolution of consumer preferences linked to income elasticities. In short, 'Engel's law' on the declining share of basic necessities, and in particular clothing, within rising consumer expenditures *at current prices* continues to be broadly valid in OECD countries' (original emphasis), France being no exception to this rule. In other words, the 'apparent income elasticity of demand for clothing (i.e. the percentage rise in demand for clothing which corresponds to a 1 per cent increase in total consumer expenditures) at current prices appears to be well below one.'[4] Clothing thus passed from the 'intermediary' to the 'inferior' goods category during this period. The OECD analysis notes, however, that the fall in shares partly reflected a decline in the relative price of clothing. *Real* income elasticity thus may have been about one. It is considered difficult to separate demand elasticities from price changes, though it is admitted that there were considerable variations from country to country.

In France, price evolution apparently had a definite effect on income elasticities. Although clothing prices did not outstrip the growth of the overall consumer price index from 1972 to 1978, this price index of course includes such elements as the enormous rise in energy and certain commodities prices. Clothing prices did, on the other hand, outstrip the manufacturing prices index in the same period. It is estimated that this slowed consumption by up to 0.6 per cent, indicating a real income elasticity of less than one.[5] Income elasticity for textile products in France was estimated at an average of 4 per cent from 1960 to 1972, 0.8 per cent from 1972 to 1978, and by 1981 had fallen to 0.2 per cent.[6] This development combines with the slower growth in per capita disposable income after the 1974 crisis. Of course, the evolution varies among types of garments or products, but in all, the trend is clearly towards declining income elasticities, below one, with slower income growth compounding the situation.

The problem of elasticities was aggravated by the relationship of *consumer* demand to *total* demand for textiles. The production stream in the sector is long, with each stage dependent on the others for either its inputs or its markets:

The traditional aggregate demand analysis conducted in terms of price and income elasticities does not fit well a complex sector with considerable product differentiation and several distinct stages of production and distribution...The link between *final consumer demand* and *total demand* is far from straightforward. (Original emphasis)[7]

This complex link between final and total demand results in what is called the 'textile cycle', over and above normal business cycles. The textile and clothing industries, in particular the upstream portions, suffer disproportionately from downturns in business activity at the downstream and retail level. A slowdown in final consumption creates a disproportionate accumulation of stocks in upstream production; put differently, a given percentage drop in final consumption of finished textile products, in particular clothing, leads to a more than proportionate decrease in demand for fabrics, and the situation becomes even worse for yarns or fibres: 'the *long run* income elasticity of total demand for textile products will be significantly below that of final demand;' thus, the 'textile cycle' is more severe than the general business cycles, and due to the highly volatile influence of fashion and climatic conditions on purchases it is not always synchronised with general downturns in business activities.[8] Demand may not only be in decline, but is also capricious where fashion holds sway, with upstream producers usually bearing the consequences.

The nature of the fashion market made these quantitative relationships yet more difficult for textile and clothing producers. Once intermediary textile products are assembled as clothing or even finished cloth, they are no longer transformable into other products. Stockholding risks become high for fashion-related items whose market is never guaranteed. There is, therefore, a constant pressure to push the risk of stockholding upstream to the intermediary spinning and weaving activities which serve as inputs for finished fabrics or garments.[9] This can increase the volatility of the textile cycle.

Second, these quantitative demand relationships (elasticities and the textile cycle) were underpinned and aggravated by the socio-cultural developments of the decades since the last war, especially since the 1960s. Qualitative changes in textile demand structure constitute the second major development in shifting consumer priorities among categories of consumption. 'Engel's law' predicts changing priorities among broad groups of products (food, clothing, shelter, leisure, etc.) related to overall levels of prosperity. The sociological changes which have taken place have, however, had repercussions for the clothing habits of society. Changing social structures and lifestyles led to a certain 'democratisation' of fashion and a convergence of preferences for relaxed and leisure-oriented garments.

These trends must not be exaggerated: men and women still wear suits to the office, and high fashion still thrives. However, the latter in particular has had to adapt to new realities in the market, specifically through the birth in the 1960s of ready-to-wear fashions. Design has not disappeared, but it has had to be produced in greater quantities to satisfy new groups of consumers – hence 'democratisation'. Moreover, weekends which in France (and other countries) used to be a 'synonym for ceremony' (churchgoing, family luncheons) are now a synonym for leisure and relaxation.[10] Dress has adapted to changes in lifestyle and a breakdown of social hierarchies. Hence the radical shift to 'sports-wear'; fashion continues to exist but it has taken on new forms.

Research has also uncovered a diminished desire for purely aesthetic qualities in clothing in favour of the utility of the article and its ease of maintenance. These societal changes, reflected in clothing preferences, forged changes in the internal workings of the fashion industry since from the late 1960s onwards which challenged the existing production and distribution structures.[11] Consumers buy smaller and less elabo-rate articles of clothing to 'mix and match'. Lifestyle and individuality could be expressed through greater variety, and so certain aspects of fashion became more volatile. The search for self-expression in a mass fashion market can result in waves of fashion which no longer corre-sponded to the old designer-dictated autumn/winter and spring/sum-mer collections. Furthermore, as clothing increasingly became an 'inferior' good (Engel's law), consumers displayed greater sensitivity to price and their level of disposable income as factors in determining purchases. There was a search for relatively declining prices as well as less elaborate articles, once again indicative of changing elasticities and other functions of disposable income, closely linked to sociological developments.

In other words, the market became more volatile. Adaptation to these changing tastes was crucial to success, and the losers were pushed out sooner by falling growth rates in consumption. However, these changes need not have represented liabilities for local producers. These firms were, after all, closest to these market changes which facilitated the expansion of certain subsectors, in particular knitwear or single-piece garments such as skirts or blouses. In reality, however, change too often led to increased opportunities for import penetration, with

French manufacturers apparently unresponsive. Changes in markets required adaptation, presenting new opportunities for those who seized upon them. The changes also drew attention to the importance of marketing in the strategies of firms. Manufacturers must have adequate knowledge of market trends (information), produce for these volatile markets (flexibility), and be capable of manipulating consumer choice (anticipation/creation of fashion).

(b) International Trade

International trade was defined as the other parameter of industrial change. The principal pressure on French firms came from high-wage producers, and the French trade balance has proven weakest in capital-intensive textile manufactures. In clothing low-wage competition is more important but not paramount. However, the pressure of international markets exerted itself in many ways. Abuses of the trade regime (frauds with respect to country of origin, dumping, export subsidies, abusive protectionism) were a much remarked upon but relatively minor phenomenon. More importantly, the analysis of the previous chapter revealed that not only had import levels increased, as might be expected in a progressively liberalised trade regime, and trade surpluses turned into deficits (a less inevitable development), but also that increases in consumption, for example in 1981–2, tended disproportionately to benefit imports.[12] How exactly did this process take place? A study carried out on the UK industry provides a useful illustration.[13] The interplay of shifts in demand, trade competition, and the textile cycle worked seriously to reduce the capacity of the domestic industry.

Initially, minor downward shifts in consumer demand for textile products, perhaps affected by minor changes in fibre prices (operating through relevant elasticity mechanisms) probably lay at the bottom of the problems encountered by domestic producers on their own markets. This was predictably accentuated by the textile cycle.[14] The failure of firms to respond to changing demand functions rendered them by definition steadily less competitive. In addition, international trade competition constituted a dynamic of its own. Regression analysis of the UK industry showed that imports had come in surges, when increases in domestic consumer demand outstripped the capacity of the already compromised domestic producers.[15] The evolving inability of domestic industrialists to supply their own markets accelerated the initial decline in a downward spiral, and supply bottlenecks increased as domestic capacity fell after the ravages of each successive crisis. Demand functions are thus at the bottom of the surge in import penetration. Domestic firms responded poorly to market changes, putting themselves in difficulty, which in turn led to their inability to supply the home market as the industry was forced to contract. The domain of international trade became a hammer, not a haven, for the national producer. Foreign manufacturers filled the vacuum left by unresponsive home industrialists.

This picture was perfectly applicable to the French industry, though the clothing sector resisted somewhat better than in the UK The domestic market share (percentage of the market furnished by domestic producers) had constantly diminished since the late 1960s when the market changes began to be felt. From 1970 to 1979, of the 37 textile products classified by French statistical authorities, which represent 96 per cent of textile employment, 26 products saw their domestic market share diminish.[16] It is interesting that this drop in domestic supply began in the late 1960s to early 1970s: the market was still growing rapidly at that time, though major qualitative shifts in demand were taking place. This appears to indicate that the competitive problems of the sector and the unresponsiveness of firms to markets goes back some time before market growth actually began to slow down. Firms thereafter became trapped between continuing market change and the growing competitive pressure of overseas producers. Demand and trade have translated as cumulative pressures on French textile and clothing industrialists, with only a few firms using the changes as opportunities to fill the vacuum left by failing firms.

(c) Firm Strategies and the 'Textile Problematic'

The key variable at this stage of the argument, then, was the particular production and market strategies adopted by firms in the sector. *It was the aggregate reaction of firms-as-agents to changing markets, international competition, and the trade regime which would determine the fate of a national textile and clothing industry.* What specifically went wrong with the French textile and clothing industry?

(i) Investment, Productivity, and Profitability
First, a chronic lack of investment was perhaps the most important factor in the sector's failure to adjust to changing markets and intensified competition. Modernisation presupposes investment, but

French textile and clothing firms were among the lowest investors of the industrialised countries throughout the 1970s, and performance deteriorated further in the early 1980s.[17] If low investment in the clothing industry was perhaps partially excusable (lack of technological progress, low capital stock, need for low overhead), the continuous drop in textile investment since 1970 was the less so as levels began to fall well before demand tapered off.[18] Given the way falling domestic supply propels import penetration, it is not surprising that the upstream trade balance deteriorated.

Growth in the productivity of labour in the industry, though not inconsiderable,[19] was also inferior to other industrialised countries. With France at an index level of 100 in 1978, Italy was at 103, Germany at 118, and the United States at 135. Of the major industrial powers, only Great Britain was below France, at 79.[20] Though the precise link between productivity growth and investment is difficult to establish,[21] investment remains a precondition of success in practical terms. Industrialists in the sector at the time pointed out that successful firms invested 5 to 8 per cent of their annual turnover, some even more, often over a period of up to twenty years or more.[22]

In France, the situation seems to be clear. On the whole, chronically low investment levels have fed vicious circles in which antiquated equipment and strategies reduced competitiveness while maintaining overcapacity. Small, marginal firms had low fixed costs. In the case of modern, capital-intensive firms, high overheads meant that low capacity utilisation led to a sharp rise in unit costs. A poor economic climate can therefore have a paradoxical effect on the industry. Old, traditional production units could survive in poor market conditions for relatively long periods. The overcapacity they represented constituted a barrier to modernisation. There was a strong disincentive to modernise as long as crisis conditions prevailed. The actual pace of contraction was therefore accelerated.[23] Profit levels were correspondingly low for over a decade, severely compromising the self-financing capacity of firms,[24] which concomitantly redoubled the decline of investment levels.

Investment and improvements in productivity are not, however, a sufficient condition of success in a volatile market. Integration and modernisation is not justifiable unless a particular technology adds something at each phase[25] and is linked to a clear strategy of responding to shifts in demand. The modernisation of production serves little purpose if the products produced do not relate to identifiable markets.

(ii) Linking Markets to Production

Much weight has been placed on demand as a factor in the industry's evolution. Adaptation to markets was, correspondingly, a key element of a successful firm strategy.[26] How did French industrialists see the question?

In the case of the textile and clothing industry, where economic actors were many in a long and heterogeneous manufacturing process, the independent decisions of actors were often poorly informed of the overall workings of the system. Wholesalers and successful industrialists alike complained that, in general, French manufacturers of textiles and clothing maintained their distance from the day to day realities of the market. It is difficult to overestimate the damage this did to the competitiveness of French firms, given the enormous changes in the market. Many articles in the business press recognised it as a problem. Distributors complained that they could not find what they wanted from French manufacturers,[27] and that producers would not send samples or show a desire to respond to distributors' needs; 'it doesn't interest them to know what the client wants. They never come to us to find out whether an article has sold well or not, and why.'[28] Likewise, a report by the National Assembly on the problems of the sector stated clearly that the lack of cooperation between distributors and producers was one factor which led, among other things, to a preference for imports.[29] It was noted that firms in trouble often sacrificed quality to cut corners, that distributors had trouble getting reliable supplies of French products which suited their needs, and that there was little attention to the respect of delivery dates.[30]

That firms must concentrate on following market trends appears self-evident, but the changes in the nature of demand which occurred from the late 1960s onwards rendered this otherwise banal invocation of foremost importance. Lower absolute consumption levels meant the battle was often for market share, not just for a share of growth. This was a fight French firms were losing on the whole, especially to Italian competition. The change in tastes – to a considerable extent a move down-market to less expensive, more casual products and a greater concentration on textile products for home furnishings and decoration – meant that attempts to fill the demand of yesterday's market were bound to meet with ever-diminishing success. 'They did not know how to adapt to what people want today',[31] noted B. Labouerie, an importer. There developed a certain qualitative misalignment of supply and demand.

If these difficulties were to be overcome, the market not only had to be mastered, but a firm's production activities had to be complementary, straddling several types of markets, in order to fill the gaps left by the risky and speculative nature of fashion production. Various solutions were practised. A firm such as Diroco (the result of a merger between several smaller firms) exploited the possibilities of automation in its domestic plants, searching for ever-higher productivity and rationalisation of its facilities to save costs, while contracting some 20 per cent of its production out to the then East Bloc. Some of the risk thus fell on the subcontractors. Others, for example Thiéry SA and Mathelin, tried to avoid the problem of seasonal variations through complementary product lines. Mathelin began producing auto seat covers to fill the slack seasons, and Thiéry ended up doing the same after the initial success of its new furnishings department.[32] None of these firms were large, and all experienced fast growth. If investment was one common element of their success, an attention to markets was another.

Price factors were also important. The higher prices (relative to imports) of inefficient French producers contributed to decline of the national industry. As consumers devoted declining shares of total disposable income to textile and clothing products, research has shown that they became increasingly sensitive to price in their choice of articles.[33] Where aesthetic values were dominant, consumer judgement could range from the subjective to the outright irrational. In such a case, price (within a given range) may have little incidence on choice. Sensitivity to price decreases as the purchaser seeks appearance value or acts on impulse, which is often the case in the short run. In the long run, however, the average consumer was seeking a downward relative price evolution, which should have been the result of productivity improvements. Furthermore, consumers became more sensitive to considerations such as utility and durability in their choice of articles. Where these qualities are sought after, impulse-buying (and therefore insensitivity to price) was relatively reduced.

In many cases price played a significant part in determining aggregate demand for various garments. As the price level became important in product substitution, it constituted a vital factor in the process of import penetration. The retreat of domestic supply can be partially explained by the differential evolution of the prices of domestic production and imports.[34] In the textile and clothing sector there was apparently a particularly high sensitivity to price as a factor in substituting imports for domestic products.

A 1 per cent drop in the *relative* price of imports resulted in a 0.5 per cent rise in the import penetration level (as opposed to 0.2 per cent for the manufacturing average). Or, if one prefers, a 1 per cent divergence between the growth rate of import prices and those of domestic producers created a gap of 5 per cent between the growth rate of imported and domestic production sales (a gap of only 2 per cent for industry taken as a whole).[35]

The elasticity of substitution of imports was thus extremely high. The difference between import prices and those of domestic supply continued to grow, but was especially striking from 1970 to 1973 when the import surge began (see Table 2.1). Though relative clothing prices were on the decline throughout the OECD, owing to productivity gains and cost savings in the industry, in France prices rose 10 per cent per year in 1973–6, and this did not slow in the later 1970s (current prices).[36]

Table 2.1   Evolution of relative prices of textile products in France, 1960–80 (average annual change, %)

Price index ratios	1960–70	1971–80	1971–73	1974–80
Export prices/import prices				
Spun Yarns	−0.2	−0.3	+1.4	−1.1
Knitting	+0.7	+1.4	+6.1	−0.5
Weaving	−1.0	+0.5	+0.1	+0.6
Clothing	+1.2	+0.3	+1.2	−0.1
Total textiles and clothing	0.0	+0.5	+2.4	−0.3
All Industry	0.0	+1.4	+2.0	+1.1
Import price/domestic supply				
Spun Yarns	−1.6	−3.0	−4.1	−2.6
Knitting	0.0	−5.0	−10.2	−2.7
Weaving	−1.3	−2.3	−4.4	−1.4
Clothing	−0.8	−2.2	−5.2	−1.0
Total textiles and clothing	−1.4	−3.2	−6.1	−1.9
All industry	−0.8	−3.1	−5.1	−2.2
Export price/domestic supply				
Spun Yarns	−1.8	−3.4	−2.8	−3.6
Knitting	+0.7	−3.7	−4.8	−3.3
Weaving	−2.4	−1.9	−4.3	−0.8
Clothing	+0.4	−2.0	−4.1	−1.0
Total textiles and clothing	−1.4	−2.6	−3.9	−2.1
All industry	−0.8	−1.7	−3.3	−1.1

Source: Micheline Vincent, 'Vingt Ans du textile-habillement', *Economie et statistique*, no. 138, November 1981, p. 25, after Compatibilité Nationale.

To conclude, the relatively high retail prices of French domestic products were a curb on the growth of consumption and engendered certain patterns of substitution among different types of clothing articles: towards cheaper garments (especially imports) and towards other categories of goods altogether (travel and leisure activities, for example). The effect was felt by domestic producers, particularly where imports were substituted for their products. The 'textile cycle' effect exacerbated the problem.

The functioning of the distribution sector also tended to aggravate the problem of rising prices. The French distribution sector was highly atomised.[37] In 1975, small independent retailers accounted for 70.4 per cent of sales, franchise chains and the like for about 2.5 per cent (total small commerce: 72.9 per cent) and large-scale outlets for only 27.1 per cent (department stores, mail-order firms, hypermarkets, divers). In later years there was a resurgence of these small outlets and over time (at least until the mid 1980s), independent retailers more or less held on to their share of total clothing sales. There was therefore an increasing number of small sales outlets chasing the same or a slightly diminishing share of business. What effect has this had on the overall fortunes of the industry?

First, the atomised distribution sector tended to restrict the size of clothing production runs ordered by retailers. Small shops ordered a few articles at a time. This prevented many producers from employing the economies of scale which could reduce costs and justify the pro-curement of expensive new technology. It is estimated that in clothing assembly this increased costs by about 20 per cent on average, or up to 50 per cent in extreme cases.[38] As pressure on small shops mounted, shop-owners attempted to maintain their living standards by raising profit-margins on their sales.

Second, as fashion became more volatile, small shops increasingly refused to hold large stocks owing to the risk involved if an article did not sell well. Retail price multipliers initially increased to cover the risks, but eventually orders were simply reduced in size and, as retailers still demanded rapid reprovisioning in the case of successful items,[39] the risk of stockholding was steadily transferred upstream, onto the manufacturer. This increased producer costs and amplified the po-tential effects of the already fickle textile cycle.[40]

These developments constituted a cumulative series of price increases for French domestic textile and clothing articles. This elimi-nated many of the cost-saving productivity gains of producers, and the reduction in the size of production runs also acted as a restraint on further modernisation. Pricing practices appear to have exacerbated the long-term problems of the sector and spurred import substitution as large-scale distributors turned to imported products.

This again raises the larger problem of *links between the various segments of the production stream, and especially the question of linking production to markets.* Large-scale commerce could as easily have been harnessed to the needs of the French sector as to those of foreign producers and their importer intermediaries but close relationships between distributors were not fostered. Producers first needed to respond to market changes and the needs of large retailers, thereby laying the basis for potential cooperation. The cost/price difficulties of the sector were cumulative, and required subtle responses from industrialists. A failure to adjust to markets led to a vicious circle in which producers were unable to make the necessary investments, and imports were substituted for French products on the domestic market. Innovative firms were nonetheless able to prosper, proving that the circle could indeed be squared.

(d) Corporate Structures and Sectoral Performance

The preceding discussions have attempted to situate the difficulties of the French textile and clothing sector in the strategies of firms. The analysis centred on how manufacturers have failed to meet the exigencies of changing demand and international competition, and how their behaviour tended to accelerate their own decline through a lack of investment, isolation from markets, and the operation of complex price mechanisms in the production and distribution of textile products. It has also been made clear that alternative strategies were available to French entrepreneurs, as is illustrated by the success of Italian, American, and German producers, to say nothing of those French firms which were successful as well.

What, however, is the role of corporate structure in sectoral performance? The argument here is that *structure was not nearly as important as strategy.* For many years it was the contention of state policy that larger firms increased the chances of success in the sector. In order to understand better the policy debate in the context of the industry's evolution, some notion must be developed of the capacity of the firm as an institution which can vary in size and level of integration.

The textile and clothing sector in France remains an industry of small and medium firms, despite the existence of large conglomerates in most activities, a feature shared with other countries. A movement towards greater concentration in the 1960s was somewhat reversed in the early part of the following decade. The sector remained less concentrated than manufacturing industry as a whole, and less concentrated than a number of other national textile and clothing sectors. There is also a low level of vertical integration in the industry. Large groups have tended to expand horizontally within their chosen activity rather than integrate the various activities and fibre types in the industry.[41]

The reversal in the trend towards concentration in the sector was apparently common to most OECD countries.[42] However, it is difficult to establish a clear relationship between the continuing below-average profitability in the French sector and either firm size or level of vertical integration. For example, the profitability of the highly concentrated Finnish industry was above-average among manufacturing activities, but in the UK, which had the most concentrated textile industry of all, this was not the case in the years after the 1974 crisis. The largest Italian firms were confirmed loss-makers and major consumers of state subsidies, whereas in Germany and Italy many small and medium firms obtained good results. In Italy a trend towards the 'deverticalisation' of the sector proved quite successful.[43]

In France, the Boussac/Agache-Willot saga of the 1970s demonstrated that size was no insurance against complete collapse, whereas the constant troubles and bankruptcies of many small firms throughout the textile and clothing sector pointed to their continuing fragility. Successful firms were few, but their success was often great, putting some firms in the sector among the fastest-growing industrial concerns.[44]

In an industrial milieu undergoing rapid restructuring, as in the case of the textile industry from the 1950s onwards, opportunities for financial and industrial success were great for those groups capable of seizing upon them.[45] Successful firms were spread evenly among small, medium, and large corporate structures,[46] in a sector where average profitability[47] in constant prices represented only 30 per cent of the 1972 level in 1981.[48]

Size was not necessarily, therefore, an advantage, but it may have been helpful where large investments were required. It is unlikely that a more direct relationship of size to success exists in the end. Success was determined by the flexibility of the firm's productive capacity, by their capacity to respond to the exigencies of the market, and the difficulties of competition on global markets. What *kind* of concentration –

industrial structure related to industrial strategy – is of far greater relevance, and this continues to be the case into the 1990s.

This raises the question of the institutional capacity of firms and of management attitudes. The capacity of a firm's structure to yield strategies which successfully confront production and market problems is the relevant factor. For example, in Italy, 'deverticalisation' led to new forms of 'centrally-controlled coordination of design, output, and marketing [which] took the place of oversized enterprise,' which had run up huge losses.[49] The type of firm, style of integration, and the appropriateness of structure to the exigencies of demand, trade competition, and production problems are the important variables, not size.

It would therefore be useful to look at concrete examples of firm strategies, particularly those which have been least successful. It will become clear how the process of concentration in France did not lead to a strengthening of competitiveness in the sector. The notion of the 'traditional firm' will provide a starting point, beginning with some remarks on what distinguished them from more successful concerns.

Textile and clothing firms are often described as 'traditional' – small, family-owned and managed, simple production technologies – with implications of decline, decay, and backwardness. It is important to emphasise that it is not the sector or industrial processes *per se* which made the firms 'traditional', but their practices and behaviour when confronted with the industry's problems.[50] Their behaviour was indeed linked to decline, but to call textiles and clothing traditional *industries* is inappropriate. Many textile firms, in terms of their production structures, management attitudes, and industrial strategies alike were decidedly not 'traditional', whether or not they experienced difficulties at any given point in time.

The traditional firm constituted the vast majority of enterprises in the French textile and clothing industry. The firms were small, numerous, very often long-established and usually family-owned and managed. The predominance of traditional firms accounted for the fragmentation of the textile sector, as much a result of their independent, disaggregated behaviour as of the high number of firms. It was against the traditional firm that most accusations of ignoring markets were directed.

In clothing, traditional industrialists had high (relative to other types of clothing firms) overheads and a labour-intensive production process. In later years, competition and the inflexibility of their organisation conspired to push them up-market. The quality of products could be high, but even allowing for modernisation, inflexibility and lack of response to markets often condemned them to financial losses, particularly in poor economic conditions.[51] Their position was fragile, and sometimes a counterproductive compromise on quality was used in a despairing bid to cut costs. In textiles, the situation was similar, but production was more capital-intensive on average. This did not necessarily mean that extensive modernisation had taken place; in 1981, the majority of the industry's plant and equipment predated 1973.

Family ownership and management structures were important factors denoting the traditional textile and clothing firms. Family ownership, in itself neither good nor bad, was historically associated with backwardness in the French textile and clothing industry. Family decision-making could frustrate efficient management, especially where a concern for personal prosperity, dependent on the fortunes of the firm, obliged directors to siphon off dividends which would have been better used if reinvested. Family and business were 'inextricably united economically in the sense that business treasury and household purse [were] simply one, just as national treasuries were once inseparable from the king's personal fortune'.[52] Independent industrialists jealously guarded their own destiny, often to their peril.

Thus the traditional firm was very much a legacy of the past. The *Patron* often learned his craft from his father, under a long apprenticeship, and lacked professional management skills. He responded to pressure for restructuring and modernisation as best he could: by either raising prices or cutting costs, sometimes by investing in more modern machinery, but with little or no knowledge of how to use it in an integrated production/marketing strategy. Considerable effort at modernising industrial plant was therefore expended, to little long-term effect other than to add to the level of fixed costs in times of crisis. The atomisation and separation from markets remained: 'structures ... equipment ... mentalities, are archaic.'[53]

The relatively low fixed costs associated with fully depreciated capital permitted many traditional firms to survive through a sort of price dumping, augmented by worker lay-offs or short-time to ride out a storm. In the 1974–5 crisis many Vosges cotton firms simply closed for the last months of the year, waiting for orders to pick up.[54] This put additional pressure on those who had invested heavily and who found their fixed costs relatively high and their self-financing capacities reduced by recourse to external debt financing for investments.

One of the responses to growing difficulties was the birth of new types of textile firms – manifested in the steady concentration of the late 1960s. Firms increased in size through mergers and takeovers in a largely horizontal process of concentration, often yielding spectacular growth in turnover actually more attributable to absorption of smaller firms than to self-generated industrial expansion. Government policy encouraged the takeover of weak and failing traditional enterprises.[55] The remarkable growth of these new textile groups resulted in the creation of some of Europe's largest textile firms. The Prouvost group, for example, became the largest woollens manufacturer in the world, and (measured by size of turnover) Europe's fourth largest textile group.[56] The Agache-Willot concern became the largest textile group in France through spectacular growth by absorption. European and even world-size enterprise was not lacking in the French sector.

However, the quality of firm strategy was far more important than corporate concentration as a factor in successful competition. Putting aside the Agache-Willot case (see below) for a moment, the process of absorption and takeover resulted in an almost exclusively horizontal expansion of firms. They developed into huge conglomerates with little attention to the rationalisation of internal structure.[57] The conglomerates were a series of financial links wherein the juridical existence and autonomy of the acquired company often remained.[58] When failed ventures were absorbed by a conglomerate, the former *Patrons* were often established as the managing directors of the new and relatively intact subsidiaries. In the case of Dollfus-Mieg, this resulted in a lack of overall commercial logic and management 'whose interest in their former firms [was] greater than in DMC as a whole.'[59] In the case of the Lainière de Roubaix, the family board members, over and above the objections of the firm's very professional president of the 1970s (Claude-Alain Sarre), continued to make unprofitable acquisitions of failing firms. Profits were correspondingly low.[60]

To summarise, these large firms (though by no means all) simply juxtaposed many aspects of the traditional enterprise on a vastly expanded industrial base, with relatively little regard for internal rationalisation or advanced management practices. This appears to be analagous to the situation in the steel industry, where the state likewise encouraged mergers and concentration. Mény and Wright point out that concentration 'rarely prevented conflict between the merged corporations.' in the steel sector.[61]

Another example is that of the firm of Marcel Boussac, the 'King of Cotton'. After the last war, Boussac created a vast integrated concern which manufactured cotton from raw fibres to finished garments, with production situated mostly in the traditional cotton region of France, the Vosges. A large network of Boussac's own retailing outlets completed the picture. By launching Christian Dior, Boussac was part of the post-war resurgence of the *haute couture*, and his interests expanded into the French colonies, particularly Africa. The firm was a remarkable affair, exercising paternal responsibility for workers under its command by providing housing and social services for them, and Boussac expressed a constant wish to use the best machinery, engineers, and sales managers for his company. Exceptionally high productivity, investment (thirty million francs a year in the decade of the 1950s), and the use of long production series for an integrated large-scale distribution network, trading at low prices, made it an exemplary company.[62] Why, then, did it experience the financial difficulties which led to its eventual demise in 1978?

The Boussac collapse seems to be a case where rigid and antiquated management structures confronting radically changing patterns of consumer demand in the market weighed too heavily on a first-class industrial plant, and hence on the company's fortunes. An ageing Marcel Boussac, the once 'richest man in France', stubbornly held to a strategy which had less and less to do with the wants of consumers. 'Boussac didn't change his habits and attitudes one iota...and the stocks began to accumulate. By 1971 they were worth six months' total production or 300 million francs.'[63] Producing more cheaply than competitors was not sufficient; nor was the high quality of 'guaranteed Boussac' merchandise. It was some ten years after the introduction of synthetic fibres as an important element in textile production that Boussac, in the 1960s, finally consented to produce mixed-fibre products, the fastest-growing market at the time.

Boussac's old, paternalistic style of management likewise presented problems. The firm was never transformed into a professionally managed concern.[64] As the financial black hole gobbled up most of his own considerable fortune, there were some attempts to impose a state-chosen manager. Boussac refused all offers, maintaining his own dominance by substituting his incompetent nephew as heir apparent. Restructuring plans were drawn up, with job losses, swallowing state aid, bank loans, and more Boussac fortune, but these plans failed. Finally, the state was exasperated and pressed things to a climax by withholding all further aid (the banks became commensurately worried) in the absence of a new manager which the state could not impose.[65] There was a clear identification of ill-conceived and poorly structured management and a failure to adapt to markets with the collapse of an otherwise promising industrial enterprise.

Agache-Willot (the company which eventually bought the failed Boussac empire) presents a rare case where constant rationalisation and vertical integration, from upstream activities all the way to distribution of finished products, was the guiding principle and operated successfully over a number of years.[66] Contrary to many accounts, the group underwent a continuous rationalisation of its industrial structure. Over ten years, and in three separate stages, the group was restructured, coinciding with major industrial and commercial acquisitions. The principal investment imperatives of this restructuring[67] were the search for increased productivity and the mastery of modern technology on the one hand, and the substitution of vertical integration patterns for traditional horizontal ones on the other. Each sub-branch of the sector was regrouped, and subsidiaries were obliged to remain competitive. The emphasis was on the coherence of industrial strategy.

Unfortunately, industrial logic eventually became subordinated to financial logic,[68] with constant and substantial financial flows (dividends, capital gains, etc.) from the productive sector to the parent holding company. External expansion (acquisitions) came to hold sway over internal development and the stream of mergers became too large to swallow. The profitability of the industrial concerns was not in question, but the strategy came to grief. A convergence of factors, including rising interest rates paid on the heavy external debt which the industrial sector was obliged to carry (for lack of self-financing siphoned off by the parent holding company), led to its collapse and declaration of bankruptcy in 1981, just in time to greet the new Socialist government as it came to power. The financial strategy of the holding company eventually destroyed its own source of capital.

To summarise this section, there is no fixed relationship between corporate structure and success in the textile and clothing sector. What counts is strategy, for firms large, small, or medium. A weak corporate entity, in the form of poor management, poor communication between departments of firms, and isolation from rapidly changing markets, can definitively compromise the future of whole segments of the domestic industry. Financial losses reduce investment on a slippery slope towards collapse.

(e) The Labour Force

Up until now little has been said about the textile and clothing industry's workforce. The characteristics of the labour force nonetheless had considerable bearing on the competitive position of the industry. New technologies and firm strategies required new labour management techniques in a tradition-bound industry, and new working conditions to which workers adjusted uneasily.

There were characteristics of the labour force traditionally employed in the textile and clothing industry which hampered the process of adaptation to the new conditions prevailing in the global industry. These were the high proportion of women and young workers employed, who tended also to have a low average level of worker qualification,[69] and salaries well below the manufacturing industry average. These tendencies, already present in the textile sector, were more pronounced in the clothing industry.[70]

The recruitment of this 'marginal' workforce emphasised the unattractiveness of the sector in the eyes of those seeking employment. Low salaries were not the only issue: the often poor working conditions and the general unpleasantness of the work involved in traditional factories must be added. There were considerable health hazards, such as noise, dust and fibre inhalation. These features, combined with the general insecurity of employment in an industry plagued by constant cyclical fluctuations, and labour practices which often emphasised the intensification of the work pace as a substitute for productivity gains (particularly in clothing manufacture) rounded out an image of a generally undesirable job. Unattractiveness led to recruitment difficulties, which led to increasing marginalisation of the textile workforce in a vicious circle which was manifested often in chronic labour shortages.

The problem has of course declined in importance since the general rise in unemployment in the western economies, but old recruitment patterns still existed into the 1980s and the weight of past hiring practices was heavy. In order to alleviate labour shortages in the 1950s and 1960s, textile firms resorted increasingly to immigrant labour. As this proved insufficient, a rural female workforce was brought in daily (often from fifty to a hundred kilometres away) to factory centres. This was particularly true in the textile regions of the Nord and the isolated valleys of the Vosges. There, female labour from the mining basins of the Nord-Pas-de-Calais and the Lorraine was available from outlying areas. These recruits topped up the local pool of male and female workers, creating a two-tier labour force: the fringe, recruited among immigrants and women, who often bore the brunt of the textile cycle's downturns, and a core of local, mostly male, workers.[71] The women recruited were often young, and they withdrew from the workforce at an early age to marry and raise families. Immigrants were usually single males and therefore migrant. Both categories became expendable when lay-offs were in order, while the core workforce was maintained intact.

The result was an unstable and fluctuating workforce. The rising level of economic redundancies in the 1970s was disproportionately borne by women in the workforce.[72] This development can be confirmed in textiles.[73] A truly marginal and dispensable pool of labour developed throughout the industry in a process of labour market segmentation.

These developments resulted in a deterioration of the quality and stability of the labour force. This situation aggravated the problems associated with economic crisis in a period of intensifying international competition and rapid technological evolution. The existence of a poorly paid, poorly qualified workforce and pool of excess labour may have its advantages for a labour-intensive industry competing with low-wage countries by keeping salaries down and resisting unionisation, but the battle was not in fact there. Competition was principally with the capital-and technology-intensive textile industries of the industrialised countries such as Italy, the United States, or Germany, and the introduction of more complex technology and changing factor mixes required the recruitment of a competent workforce.

A major study on the composition of the textile labour force and its consequences for the sector concluded that there was a link between the low level of worker qualification and the difficulties involved in the reorganisation of production and productivity growth. A marginal labour force rendered firms less able to adapt to competition and the new technology. A greater focus by firms on raising the general skill level and flexibility of their workforces was seen as an important plank in an overall restructuring/revalorisation effort.[74] A focus on design and product development presupposed specialised and skilled personnel, which had to be trained within the industry. The introduction of new technology also increased the need for highly skilled technicians for machine maintenance, and changed the nature of work for most of the labour force. The high cost of a breakdown in rapid, capital-intensive production placed a premium on attention span and fast and precise intervention when necessary.[75] The work required was more complex, with a greater interchangeability of workers becoming desirable.[76] Traditional strategies which treated the workforce as the principal expendable cost variable were therefore ill-suited to the increasing complexity of textile processes.

CONCLUSION

It should by now be evident that single factor explanations cannot account for the difficulties of the textile and clothing sector in France, nor in other countries where firms found themselves in comparable difficulties. The story of the French industry could be repeated in a number of advanced economies, even where in aggregate the adjustment has been relatively successful. If the international division of labour appeared to be shifting to the advantage of low-wage producers, this was not because of the inherent structure of comparative advantage, but because firms-as-agents, on a background of state policy and the changing international trade regime, often failed to take advantage of competitive factor mixes and to seize the opportunities offered by changing markets. *Explanations focusing on economic structural factors and omitting the crucial agency of firms are misleading.*

An account has been presented wherein the markets for finished products (demand) and the terms of international competition continuously formed and reformed the structures of the industry, fashioning the future through the responses of firms as the 'bearers' of structure in the international division of labour and of competitive industrial activity. Demand was revealed as an essentially a social construct, evolving continuously and affected as much by long-term socio-economic trends as by fluctuating conjuncture in changing patterns of needs and wants. International trade, through the institutions and rules of the trade regime, translates the terms of competition of an international economy, which increasingly consists of the responses of enterprise to a multitude of international markets. The relation of demand to international trade in this view is evident and important. Domestic firms with reduced competitiveness constantly face having their traditional markets usurped by foreign competition, which becomes more intense in a period of slower growth. The tension between internationalisation and domestic industrial structures remained a key interface of industrial development in the sector.

The major social changes of the post-war era, their effect on fashion and consumption patterns, the constellation of elasticities of demand which result in the textile cycle, and complex price effects greatly changed patterns of textile and clothing consumption in France and the other advanced economies. Liberalisation of international trade, initially through the EU but also at the global level through GATT, intensified competition among producers. The particular practices and structural features of the French industry failed to confront these challenges and so contributed to industrial decline. The dynamics of demand and international trade called for change and adaptation; organisational ineptitude and the traditional practices of firms resulted in inertia. Some firms broke out of the circle, perhaps to the greater peril of others with whom they were competing. The crisis of competitiveness became very real for the national economy – fostering unemployment, industrial collapse, and trade deficits.

The previous two chapters have therefore sketched out the material basis of policy preferences among textile and clothing interests in a context of crisis and decline. Successful adaptation to new markets and international competition was possible, but inadequate firm strategies meant that the liberalisation of trade often translated as industrial crisis. This crisis was inherently linked to the political decisions taken to move towards a liberal trade regime, in manufactured goods at least.

In such a situation, distributional conflict over the terms of adjustment may be predicted. When the firms of a domestic industry emerge in the newly liberalised context as economic liabilities, this provides fertile ground for protectionism and subsidy. As Chapter 3 will demonstrate, there is nearly always room for manoeuvre. In this case, distributional conflict played itself out as much through the state policy process as through what one strictly regards as economic competition. The political strategies of firms and their associations need to be added to the picture represented so far.

As this book has insisted, process is more interesting than structure, where process does not necessarily concern equilibrium, and where the tensions of distributional conflict become fundamental to the pattern of industrial adjustment and the rules of international trade. Political interaction shapes and defines many of the crucial structural and institutional variables. A market is not a market without the political authority and structure which defines it, whatever the abstract dreams of neo-classical economists. Also, of course, when referring to the management of adjustment and its socio-economic consequences, it is the state which is principally implied. Without the institutions of the state as a political focus for the conflicts implied by economic structure, the tensions which have been described would undoubtedly manifest themselves in a radically different fashion.

The next step, then, is to understand how this material economic base of the textile and clothing sector became articulated within the policy processes of the state, the EU, and the GATT. In this regard the textile and clothing sector may be seen as exemplifying the problems of post-war industrial evolution. The development of the sector raises all the familiar questions: managing saturated markets, shifting revenue and expenditure patterns, related business and product cycle evolution, changing factor mixes and production processes, and the introduction of new technologies. To these are added the difficulties of adjustment and its social consequences, against a background of generalised economic recession, monetary instability, volatile trade patterns and international divisions of labour.

Notes

1.   See this volume, 'Introduction'.
2.   N. Thiéry, in Alain Bienaymé, *Stratégies de l'entreprise compétitive* (Paris: Masson, 1980), p. 4.
3.   See Union des Industries Textiles, *L'Industrie textile française* (annual), (Paris: UIT, 1982), p. 6; Senate Report, p. 212.
4.   Quotations from Organisation for Economic Cooperation and Development, *Textile and Clothing Industries: Structural Problems and Policies in OECD Countries* (Paris, 1983), p. 29; hereafter referred to as 'OECD Report'.
5.   France, Sénat, *Rapport au nom de la commission d'enquête parlementaire chargée d'examiner les difficultés de l'industrie du textile et de l'habillement*, 2ᵉ session ordinaire de 1980–1981, no. 282, 6 June 1981, p. 212 (hereafter referred to as 'Senate Report'), p. 224.
6.   Ibid., p. 221. Another study on the garment industry only (P. l'Hardy and A. Trognon, cited in Micheline Vincent, 'Vingt ans du textile-habillement', *Economie et statistique*, no. 138, November 1981), more or less confirms the findings, pointing to an income elasticity for clothing of 0.6 per cent in 1962, and 0.4 per cent in 1973. Relative clothing prices dropped *vis-à-vis* the consumer price index, accounting for some of the difference, but this slide slowed to only 0.6 per cent a year 1974 to 1980.
7.   OECD Report, p. 34.
8.   Ibid., pp. 34–5.
9.   Senate Report, pp. 276–7.
10. Ibid., p. 228.
11. See Jean-François Boss and Alain Boudon, *La Formation du prix des vêtements à la consommation*, Les Cahiers de Recherches de la CESA, 2 vols, 1978, pp. 119–45, for an excellent discussion of the fascinating 'psycho-sociology' of modern fashion and clothing consumption trends. Though men and women respond to different imperatives in clothing purchases, several conclusions applied to the behaviour of both: clothing purchases are increasingly related to lifestyles and expressions of

individuality, rather than to the old sociologically-determined [class] definitions of fashion.

12. The statistics used in support of this study clearly indicated a decline in production in 1981–2 which coincided with rising consumption and import levels.

13. T.G. Taylor, *The Role of the Textile Industry in a Developed Economy* (PhD thesis, University of Wales, Swansea, November 1981), op. cit., pp. 445–6.

14. Ibid.

15. Ibid., p. 440.

16. Senate Report, p. 130.

17. Based on nominal investment figures and calculations of investment growth rates, investment measured against turnover and value added, and comparisons to the average for manufacturing industry. For comparisons with other countries, see OECD Report, p. 63 (table 29); France, Assemblée Nationale, *Rapport fait au nom de la commission d'enquête parlementaire chargée d'examiner les problèmes de de l'industrie textile et les moyens à mettre en oeuvre pour les resoudre*, 6ᵉ législature, no. 2254, 18 March 1981, vol. I, p. 59; hereafter referred to as 'National Assembly Report'.

18. National Assembly Report, vol. I, p. 62.

19. From 1960 to 1980 roughly equivalent to the average for manufacturing industry. See Vincent, 'Vingt ans du textile-habillement', op. cit., p. 23. Some figures however disagree and state that clothing brought the sectoral average below that of industry throughout the 1970s. The important point is that productivity gains were far from negligible. For an excellent long-term study of the returns on factors of production in textiles and clothing, see France, Institut National de la Statistique et des Etudes Economiques (INSEE), *Emploi, qualification, et croissance dans l'industrie*, vol. II, Les Industries de Consommation, concerning the period 1959–74.

20. France, Conseil Economique et Social, 'Le Devenir des Industries du Textile et de l'habillement,' *Journal Officiel* (Avis et Rapports du Conseil Economique et Social), 25 February 1982, p. 239; hereafter referred to as 'CES Report'.

21. See Centre d'Etudes et de Recherche sur les Qualifications (CEREQ), *L'Evolution des emplois et de la main d'oeuvre dans l'industrie textile* (Paris: La Documentation Française, Dossiers du CEREQ), no. 20, 1979, pp. 54–69; hereafter referred to as 'CEREQ Report'.

22. Hélène Pichenot, 'Textile: et pourtant ils réussissent', *L'Usine nouvelle*, no. 23, 4 June 1981, pp. 96–7. This article cites a number of cases of successful firms, commenting on their strategies.

23. This account of fixed and variable costs from Taylor, op. cit., pp. 443–4.

24. See Annie Lecompte, 'L'Evolution économique et financière du textile entre 1972 et 1981', *Bulletin de Crédit National*, 1ʳ trimestre 1983, pp. 59–74.

25. Thiéry, in Bienaymé, *Stratégies de l'entreprise*, op. cit., p. 5.

26. Pierre Dubois and Giusto Barisi, *Le Défi technologique dans l'industrie de l'habillement: les stratégies des entrepreneurs français et italiens* (Paris:

CNRS, Groupe Sociologie du Travail, 1982), pp. 253–6, emphasise that the key element in the success of Italian clothing manufacturers throughout the crisis period was their attention to the laws of the market, even though many successful firms were well below the minimum optimal size required to benefit from economies of scale or new technologies.

27.   Frédérique Lorrain, 'La Longue Marche vers une nouvelle distribution', *LSA Libre Service Actualités*, no. 822, 27 November 1981, p. 73.
28.   Gérard St Albin, President of a clothing assembly firm, quoted in Claude Villeneuve, 'Textile: la débandade', *Le Nouvel Economiste*, no. 91, 25 July 1977, p. 29.
29.   National Assembly Report, vol. i, p. 38.
30.   Ibid., pp. 45, 47.
31.   Villeneuve, 'Textile: la débandade', op. cit., p. 29.
32.   Hélène Pichenot, 'Habillement: Comment se retailler une place?', in *L'Usine nouvelle*, no. 26, 24 June 1982, pp. 97–98.
33.   The principal sources for the following discussion are A. Boudon, 'Une Analyse de filière: la formation des prix dans le secteur textile', *Revue française de marketing*, no. 3, 1979, pp. 73–102, and Boss and Boudon, *La Formation*, op. cit.
34.   Vincent, 'Vingt ans du textile', op. cit., p. 30.
35.   Ibid., p. 32.
36.   Boss and Boudon, *La Formation*, op. cit., p. 249.
37.   Once again the discussion draws principally on Boudon, 'Une Analyse', op. cit., and Boss and Boudon, *La Formation*, op. cit.
38.   Boss and Boudon, *La Formation*, op. cit., p. 253.
39.   This led to the accelerated development of the Sentier, a parallel manufacturing sector in major urban areas (particularly Paris, where it began around the rue du Sentier). The Sentier often resorts to poorly paid undeclared labour or home workers, and is able to reprovision small shops within the week, outdoing traditional manufacturers. It is extremely dynamic, in a process of 'perpetual reconversion'. See Villeneuve, 'Textile: la débandade', op. cit., p. 29.
40.   Boudon, op. cit., p. 101. These cost increases were partially manifested in the increase in supplier credit to retail outlets, which was up some 40 per cent from 1970 to 1975.
41.   See Laurent Benzoni, 'Le Textile: industrie de l'avenir', in Bertrand Bellon and Jean-Marie Chevalier (eds), *L'Industrie en France* (Paris: Flammarion 1983), pp. 100–02.
42.   OECD Report, p. 27.
43.   Meaning the undoing of vertical integration in corporate structures; OECD Report, pp. 27–8.
44.   Pichenot, 'Textile: et pourtant', op. cit., p. 95.
45.   Benoît Boussemart and Jean-Claude Rabier, *Le Dossier Agache-Willot: un capitalisme à contre-courant* (Paris: Presses de la Fondation Nationale des Sciences Politiques, 1983), p. 19.
46.   CEREQ Report, p. 55.
47.   This is measured by the French accounting equivalent to gross operating profit, known as *résultat brut d'exploitation*, or value added minus

labour costs and taxes (excluding VAT and corporate income tax) minus net financial costs.

48. Lecompte, 'L'Evolution economique', op. cit., p. 67.
49. OECD Report, p. 27.
50. See David S. Landes, 'French Business and the Businessman: A Social and Cultural Analysis', and John E. Sawyer, 'Strains in the Social Structure of Modern France', particularly p. 301 and pp. 304–11; both in Edward Meade Earle (ed.), *Modern France: Problems of the Third and Fourth Republics* (Princeton University Press, 1951), for an account of traditional French business behaviour.
51. Robert Weisz, 'Stratégies d'entreprises et modes de gestion dans l'industrie de l'habillement', *Revue française de gestion*, no. 39, January–February 1983, p. 92.
52. Landes, 'French Business', op. cit., p. 336.
53. Quote from B. Labouerie, importer, in Villeneuve, 'Textile: la débandade', op. cit., p. 29.
54. *Le Monde*, 21 November 1974.
55. OECD Report, p. 27, note 14.
56. M. Damien, 'L'Industrie textile', *Profils économiques*, no. 13, Autumn 1983, pp. 97–100. The best up-to-date reference on major firms in France is the annual supplement on the largest firms in each sector, published by the *Nouvel Economiste*.
57. Erhard Friedberg, in *L'Etat et l'industrie en France: rapport d'enquête* (Paris: CNRS, Groupe Sociologie des Organisations, mimeo, 1976), using the example of the Prouvost group, points to the compartmentalised company structure and 'closeted' nature of the various production divisions.
58. Friedberg, p. 110.
59. Berrier, *The Politics of Industrial Survival: the French Textile Industry*, unpublished PhD thesis, Massachusetts Institute of Technology, 1978, p. 227.
60. Ibid., p. 196.
61. Yves Mény and Vincent Wright, *La Crise de la sidérurgie Européenne 1974–1984* (Paris: Presses Universitaires de France, 1985), p. 100.
62. Alain Jemain, 'L'Affaire Boussac', *Entreprise*, no. 968, 28 March–3 April 1974, pp. 56–65, is a good summary account of the company's growth and demise. There was also substantial press coverage of the lead-up and actual collapse.
63. Ibid., p. 59.
64. Berrier, *The Politics of Industrial Survival*, op. cit., pp. 202–203.
65. Statement by the Minister of Finance, *Le Monde*, 12 May 1978.
66. See Boussemart and Rabier, op. cit.; the following discussion is taken from their work.
67. See ibid., ch. 4, particularly pp. 163–98.
68. See ibid., ch. 6.
69. These were actual tendencies; it is not being suggested that women or young workers are by definition poorly qualified.

70. This use of female and often immigrant low-paid labour was a feature of much of the global fashion industry. See Annie Phizacklea, *Unpacking the Fashion Industry* (London: Routledge, 1990).
71. See Berrier, *The Politics of Industrial Survival*, op. cit., ch. 6, pp. 241–301, for a discussion of these labour practices in textiles.
72. Pierre Dubois, 'Mort d'une industrie? L'emploi dans l'habillement', *Revue française des affaires sociales*, 35–1, April–June 1981, p. 148.
73. Berrier, *The Politics of Industrial Survival*, op. cit., p. 253.
74. CEREQ Report, p. 175.
75. See discussion in Boussemart and Rabier, op. cit., pp. 189–95.
76. Boussemart and Rabier, p. 194. Also CEREQ Report, p. 174. This point is not without controversy.

3 State, Market Governance, and Particularistic Interests: The Political Economy of Capture

The aim of this chapter is to demonstrate the power of particularistic interests in the policy-making processes which govern the overall pattern of distributional conflict in the textile and clothing sector. In this sense it will build on the analysis of the material economic base underpinning these conflicts of interest which was presented in Chapters 1 and 2. To accomplish this, the chapter will examine the political strength of the textile and clothing sector in the UK and the US, and will then look in detail at the pattern of state–industry relations in the French sector. The French case provides evidence of how textile interests were able to dominate and indeed 'capture' the policy agenda, a detailed and extended example of the political economy of capture.[1] The employers' organisations were able to commandeer industrial and trade policy resources and so as to attenuate the impact of rising import competition, a process repeated across a broad range of industrialised economies, demonstrating the ways in which policy processes are part of market structuration. The chapter will then demonstrate how a very different industrial culture and pattern of interest intermediation in Italy led to a dynamic strategy of successful market-led adjustment to the new transnational competitive pressures of the global market. Italian firms organised themselves so as to increase their competitiveness through a collectively sponsored strategy of flexible specialisation and became the leading textile and clothing exporters in the global economy. The associational patterns and mechanisms of state–industry relations were crucial to this outcome.

The underlying assumption is drawn from the arguments of Chapters 1 and 2 of this book: that the policy preferences of particularistic interests are based on a particular set of economic structures prevailing at a particular time, and on the competitive practices peculiar to firms as 'bearers' of this structure. Structural change in the market results as much from changes in policy as from changes in the practices of firms in a particular sector; there is an ongoing dialogue between the two. Particularistic interests were able to cloak themselves in the mantle of the public interest through their command of the institutions of political authority, at least partially compensating for their unwillingness to adapt to the competitive realities of liberalisation and adjustment.

An understanding of economic structure and market relationships is therefore inadequate for explaining the international political economy of industrial production and its manifestation in terms of trade. One cannot draw teleologically on the laws of market dynamics such as the international division of labour or the logic of accumulation in the global economy. It must be demonstrated systematically how those interests which derive their social and political position from the control of the means of production are integrated into the body of the state in a state–market system of governance, and thus convert their private power and interests into the dynamics of public policy. Policy preferences must be successfully articulated and translated into state action, and political economy analysis must systematically demonstrate this connection if we are fully to understand how dominant social forces in turn dominate the world of official policy as part of the ongoing distibutional conflict of interests across the globe as carried out through state institutions.[2]

The successful implementation of an economic strategy through a particular set of political institutions

> reinforces the political resources of those who have power in those structures [institutions]. This gives them both a stake in preserving those structures and the means for doing so, even in the face of economic costs or political tensions that might result.[3]

In other words, institutional patterns which articulate particularistic interests facilitate the implementation of corresponding policy preferences. Victory in the battle to influence the regulatory structure of the market reinforces the political power of those who are already well-placed in these institutions of governance. The pattern of state–industry relations which emerges is the embodiment of this process. Market and state become fused in an integrated set of socio-economic institutions, formal and otherwise. Furthermore, the policy issues at stake evidently cut across local, national, regional, and international policy-making institutions, thus transcending the traditional conceptions of levels of analysis in international relations.

This chapter will demonstrate these arguments by beginning with a brief look at the American textile coalition and its strong ties to senior politicians on Capitol Hill. While their influence has declined over time, the late 1980s demonstrated their continuing political clout in the structuring of international markets. The focus will then shift to the UK industry, which throughout the 1970s was able to press the government for both subsidies and protection. Then the key position of France and the peculiarities of French textile interests and their relationship to the state will be highlighted once again. French textile and clothing industrialists came to control the policy agenda with respect to adjustment and restructuring in the face of intensified competition and transnationalisation, which permitted it to preserve for some time the balance of interests in favour of competitively weak firms. Finally, by way of contrast, the analysis will focus briefly on organised interests in the Italian textile and clothing industry and the ways in which these associational groups actually facilitated and accelerated adjustment to international competition. The industry evolved an export-led strategy based on flexible adaptation to changing market demands, and then benefited from EU protection to dominate the EU home market for textile and clothing production.

TEXTILE AND CLOTHING INTERESTS: THE US AND UK

A classic argument which is often advanced to explain the prevalence of protectionist policies despite the high aggregate costs of trade discrimination has to do with the differential economic incentives of key groups of socio-economic interests in the market. The costs of protectionism remain relatively diffuse, usually manifested in terms of higher prices for consumers. In contrast, the interests of producers (labour or capital) are much more focused.[4] Producer groups directly bear the cost of adjustment to the intensified competition implied by liberalisation: 'it therefore pays them to influence trade policies through voting and lobbying.'[5]

This is nonetheless only part of the equation: while the incentives for each group might remain broadly similar across the industrialised economies, the policies of some countries are highly protectionist, others are much less so. The United States, despite its general declaratory policies in favour of trade liberalisation, has been a consistent sponsor of protection in the textile and clothing sector since the mid 1950s. Protectionist fervour has waxed and waned in degree, but the objective has remained the same. Germany has suffered substantial job losses in the textile and particularly the clothing industry, yet remained resolutely liberal in terms of trade policy from the 1970s onwards. These differences mean that the intervening variables of contrasting economic structures in the domestic economy and the associational patterns of organised interests must be brought into the equation. The main point of the following discussion is to demonstrate that textile interests commanded substantial political resources in two number of key OECD countries affected by low-wage imports. The power of these groups varied across domestic political systems but all were capable of mounting a serious campaign to capture the trade policy agenda. As will be demonstrated, a number consistently succeeded in doing so.

(a) The United States

Textile interests in the United Sates have long been organised. Nevertheless, US textile producers were historically fragmented into a variety of regionally based organisations which represented the various subsectors of the industry (wool, cotton, knitting, spinning, weaving etc.), sometimes with overlapping membership. They have tended to become more centralised and inclusive over time, the result of several crucial mergers of associations across the industry.[6] The two most influential organisations are without doubt the American Apparel Manufacturers Association (AAMA) and, especially, the American Textile Manufacturers Institute (ATMI). 'Since 1983, nineteen producer associations and two labour unions have sought to coordinate action on trade policy issues through the American Fiber, Textile, and and Apparel Coalition (AFTAC).'[7] AFTAC remains, however, a coordinating body encompassing the AAMA and ATMI among others, and not an association in the strong sense of the term.

Even though the textile coalition has appeared fragmented, it has nonetheless maintained substantial political influence. In terms of votes, the textile and clothing industry in the US still claimed (in the early 1990s) to be the largest employer in the manufacturing sector.[8] While these votes tend to be concentrated in key southern states such as the Carolinas, Georgia, Alabama, and to a very much declining extent, New England,[9] nearly every state in the Union has some element of textile and clothing industry present.

The lobbying strength of the textile coalition is yet more impressive, especially when combined with its capacity to mobilise Congress in favour of protectionist legislation.[10] As mentioned, there remain pockets of the textile and clothing industry in nearly every state of the Union and therefore nearly every congressional constituency. Although the congressional strength of the textile coalition has declined along with employment levels and the increasing transnationalisation of the industry, it nonetheless remained capable of mustering a 'substantial majority in both houses of Congress,' including some sixty votes in the Senate.[11] This is more than sufficient to pass legislation proposed by the industry, but was just short of the necessary two-thirds vote to override a presidential veto. The dominant force behind these efforts is the American Textile Manufacturers Institute, which represents the fabric producers and their substantial wealth,[12] but all segments of the coalition were very much united on the issue of protection,[13] at least up until the closing stages of the Uruguay Round itself.

A substantial number of congressional representatives in both Houses see textile and clothing issues as 'the number one trade topic; maybe the number one topic overall'.[14] In the House of Representatives there is an ongoing and well-organised 'textile caucus' typically animated by representatives from southern states. Prominent Senators supporting the textile coalition are also senior and powerful members within the Senate committee system, names such as Strom Thurmond of South Carolina, Senator Fritz Hollings of South Carolina, or Jesse Helms of North Carolina. These Senators and equivalent members of the House of Representatives were often backed by wealthy mill owner individuals such as Roger Milliken of South Carolina who is a substantial donor to and supporter of the Republican Party.[15] During the 1980s, there was a parade of protectionist textile trade bills from 1985 through to 1990.[16] These congressmen were 'willing to go to the very end on this issue',[17] despite just as many presidential vetoes.

In addition, the textile coalition has had ongoing and intimate connections with the US Administration itself. Contact between the employers' associations, the US Trade Representative's office (USTR), the Departments of Commerce and Labour, and Capitol Hill is daily during trade negotiations. This is chanelled through a policy committee which draws together representatives of the departments of Commerce, State, Labour, Treasury, and the textile negotiator of the USTR. This committee, called Committee for the Implementation of Textile Agreements (CITA), is chaired by the Deputy Assistant Secretary of the Commerce Department. These issues are most important for State, Commerce, and the USTR, and each one has a different constituency. Historically, the Commerce Department Chair has been the dominant member,[18] and Commerce has close connections with the industry and its protectionist lobbies. Industry lobbyists would meet 'usually every day'[19] with the USTR reps during MFA or other negotiations. This did not mean that US policy was dictated by the industry's lobbyists, but contact was intense and ongoing; negotiators got the industry's advice whether they wanted it or not. US importers and retailers in favour of textile and apparel products eventually became active, but were of little influence relative to their producer rivals.[20]

It is therefore far from an exaggeration to claim that protectionist interests of the US textile and clothing industry were systematically institutionalised into the policy process. State policy-makers often had differences of opinion with these groups and had to defend a wider array of interests than the textile coalition. Nonetheless, negotiators and policy-makers across thirty years of changing US Administrations recognised that, overall, textile trade policy decisions required legitimation through the textile coalition, and that the MFA was a system run at the behest of the industry itself. The accord was in outright contradiction to the longer-run liberalisation aims of these same post-war US Administrations, all of which have consciously sought 'as much liberalisation as the traffic would bear, but the traffic wouldn't bear much liberalisation in textiles and clothing.'[21]

(b) The United Kingdom

The British state is at first glance far less permeable to particularistic interests than the American system of government. The long tradition of independent Whitehall civil servants and the extraordinary power of the executive, at least if supported by a Parliamentary majority, is well known.[22] The UK, furthermore, had as long a history as any in support of a generally liberal trade policy. Nonetheless, the UK became a strong proponent of sectoral protectionism and subsidy in the post-war period,[23] lending crucial support to more traditionally protectionist countries such as France and Italy within the EU. This came on a background of several post-war government programmes aimed at modernising and rationalising the UK textile and clothing sector. Despite these programmes, the competitiveness of the UK industry remained weak,[24] an ongoing invitation to play the protectionist card. Rising unemployment in the 1970s resulted in policies aimed at encouraging firms to hold onto their workforce despite the problems of consistent overcapacity.[25]

Large companies and textile and clothing industry associations played their part in lobbying for protection and public subsidy. As the UK had the most concentrated industry in terms of firm size, the 'big three' of Courtaulds, Coats Viyella, and Tootal enjoyed privileged access to the Department of Trade and Industry,[26] as did the chemical fibres producer ICI. There was also a complex and fragmented system of employers' organisations. They were organised on the basis of both region and/or industry segment into associations such as the British Nylon Spinners or the Federation of Master Spinners Associations. The peak association for the textile producers was the Textile Council, which was renamed the British Apparel and Textile Confederation in the 1970s. In addition one should not forget the role of trade unions as organised interests representing the textile and clothing industry, particularly on questions of subsidy and trade protection. The influence of trade unions was particularly strong in the Labour Party when in government, but jobs were votes to both major political parties.

These interest organisations were important interlocuteurs for the Department of Trade and Industry. When combined with the large producer companies, there was a prevalence of informal state–industry contacts and *ad hoc* commissions looking into the plight of the industry.[27] The result was a pattern of self-governing organisations in charge of various industry restructuring funds and programmes over the years[28] (not unlike the pattern in France discussed in detail below). There was also an attempt to introduce an element of more formalised corporatism in state–industry relations through the National Economic Development Council, which had sectoral divisions such as the Cotton and Allied Industries Economic Development Council but it seems that informal relationships remained central to the pattern of governance in the sector.

Nonetheless much of the pressure appears to stem from the nature of the political balance in Parliament and the rising concern with unemployment throughout the 1970s and early 1980s. The Heath Conservative government (1970–4) was dismissed by the electorate following confrontations with the unions, particularly the miners. The Labour Party won the election with a minority in Parliament, relying on support from the Liberal Party and others. Rising unemployment in key constituencies became a serious concern. In 1975 the Trades Union Congress (TUC), a national body with close links to the Labour Party, opted for a trade policy consisting of selective import controls.

This was to include a substantial reduction in imports of clothing and textile products.[29]

As mentioned, there was a long history of state intervention in the textile industry.[30] From 1972, the UK had responded to these pressures with programmes of subsidies to the industry.[31] When Britain joined the European Community in 1974, pressures on the textile and clothing sector intensified. As the newly elected Labour Party struggled from 1974 onwards to balance a diverse set of socio-economic constituencies, a growing balance of payments crisis, and a hung parliament, the government found itself confronted by a Confederation of British Industry (CBI)[32] temporarily united with the TUC. They claimed that the 1974 MFA (as negotiated and implemented by the EU Commission) was entirely inadequate.[33] The government responded firmly during the 1977 MFA renewal negotiations, seeking to strengthen the system of quotas. The Prime Minister was no doubt all too aware of the importance of marginal constituencies in Lancashire, home of the cotton industry, and other centres of textile production in the northern counties and Scotland. As textile interests were lobbying constantly in London, Brussels, and their local constituencies, it is not surprising that under the circumstances the government found itself obliged to lend an ear. The influence of these textile interests lasted even into the Thatcher government years, a period dominated by neo-liberal ideology with the apparent exception of textile trade policy.[34]

The discussion of the power of textile interests in the UK and the United States provides clear evidence that coalitions of textile and clothing interests maintain considerable political resources despite the relative decline of the sector. However, the above analysis of the UK and US does not fully illustrate the ways in which the organised interests of the market can become institutionalised in the trade policy process to the exclusion of other interests of equal economic significance. In order to understand the political economy of capture, a closer look at the political articulation of economic interests within the body of the state is necessary. It is necessary to establish precisely how organised interests succeed in capturing the very agenda of policy-makers, infusing the decision-making process with their values and industrial culture over time. This chapter now turns to analysing the example of associational patterns and state–industry relations in the French textile and clothing sector under a microscope, demonstrating through historical analysis how capital, as agency, can articulate its structural economic power in terms of political outcomes. The history and practices of these associational groups and their member firms *do count* as the control of the business commmunity over the system of production becomes translated into notions of legitimate public interest and policy.

FRENCH TEXTILE AND CLOTHING INTERESTS

It has been argued in chapters one and two that the competitive equation in the global textile and clothing sector in the 1970s and 1980s provided opportunities for the development of the industry, as well as the all-too-familiar difficulties upon which this development might founder in the rising tide of transnationalisation. This suggests that there was room for both firms and the state to influence the economic destiny of the industry through their respective strategies or policies. This assertion is based on several presuppositions: that there existed a relationship between state and industry; that the sector was of sufficient economic and political significance to attract the attention of policy-makers; and that the interests of the industry were, in fact, successfully articulated and promoted within the policy-making apparatus.

This section seeks to establish that there was such a relationship in the French sector, and to examine its nature and substance, showing that it was grounded in long-run historical developments. It will then go on to analyse how the perceived interests of these groups were articulated as political demands in practice, and how state attitudes and interventions developed over the post-war period in an elaborate game of market structuration. From this basis, combined with earlier analysis of the nature of competitiveness in the sector, it should be possible to ascertain how crisis and transnationalisation affected the established relationship between state and industry and what policies resulted.

(a) The Question of Political and Economic Significance

The textile and clothing industries were old-established sectors which helped form the very backbone of the French industrial revolution, as in Britain and elsewhere. They were, therefore, firmly anchored in the historical process of national economic and institutional development. Although their share of national output and employment tended to diminish relative to other sectors of the industrial economy, in 1980 they still represented roughly 10 per cent of industrial jobs, making the social consequences of a collapse of the sector politically difficult to contemplate.

The structural features of the sector's development in post-war France can perhaps be reviewed briefly. To start with, the development of the textile and clothing industries took on particular patterns of regional implantation. Those regions in which it forms a high proportion of local industrial employment were of particular importance.[35] There, the decline or prosperity of textiles and clothing was an important political and social issue, especially where large numbers of jobs were concerned.

The Nord-Pas-de-Calais region held the largest portion of the national textile industry of any region. Most textile activities were represented, but the wool manufacturing industry was dominant. Just to the south, Picardie was the traditional home of the jute industry and certain cotton manufacturing activities. The main cotton manufacturing centres, however, were traditionally in the Lorraine, particularly the rural valleys of the Vosges. Neighbouring Alsace was likewise involved in cotton activities, but became increasingly oriented towards dyeing and printing processes (this was important for these regions, for cotton-based products were most directly affected by low-cost international competition).[36] The region around Lyon was famous for its silk manufacture, and in modern times the Rhône-Alpes industrial complex which encompassed Lyon became the centre of both silk and man-made fibre production (this was not coincidental, as artificial fibres were originally an attempt to imitate the qualities of natural silk). Finally, the knitting industry was traditionally centred on the city of Troyes, and spread throughout the Champagne-Ardennes district.

There were other less important pockets of textile industry concentration, particularly wool and cotton manufacture in Normandy and wool production and manufacture in the south-western Midi-Pyrénées. For all these regions, the textile industry was part of the established industrial base, and the sector formed an important proportion of regional industrial activity.

The clothing industry, requiring less capital and being therefore more 'mobile', was generally more scattered. Outside a considerable concentration in the Nord, Rhône-Alpes, Pays-de-Loire, and in particular the Paris region (centre of the fashion industry with, 20 per cent of national clothing output at the dawn of the 1980s) the industry was fairly evenly but sparsely distributed throughout France. It often benefited from close contact with particular centres of textile production but could also be relatively isolated in what were essentially rural or non-industrial areas.

The sector (textiles, and to a lesser extent clothing) was thus firmly attached to the local and regional economic development of many areas, but the simple fact of economic significance to a regional industrial economy gives few clues to the substance of state–industry relations. Regional distribution was only one of several structural features of the industry which tended to shape the sector's political significance and eventual relations with the state.

First, the textile and clothing industry often subsisted as the only industry in essentially rural communities where it was the only source of non-agricultural employment. The difficulties for rural localities which might follow the closure of the local clothing or textile factory should not be underestimated in relation to the politics of isolated electoral constituencies. Relatively small economic upsets could have a great impact on the small communities which were affected, and local representatives and officials could find that their political future in the area depended on some form of solution.[37] As local elected officials in France were usually active at the national level as well, local difficulties soon translated into pressure on the Paris authorities.

Second, the sector (particularly textiles) often constituted major regional manufacturing complexes which were essentially mono-industrial. The decline of the sector, and the adverse effects which intensified competition tended to have in France, were thus felt the more acutely as there was little by way of alternative industrial activity and jobs to turn to as factories contracted or shut down altogether. Particularly in the Vosges, the crisis left few alternative economic activities. There, the hundreds of small cotton spinning and weaving establishments, which were usually the only sources of employment in the isolated valleys, were under pressure for decades. This pressure greatly increased after the early 1970s. The economic vulnerability of the region was reinforced as it became more and more specialised in cotton spinning and weaving activities, despite continuously slipping production levels since 1975.[38] The decline of the Vosges communities in isolated mono-industrial valleys thus became a significant political issue during the 1970s, to say nothing of earlier in the post-war period.[39] Other examples would be the Roubaix-Tourcoing area of the Nord, where textile and clothing activities had long been dominant among local industries, several localities in the Rhône-Alpes (for example, Roanne[40]), and the Franche-Comté, including those which suffered from the contraction of Rhône-Poulenc's artificial and synthetic fibres manufacturing activities.[41]

Perhaps the highest profile was given to the collapse of the Boussac cotton empire (centred in the Vosges) discussed in Chapter 2 and its subsequent takeover, contraction, and second collapse under the controversial management of the Willot group. This caused considerable political, and particularly trade union, turmoil.[42] Likewise the closure of the Italian multinational Montedison's Montefibre plant in the Vosges led to the direct intervention of the French government with the Italian authorities (unsuccessful as it turned out).[43] The bankruptcies of old-established firms such as the Schlumpf concern in Alsace seldom failed to provoke controversy in the press and in Parliament.

The problem of decline was exacerbated by the fact that the textile and clothing industries were often located in the older industrial areas of France. These regions were already suffering the pains of adjustment problems in other declining industrial sectors. This was particularly true of the Nord and the Lorraine, where the steel and mining industries had faced continuous and increasing pressure for many years.[44] The existence of a declining textile industry in these regions compounded the problems of economic management involved. These regions became 'crisis zones', where the problems of older industrial societies were concentrated, and the difficulties of textiles and clothing were no small part of the dilemma. In the Nord-Pas-de-Calais, textiles and clothing constituted a quarter of the region's industrial employment, some 12 per cent in the Lorraine (though this was much more concentrated in the Vosges taken alone), and 13 per cent in Alsace.[45] These regions were all hit by the mining, steel, and (Pas-de-Calais) shipbuilding crises as well. This accumulation of sectoral crises in certain key industrial regions could potentially increase the sensitivity of the state and local authorities to the problems of managing the socio-economic consequences of decline. Highly publicised bankruptcies contributed to the impression of an unacceptable pace of decline in the sector,[46] and as the troubles accelerated in some areas the textile crisis became a constant issue in the press and Parliament.[47] The ability of political authorities to find solutions or at least to be perceived to cope with the problems could reflect on the fortunes of governing coalitions in the relevant areas and of its representatives at the national level.[48]

There were two more features which affected both the industry's political profile and the difficulties of managing its economic development. These also had an effect on the sector's relations with the state. The first of these was *corporate structure*. A few large and often transnational firms capped a mass of small- and medium-sized enterprises which were more often than not family-owned and operated. The majority of firms in the sector therefore shared the concerns of small- and medium-sized business in France.

This small- and medium-sized firm structure was significant. The rising pressures of competition had turned small and medium firms in France into vociferous (and sometimes violent) defenders of a waning status quo. Also, small firms were incapable of themselves paying for the social consequences of lay-offs, retraining programmes within the sector, and the reconversion of workers for other industries. Various schemes to cope with this problem, such as early retirement benefits, retraining, and short-time[49] working practices in fact proliferated throughout the 1970s.[50] In the case of smaller firms, the state and local authorities tended to find themselves alone in dealing with the consequences of redundancies and plant closures. Though the subsequent concentration of industry somewhat altered affairs in the 1970s, the small business lobby in France, with which these firms identified, remained powerful and actively promoted its clients' needs as distinct from those of large corporations.

The second feature was *the historical sociological practices of the textile* patronat *itself*.[51] In the first place, family rivalry could prevent mergers and the eventual restructuring of uncompetitive branches of the industry. The employers' associations sought to attenuate these pressures, though not always successfully.[52] Second, the family firm was not seen simply as an economic unit but, to a degree, as an extension of the family as a social unit.[53] This implied that family and firm had a role to play in the local community, which included paternalistic attitudes towards workers, social welfare, and the economic prosperity of the locality.[54] Such perceptions affected the political and economic behaviour of entrepreneurs towards market pressures.[55]

(b) Associational Patterns and the Articulation of Interests

If the political significance of the industry and the structural features which affect it are easily enumerated, a further and vital element of state–industry relations concerns associational patterns and the articulation of interests in the sector. The institutions and organisations which arise for systematically voicing positions on matters affecting the sector's interests are important in mediating this process of articulation.

It is useful to begin by sketching the role of textile and clothing interests in the wider game of local and national politics. The fact of local and regional economic implantation tended to lead to a certain integration of the industry into local and regional political structures and to participation in patterns of regional representation at the national level. As a sector of traditional and often long-standing family-owned firms, the textile and clothing industry played a considerable role in the formation of the local bourgeoisie of many regions in France. Labour unions of the textile sector usually formed an important part of the loose coalition of interests opposed to the social consequences of decline and adjustment and the broad coalition of the Left.

There is no doubt that the textile and clothing interests were historically able to mobilise politically to some considerable effect. Because of the peculiarities of the highly centralised French political system, a prominent position in local society and political institutions to a certain extent ensured that the industry's interests were articulated at all levels of the body politic. The direct role of factory owners as 'notables' in local political structures included representation at the national level. These local notables could secure Senate and National Assembly seats and participate directly in government. The best example was that of Joseph Laniel, a textile manufacturer and honorary president of his trade association, who was a Deputy under the Third and Fourth Republics and became Prime Minister in the early 1950s. Raymond Boisdé, associated with the national clothing industry federation, was first elected to Parliament in 1951 and served as an undersecretary in the Laniel government.[56]

Influence came also through the personal interventions with ministers of textile magnates themselves. When Antoine Pinay's government proposed a reform of the production tax which would place a heavier burden on labour-intensive industries, it was agreed by most businessmen that 'Boussac and his cotton empire' had undermined the proposed changes.[57] In addition, textile magnates wielded national influence through their ownership of the press. Jean Prouvost of the Lainière de Roubaix (who became the largest wool manufacturer in France) owned *Le Figaro* until it was sold off to the Hersant media group in the 1970s, while *L'Aurore* belonged to Boussac until his business empire began to crumble. These papers were not necessarily industry or even business mouthpieces, but they were not above a general support for these interests and sometimes commented directly on the textile industry.[58]

More contemporaneously, the right-wing governments in France throughout the 1970s were elected on a hairline majority. Elections were won at the margins, and regional crises and consequent job losses were a sensitive issue, 'where a slight shift of votes would have been sufficient to chase the centre-Right coalition from power.'[59] Large firms constituted objects of political interest in their own rights and could form lobbies of considerable importance. In 1978, Antoine Willot (a director of the large Agache-Willot textile group) recalled with some humour how he had run into the Minister of Finance, René Monory, as the Minister stepped out of the toilets during a Paris-New-York flight on Concorde. It was the Minister himself who took the initiative to propose that the Willot group become involved in rescuing the Boussac empire, and this was neither the first nor the last time.[60]

In terms of political organisation and influence, however, the idiosyncratic cases of textile magnates in high places or general electoral pressures were not the most important. The more formal and organised pressure constituted by the textile and clothing professional associations themselves was vital in the long run. It would be useful to examine their structure before discussing their role.

The overall structure of the many textile and clothing associations was complex and interlocking. Local and regional organisations were usually mirrored in federal structures at the national level, and large firms involved in several textile or clothing activities might be active in several corresponding associations. With the exception of the metallurgy industry associations, the textile federations 'could boast the densest network of well-organised trade associations'.[61]

It is useful to begin with the textile industry, as the associational structure was the more sophisticated. Local or regional organisations tended to be distinguished by the type of raw textile fibre with which member firms worked (cotton, wool, silk, jute, etc.) and/or by the type of manufacturing process they represented (spinning, weaving, knitting, dyeing and printing, and so on). Finally, there were 'inter-textile' federations grouping the employers involved in textile production in a particular region or locality.

Organisation was, therefore, extremely dense at the local and regional level, particularly in the traditional textile and clothing areas, but at the national level groupings tended to be more broadly based. For instance, within the Nord textile complex at Roubaix-Tourcoing there were primary employers' organisations representing individual segments of the wool manufacturing industry, with the functional divisions being quite fine. In the Vosges cotton areas there was a similarily complex web of organisations for almost every segment of the production process.

These local organisations were often federated into broader associations at the regional level. They either grouped industry branch associations like SYNDIFIL (combed wool spinners) more broadly (for instance, to include all wool spinners), or they regrouped as an 'inter-textile' structure grouping all subsectoral activities (the latter usually for the purpose of sectoral wage negotiations; the Syndicat Patronal Textile de la Région Lilloise would be an example).

The subsectoral associations were then aggregated at the national level. Among others, there was a Comité Central de la Laine to represent wool manufacturers, the Syndicat Général de l'Industrie Cotonnière Française for cotton, or the Syndicat Français des Textiles Artificiels et Synthétiques for chemical fibres, and also a Syndicat Général de la Filterie and a Confédération Générale des Filateurs et Tisseurs together covering the various spinning and weaving functions. The Fédération Française de l'Industrie de la Maille et de la Bonneterie covered the knitting industry, and there was also a national dyeing and printers organisation. The role of these national subsectoral associations was to confederate the local/regional instances so as to formulate a coherent position representing members' interests at the national level, transmitting views to the state and the public. These associations were often called upon to arbitrate among conflicting interests of different sorts of firms across their particular subsector.

The entire structure was tied together by the Union des Industries Textiles (UIT), a confederal organisation of some one hundred or so associations, which was formed early this century and in the early 1980s represented about 80 per cent of the firms in the sector.[62] However, it should be noted that the members of the UIT were other industry federations (wool, cotton, spinning, dyeing and printing), *not* firms. The same held true for the national branch associations which in turn belonged to the UIT. The top end of the professional association pyramid was therefore at several removes from the firms themselves.

The UIT performed several important functions, from negotiating national collective agreements with worker representatives (textiles was the first industrial sector to negotiate such a national agreement in France), to raising issues of tax policy with the authorities. The organisation sought to unify and consolidate industry positions on these matters, and to arbitrate between diverse factions. It also collected and disseminated statistics on the sector to the government ministries. This latter function was important; it conferred control over information about the industry upon the UIT.

Here, however, a division of functions between the UIT and the national branch associations (wool, cotton, etc.) must be noted. It corresponded to a certain division of power. Where questions of economic policy were concerned, the subsectoral branch associations were usually dominant. This did not mean that the UIT did not take positions on such matters, but rather that the articulation of interests within each branch association, starting at the local level, was more important than whatever remaining discussions took place subsequently at the UIT level. It was the subsectoral branch associations which controlled the actual information-and statistics-gathering process, and each maintained its own separate rapport with its members and with the relevant state administrations. The industry branch organisations remained the stronger pillars of the house of professional associations, maintaining a vertical coherence and contact with the industrial base not matched by the *con*federal UIT.[63]

An analysis of the institutional structure of the professional organisations reveals that it mirrored the fragmented structure of the industry itself. This was not by any means accidental. Power relations within the organisations in turn helped maintain these very industrial structures and the practices of firms over time. It is clear, for instance, that to a considerable extent the professional associations were able to act as arbitrators of the process of corporate concentration in the sector. They ensured that firms stuck to their particular branch or production activity, allowing little room for vertical integration.[64] This must be examined in greater detail.

The small- and medium-firm structure made the industry relatively inaccessible to state policy-makers and difficult to impose upon. Contact with the industrialists was most easily carried out through the peak association (UIT) or the national subsectoral associations. However, atomisation of the institutional structure of the professional associations meant that the real power remained at the local/regional level. The UIT tenuously united what was an old-established and regionally based industrial/associational structure. The principal lines of cleavage were vertical, between the various subsectoral branches, calling into question the very notion of 'inter-textile unity' that the UIT supposedly incarnated. Small family firms, with strong ties to their localities, were accommodated in a structure where members and participating organisations were, on the whole, equal, *despite obvious disparities in the economic power of individual firms.* There were there-fore powers of veto for local interests throughout the system and the UIT and the branch associations tended to reflect the views of the small- and medium-firm majority in the industry as it arose from the bottom up at the local level.

This equality of firms-as-members had important repercussions, affecting the resolution of conflict over the policies which the asso-ciation would eventually promote at the national level. Member organ-isations enjoyed the possibility of posing a veto within the national federations, which prevented any departure in a direction antithetical to the interests of the effective majority of member firms.[65] The system of equal representation and the multiple levels of interlocking organ-isations thus helped attenuate or even correct actual disparities in economic power among firms; the small local associations with few members easily maintained cohesion and passed their preferences up the pyramid to the national instance.

So why did not the large firms simply break ranks? Large firms were certainly capable of short-circuiting traditional channels through their own contacts with the authorities. There is, however, strong evidence that these large firms, which grew out of the traditional milieu and often remained family-owned, were extraordinarily loyal to their original local organisations.[66] The heads of large firms often remained important notables in the local/regional and national structure of the professional organisations, clearly identifying their interests with the compromises and arbitrage which the system incarnated.[67]

The clothing industry tended to be less well organised, which reflects its greater economic instability, more dispersed firm structure and less marked regional implantation. It follows that local organisation was not as strong, but at the national level there was nonetheless a struc-ture similar to that of the textile branch associations. There was a national federation of men's garment manufacturers, the Fédération des Industries du Vêtement Masculin, a corresponding organisation for women's ready-to-wear clothing or Prêt-à-Porter Féminin, an association for *chemiserie-lingerie* or shirts and lingerie manufacturers, for *corseterie*, and for many smaller branches of the industry. These were united in the Union des Industries de l'Habillement (UIH), cre-ated in 1949 and by the 1980s including the greater part of firms in the sector.[68] The role of the UIH was similar to that of the textile union, and in the 1980s tended to increase as the state gradually focused its attention on the problems of textiles and clothing as an economic en-semble.

Transnationalisation was having its impact on the professional associations. There had long been an international committee for cotton and allied fibres and a counterpart for the woollen industry, but what is important here was the development of truly European organisations paralleling the growth in importance of the EU. COMITEXTIL[69] developed into an effective and genuinely transnational European pressure group for textile interests in various member countries during the 1970s, focusing on the crucial issue of the textile trade regime.[70] The corresponding clothing industry association, the Association Européenne des Industries de l'Habillement (AEIH, also referred to as ECLA or the European Clothing Association), likewise played a role in determining the outcome of issues within the Community domain. In 1996 COMITEXTIL and the AEIH merged to form EURATEX, but the process of integrating the two once separate organisations is in its early stages.[71] The Comité International de la Rayonne et des Fibres Synthétiques (or CIRFS) was a key performer in attempts to formulate a European policy on man-made fibres, particularly on surplus capacity reduction.

Finally, a brief note on the role of sectoral labour organisations is in order. It is difficult to characterise precisely the role of labour in state–industry relations in the textile and clothing sector in France. France's weak and fragmented system of labour unions was splintered along ideological lines as opposed to being organised according to industrial activity. It was often impossible to achieve unity of worker representation within a particular sector, activity, or even firm. This endemic weakness manifested itself in the almost total exclusion of labour from the process of economic policy-making, certainly since the advent of the Fifth Republic in 1958.[72]

Weak union organisation was especially pronounced in the textile and clothing industry. Unlike the steel or mining sector, textile workers were not organised to any great degree,[73] and the labour market was particularly unstable. Labour shortages were often endemic despite falling employment levels, and the sector was seen as an undesirable employer. This labour market instability was hardly conducive to the development of a strong tradition of worker representation.

In the post-war period the textile firms tended to contribute to this splintering of the union structure by courting the so-called independent trade unions, as opposed to the majority CGT and CFDT.[74] The major trade union federations, the CGT and the CFDT, were nonetheless present and participated in the Comités d'Entreprises

(Enterprise Committees) of appropriately sized firms, in accordance with French labour laws.[75] The role of labour in state–industry relations appears on the whole to have been marginal in the textile and clothing industry, except where workers could be mobilised in favour of the employers' demands for state resources to reverse the pattern of job losses. In general, the employers' organisations spoke for labour, presenting a united front on many policy issues, because of the political visibility of job losses as issues in the crisis which the industry was experiencing.

To summarise, the particular patterns of regional implantation of the textile and clothing sectors (especially in the case of textiles) tended to reinforce its political salience in an era of crisis in declining sectors of the economy, and the industry was organised to promote and defend its interests through a complex network of trade associations and the political contacts of notables. Thus, two essential ingredients of a state–industry relationship were present. There were not only the organisational ingredients for a state–industry relationship, but also potential issues around which this might revolve, such as unemployment, firms in severe difficulty, and declining regions.

POLICY ISSUES AND STATE–INDUSTRY RELATIONS IN FRANCE: THE POLITICAL ECONOMY OF CAPTURE

The analysis so far reveals little of the actual substance of the relationship, and even less about the state's perception of such issues and their place in the management of the wider society. This section of the chapter will now sketch out the general background to policy problems in the sector, to be followed by an extensive analysis of cases of policy formation, with a view to demonstrating how the industry was able to capture important elements of state machinery, using them to promote the policy preferences of the professional associations.

Policy-making in the sector had to confront sector-specific difficulties. The heterogeneity of the sector made it difficult for the state to grasp these problems and to attend to the difficulties of a very pluralistic production stream which nonetheless had vital economic interdependencies throughout. Equally important, however, was the problem of finding an appropriate intermediary through which to legitimate policy intervention: the small average size of firms and their sheer numbers contrasted sharply with the situation in heavily concentrated sectors such as steel, automobiles, or aeronautics. The textile

and clothing industries were poorly suited to a centralised administration often described as searching for a 'national champion' to
implement sectoral policy goals. Large firms in the sector were usually
recent creations which maintained their loyalties towards the professional milieu. The sector remained on the whole an industry of small-
and medium-sized enterprises. Therefore, the professional associations
had to be relied upon in contacts between the state and the industry.

However, it has been seen that the power of the peak organisations
(UIT/UIH) was often limited. Power remained compartmentalised
within the many subsectoral associations. The full economic and
political potential of the sector was seldom rallied; it almost always
spoke, and was heard to speak, with several voices, however close their
respective positions.[76] The UIT seldom lived up to its potential as a
reliable or unified intermediary organisation.

As long as surges in job losses could be absorbed by other industrial
sectors (as was the case until the mid 1970s), the consequences of
decline and adjustment in the textile and clothing sectors were of little
immediate significance to governing coalitions. Nonetheless, the
intensification of competition associated with trade liberalisation and
European integration, followed by the economic downturn which
corresponded to the oil shock, began to bring the industry's problems
into sharp relief. The transnationalisation of production and trade
created new dilemmas for state policy-makers as they sought to
respond to domestic interests which were in difficulty but with
diminishing means with which to affect the outcome. In textiles and
clothing, the difficulties associated with the transnationalisation of
production and trade could be particularly acute, for overseas production was a key competitive option for firms seeking to reduce costs.
As the production stream could be broken down into segments with
differing labour and capital intensities, so these segments of the production process could be, within certain limits, moved around
according to the dictates of the perceived competitive advantages
available to firms in various parts of the world. Firms which developed
genuinely multinational production strategies effectively resolved the
problem of adjustment on an individual basis. In so doing they
increased the pressure on the less-competitive, usually domestically
oriented firms.

What was traditionally a coherent, nationally based coalition of
textile interests began to fracture under the pressure of transnationalisation and the changing structural features of this fragmented
industry began to pull in several directions. These tensions took a long

time to develop and the process did not reach maturity until the early 1990s and the Uruguay Round agreements (see Chapter 5). Meanwhile, the mass of small and medium firms maintained an advantage in the fragmented institutions of the professional associations. These compartmentalised but well-organised and influential organisations continued to form the basis of state–industry relations in the sector, articulating the demands of the majority, but often least competitive, firms in the sector.

(a) Origins of Capture: State–Industry Relations in the Post-war Period

The actual history of state–industry relations in the textile and clothing sector was marked by both conflict and collaboration. In general textile and clothing interests were able to articulate demands and to appropriate state resources in favour of the industry to defend their own policy agenda. Building on the preceding analysis and by examining examples of demands and policy initiatives it is possible to develop a picture of the nature and substance of these relations of capture.

The pattern was set in the immediate post-war period and during the 1950s. The textile association in particular had been noted for its pre-war independence within the employers' movement.[77] The industry emerged from the war as an industry of traditionally managed family firms, a structure it was to maintain into the 1970s. However, despite the extensive organisation and the political power of the textile and clothing interests, the industry was not one of those chosen by France's post-war planners to lead the reconstruction effort and in particular the modernisation and growth of the national economy.[78] This did not prevent the industry affecting the course of policy while attempting to defend itself against new forms of competition and pressures for structural market change.

The most significant cleavage in the industry was between the myriad small concerns in traditional textile and clothing production and the capital-intensive artificial and synthetic fibres industry. The major producer of these man-made fibres was Rhône-Poulenc, essentially a chemicals company and dominant in a highly technology-intensive sector of large firms and few producers. The introduction of man-made fibres on a large scale raised the spectre of intense inter-fibre competition, potentially upsetting its historic relationship with the traditional textile sectors.[79] Under state pressure inspired by traditional textile interests, the company refrained from carrying out a strategy of forward integration into the downstream textile activities which could have forced the rapid restructuring of the whole industry, as occurred in the UK with the corporate strategies of Courtaulds and ICI. Rhône-Poulenc essentially remained a supplier of 'raw materials' to the more traditional firms, much like a raw cotton or wool broker. In return, the government granted the company adequate tariff protection for its activities, control over any new synthetic fibres developments in France, and development aid.

Traditional textile interests had succeeded in enlisting state help to maintain traditional structures and the stability of their industry, effectively neutralising the textile activities of the chemicals giant Rhône-Poulenc. However, this left a situation in which the increasing problem of competitiveness in the industry was simply not addressed.

Potential conflict with the artificial and synthetic fibres sector having been contained, the post-war textile and clothing sectors were left in the 1950s to contemplate their own inefficiency as post-war reconstruction and, eventually, European integration and GATT liberalisation proceeded. As older sectors, well rooted in the political system, they sought state help to defend their own agenda when necessary. The principal means was to be trade protection, but this was hardly a distinguishing feature among industrialised countries at the time. Until 1960, all European countries (except Great Britain) gave adequate tariff protection to textile and clothing products. The interesting aspects of the French case were the particular modes of trade protection and the evolution of accompanying adjustment policies.

It should be added that up until the late 1970s intervention chiefly concerned the textile as opposed to the clothing industry. In fact, one of the major political battles and strategic policy decisions concerning the two industries during the 1970s would prove to be the issue of extending aid to the clothing sector.[80] The bulk of what follows therefore refers only to textiles. It was not until the early 1980s that economic pressures and changing conceptions of the sector's problems resulted in a policy approach that saw the difficulties of textiles and clothing as interrelated.

(i) The Cotton Modernisation Act

In the early post-war period and into the 1960s, problems centred chiefly on the evolution of colonial export markets, given that domestic markets were sufficiently protected against more competitive imports. The first sign of instability in these markets was the turmoil in French Indochina in the early 1950s, confirmed by the defeat of France at Dien Bien Phu in 1954. The collapse of these protected colonial markets provoked the first of a series of post-war crises in the sector, especially in cotton manufacture.

Attempts to avoid disruption of protected markets had already proved successful on the domestic front – textile interests, in alliance with others, had in 1951 managed to abort a proposed customs union treaty with Italy.[81] However, the possible loss of the Indochina trade required more positive action to avert a full-scale crisis. Some 40 per cent of total French textile exports went to the 'Zone Franc' (essentially the colonies) at the time, and that proportion reached 60 per cent for cotton yarns and 90 per cent for cotton cloth. Indochina was the largest of the colonial markets.[82] Dumping by small, antiquated firms, using cheap labour and fully amortised capital equipment, aggravated the crisis and served to undermine incentives to modernise. These were already low in a protected market where most firms had an inadequate capital base to finance the necessary levels of investment.

With the Indochina market in the balance, the eventual reply to cries of alarm from the cotton manufacturers association (the *Syndicat Général de l'Industrie Cotonnière Française* or SGICF), was the Cotton Modernisation Act of 1953.[83] The plan was specifically designed for an industry which had hitherto been left out of the mainstream of post-war economic development efforts, with a view to modernising the sector and reorienting it towards new markets. In implementing the Act, the SGICF played a key role, acting, indeed, as an exclusive intermediary between the state and the industry. This is a crucial point. Though the state had become involved by virtue of the Act, it was not necessarily state priorities which were to prevail. The professional association, in defending its members, maintained control of the policy agenda.

The goals of the Act were to encourage greater specialisation, eliminate marginal firms or factories, and modernise plant and machinery.[84] To this end, the SGICF had established a *service de reconversion* in 1953 to survey which firms should shut down and how plants might be sold or converted to other activities. The principal policy instrument was the *Caisse de Riblonnage* (*riblonnage* meaning scrapping); it provided payments for firms scrapping old machinery and compensation for the closure of marginal firms. It was funded by a 'parafiscal' tax on sales of textile products, and the whole affair was run by the SGICF in strict secrecy.[85] *Fonds de Développement Economique et Social* (FDES)[86] funds were also available in conjunction with those of the *Caisse de Riblonnage*. The industry was to be reoriented towards the African colonial export markets and this required the introduction of broader looms to fit consumer preferences, in addition to the general need to modernise.[87]

Despite the sensible goals of the Act and the glowing expression of the will to modernise which the use of FDES funds would have symbolised in most cases, the programme cannot be considered a great success. Exclusive control of the *Caisse* funds by the SGICF combined with the secrecy surrounding the disbursement of payments were sufficient to ensure that the agenda was to preserve the basic structure of the industry while modernising sufficiently to keep afloat. It should be concluded, given the results and the troubles which were to plague the industry in the future, that the funds were used to support many marginal firms and that the aid served the purpose of re-establishing the traditional equilibrium in the sector. This serves as an illustration of how textile interests could mobilise to impose their agenda on the process of adjustment, and effectively block the changes which would lead to a more competitive industry in international trade.

(ii) The Trade Regime

The late 1950s and early 1960s saw the first and hesitant liberalisation of trade in the sector. Tariffs were increasingly seen by cotton interests as inadequate protection. Various non-tariff restrictions on cotton textile imports were added to protect markets against low-cost competition.[88] In France the period of rapid decolonisation once again threatened the system of protected markets constituted by the Zone Franc. Pressure across the industrialised countries became sufficient to ensure the convening of a multilateral conference of cotton importing and exporting countries, largely at the request of the United States. This was in addition to the many bilateral restrictive trade agreements which had developed between importers and low-cost producers over the 1950s (the Zone Franc was an integral part of this sort of policy).

The negotiations yielded what was to be the first of many multilateral framework agreements to impose non-tariff (usually quantitative) restrictions on low-cost LDC exporters with a view to protecting the industries of industrialised countries. Under the auspices of the General Agreement on Tariffs and Trade (GATT) a one-year agreement emerged: the Short-Term Arrangement Regarding International Trade in Cotton Textiles, to cover the period from 1961 to 1962, followed by the Long-Term Arrangement (LTA) which governed cotton textile trade from October 1962 to 1973, during which period it was renewed once.

Cotton textile products had proved the most vulnerable to international trade competition on industrialised-country markets, and were thus subject to an exceptional trade regime. Therefore, the inefficient French producers in spinning and weaving and in clothing manufacture were not only protected from competition from industrialised countries by traditional tariff barriers. They were also shielded from emerging low-cost producers by a (disintegrating) system of colonial markets in Africa and the newly established agreement, which covered any cotton textile product (including clothing) with a cotton fibre content of 50 per cent or more when measured by volume. This serves to emphasise the point that from early on in the process of transnationalisation which accompanied post-war economic development, textile and clothing industries were singled out for special treatment in what became an enduring exception to attempts to liberalise the post-war trade regime. Their substantial political resources were crucial to the way these protected markets were structured.

(b) The CIRIT Initiative

State–industry relations in the French textile and clothing sector became fixed on certain important policy issues, in particular the employers' attempts both to secure control of the process of adjustment and modernisation and to manipulate the trade regime. It was a clear attempt to structure the terms of global competition in their own favour, while domestic distributional conflicts were managed through the capture of state-initiated restructuring schemes. The goal of the trade agreements had been to prevent 'undue disruption of established industries',[89] and trade policy was simply one dimension of controlling the adjustment agenda. Trade protection was an ideal policy response in many respects: it cost little for the state to implement, particularly where there was international support, and such a policy left decisions on the process of adjustment to the industry itself while removing a principal incentive to adapt in the first place.

However, the rise of the trade issue signalled that the pressures of transnationalisation had begun to move to centre-stage. Decolonisation had spelt the end of the closed market system, as the newly independent countries erected their own tariff barriers to spur their own industrialisation. The industry's problems began to accumulate. Disincentives to invest resulted from the unresolved problem of dumping by small, antiquated firms. This led to a vicious circle of declining profits, compound inefficiency, and an impaired capacity to finance the investments necessary to confront the next round of competitive challenges.

The French industry was ill-equipped to confront new pressures. The rise of new producers, initially limited to the cotton trade, was in theory dealt with by the LTA. However, these new producers were by no means the only, or even the greatest, threat to the French textile industry as a whole. The spectre of increased competition from the industrialised countries of Europe through the Customs Union provisions of the Treaty of Rome began to haunt the industry.

The proposed Franco-Italian customs union had been shelved in 1951, but the European Coal and Steel Community (ECSC) had gone ahead. There was entrenched opposition to any such broadening of markets. It is not, therefore, surprising that the UIT demonstrated its opposition to the EEC project, while doing little to prepare the industry for entry into the customs union and integrated market.[90] However, the Common Market idea was in state eyes integral to the overall modernisation of the French economy, and too politically significant, for traditional sectoral interests to be allowed to stand in the way.[91] This was the larger context in which sectoral interests were unable to influence the course of events and prevent state policy from redrawing the boundaries of the market.

Accession to the Community in 1958 signalled the adoption of the policy of trade liberalisation (at least in relation to industrialised countries) as a fundamental political choice. A trade policy response to difficulties posed by the integration of the French textile and clothing industry into the Common Market was specifically excluded under the terms of the Treaty, at least once the common external tariff for the sector was phased in. An interesting dialogue therefore developed between the modernising and liberalising interests of the state, on the one hand, and attempts by traditional textile and clothing interests to maintain control of their own destiny, on the other. State priorities as expressed by the Planning Commission came to focus on the need to promote ongoing adjustment in French industry, and corporate concentration was seen as one of the principal means of achieving greater competitiveness. Tax incentives to promote mergers were established in 1965 and funds made available through the FDES to encourage the concentration of industrial firms.[92] The state clearly wished to eliminate the traditional characteristics of the industry through a market-led restructuring policy, a move which spelt doom to an entire socio-economic milieu.

The fragmented structure of the textile and clothing industries was evidently an obstacle to these state priorities, as was the success of the cotton sector in the 1950s at preserving a place for marginal firms. These were subsequently able to survive during the 1960s boom in consumption but in the long run were unable to confront the more efficient of their foreign or domestic competitors. Nonetheless, integration into the EU had to be faced one day or another. The industry, through its trade associations, tended to argue for general measures which would help all firms – including those on the margins.[93] A process of consultation began, which led to the development of the Centre Interprofessionnel de Rénovation des Structures Industrielles et Commerciales de l'Industrie Textile, mercifully abbreviated to CIRIT. The clothing industry was not originally included in this initiative, and, as will be seen, pressure to have it included was to be one of the important policy debates of the 1970s.

An examination of the establishment and implementation of CIRIT will provide considerable insights into the pattern state–industry relations which prevailed in textiles and clothing. After a long series of negotiations, the decision to establish the CIRIT was taken at the end of 1965. It should be noted that CIRIT was an initiative of the Textile Division (Direction des Industries Textiles et Diverses) of the Ministry of Industry, and an attempt to introduce a system of direct aid disbursement to firms. It was not a regime like the Caisse de Riblonnage, which had been controlled by the professional associations.[94] The objective was clearly to avoid the intermediation of the professional associations and to challenge directly the balance of economic and social forces in the sector through direct intervention at the level of corporate strategies.[95] The CIRIT initiative was thus an attempted departure from past patterns of state–industry relations and was aimed at encouraging the emergence of larger firms. By (poorly thought out) extension, large firms would be more competitive. If by-passing the traditional pattern of state–industry relations might be confounded by the fragmented corporate structure of the sector, what better way to accomplish this goal than to reorganise the sector into larger units which in the end would help the state impose its priorities of adjustment to market pressures?

Relations with the industry became a game of fine balance and deft manoeuvres for a state agency wishing to shape the course of industrial development. The new competitive pressures of liberalisation had exposed the latent state of crisis in the post-war textile and clothing industry which earlier policies had served to disguise. The employers were initially hostile to the negotiations and the still vague plan to redirect the old 'parafiscal' tax on textile products (they wanted to see it abolished altogether), towards a major restructuring the textile sector. However, the Textile Division of the Ministry of Industry was fully aware of its powerlessness to intervene in the industry without the support of its principal interlocutors, a situation which made compromise necessary from the outset. The professional associations were in a position of force as it turned out.[96]

The employers' organisations, jealous of their power over the adjustment agenda but facing a substantially restructured EU-wide market, were suspicious of any arrangement which left restructuring policy solely in the hands of the Textile Division. As representatives of the status quo within their respective branches, they had reason to be suspicious and resist the imposition of a programme of mergers and acquisitions which would adversely affect the fortunes and even existence of many small- and medium-sized member firms.

The general principle of a state aid and a restructuring programme was nonetheless accepted when the Ministry agreed that the proposed new agency should be 'largely in the hands of the profession'.[97] The governing council of CIRIT would be representative of all branches of the sector, and its secretariat would be provided by the UIT itself. Furthermore, in keeping with the employers' position, some of the proceeds of the reorganised parafiscal tax would go to the Institut Textile de France (ITF), a collective research organisation, thus making it less dependent on Ministry-of-Industry-controlled budget allocations and making it more firmly in the hands of the clients.[98]

The CIRIT project thereby became a joint initiative of the UIT and the Textile Division at the Ministry of Industry. The next hurdle was that of the resistance of the Ministry of Finance, in particular the notorious Direction du Trésor (Treasury Directorate). Here another motive of the Textile Division is uncovered – to avoid losing control of sectoral restructuring policy to the powerful Trésor. In this situation, the support of the professional associations became doubly important. The power of the Textile Division consisted essentially in its ability to use the support of one group to overcome the resistance of the other, and, one hoped, end up holding the ring. The Trésor preferred (and apparently would have been willing to pay for) the more direct control facilitated by a plan similar to the 1966 steel programme, using direct Treasury credits and the funds of the FDES rather than the parafiscal tax. This would have deprived the Textile Division of the financial autonomy afforded by the parafiscal arrangement.

To circumvent the Trésor, the Ministry of Industry relied heavily on the outside political contacts of the textile notables which short-circuited the normal bureaucratic channels to obtain the agreement in principal of the Treasury. Even the Prime Minister's office was called upon to arbitrate. The role of these extra-administrative contacts, demonstrating once again the power of textile groups in parliamentary and ministerial circles, proved decisive.[99] The Ministry of Finance agreed to the concept of a parafiscal tax and a restructuring agency under the control of the Textile Division which would manage the funds.

In the negotiations which decided the implementation and operation of the new agency, the Textile Division also managed to maintain the upper hand in its dealings with Finance. State control of the agency would rest in the hands of the Director of the Textile Division or his representative, who would have a veto over any of the Committee's operations.[100] Finance would have to be satisfied with a mere *controleur financier*[101] on CIRIT.

However, when a decision had to be made on the specific objectives of fund allocation, the game changed radically. The professional associations desired quite broad terms of reference for CIRIT interventions. This included interest-rate subsidies on investment loans, various collective actions, and a programme for the elimination of marginal firms (*assainissement*) through a sort of redundancy payment for employers willing to close shop before they collapsed, thus attenuating the competitive pressure caused by those who survived by dumping. This was the 'modernisation' agenda, as promoted by the employers, which would not disturb the competitive equilibrium among firms in the sector as much as the encouragement of corporate concentration, and would permit access by all firms, small or large, competitive or ailing, to the proposed scheme of aid to the sector.

The Textile Division, on the other hand, desired a more narrowly defined restructuring process which principally involved corporate concentration. The aim was to circumvent the power of the profession and prevent it commandeering the policy agenda as had happened in the past. In this it found itself strongly supported by the Ministry of Finance, and was quite prepared to use the entrenched position of the latter in order to resist the pressure of the professional associations in favour of 'modernisation'. Given the situation, the Ministry of Industry could maintain its legitimacy in the eyes of its industrial clients, pointing to the veto of the culpable Ministry of Finance, and still come out with its own position intact.[102]

Alliances in this game of private-public interaction, the aim of which was to determine the terms of competition in the market, remained flexible. The Textile Division constantly sought both to outwit its powerful rival in Finance and to court its industrial constituency, either of which was capable of blocking any initiative in the first place. In this way, CIRIT emerged[103] as a committee largely in the hands of the Ministry of Industry, independent of the Ministry of Finance, and dedicated to a restructuring process narrowly defined as one of corporate concentration through mergers and takeovers. The opinions expressed by sample firms clearly showed that only the largest firms, generally those with over a thousand workers (there were very few), were in favour of corporate concentration as a goal for the sector. All but the most marginal firms (which would be eliminated) accepted the 'modernisation' and *assainissement* agenda.

The policy of corporate concentration was strengthened by the strict secrecy which surrounded the operations of CIRIT. The Committee could safeguard its capacity to grant funds selectively and avoid the process being blocked by public debate or machinations within the professional associations.[104] The Ministry of Industry's power of veto over any project of the Committee, though it was never used, was also a safeguard. Nonetheless, this policy remained constrained by what was tacitly acknowledged from the beginning of the negotiations: state policies could not be forced on an unwilling profession, as the Textile Division required the active cooperation of the professional associations in order to legitimate initiatives and ensure their successful implementation.

The situation was bound to come unstuck. Large firms became, as expected, the principal beneficiaries of the aid programme, and they could maintain direct contacts with the administration without using the professional associations as intermediaries. However, the web of interlocking relationships between the Textile Division, firms (including the largest in the sector), and the professional associations, which bound them all together in patterns of mutual dependency, proved decisive. The pressure of the industry federations in favour of a redefined aid policy for the committee was great enough to lead to reforms in CIRIT after only two years, and further and more important reforms in 1971.

Despite the clear need for the sector to undergo a process of adaptation to the new competitive realities of import competition and declining domestic market share, CIRIT had encountered consistent difficulties in disbursing all its available resources. The professional associations quite simply did not distribute to their members the necessary information about the new aid programme. Many companies remained ignorant of the activities of the committee and of the assistance available for expansion through corporate concentration.[105] Furthermore (with the exception of the few large firms), the professional associations acted as intermediaries for those industrialists they did inform, giving expert advice and assistance in handling requests for aid. Indeed, about half the requests for aid came through the intermediary of the professional associations,[106] once again highlighting their influence. The professional associations played a fundamental role in maintaining the cohesion of their respective branches, and if the interests of larger firms were to be supported within the professional associations, the large firms would have to accept the game of conflict resolution which took place within the various industry federations. Large firms freely admitted that their interests remained bound to those of the professional associations in the long run.[107]

It was not long before the policy was challenged. The profession supported the idea of an increase in the amount of government funds available, and despite the fierce resistance of the Ministry of Finance a reform was obtained permitting CIRIT to finance 'modernisation' plans and the elimination of marginal firms. 'Modernisation' projects were, however, to be limited to proposals *accompanied* by mergers or takeovers. The concentration agenda effectively remained in place and financial assistance continued to go mainly to large enterprises.

However, the new Sixth Plan's (1971–5) industrial development priorities put the emphasis on productive investments in industry, a perceptible shift away from the single priority formerly accorded to corporate concentration. Though the 'large industrial groups' were seen as central to this strategy, it was recognised that the role of small and medium firms could be essential in activities where 'size is not the primary source of productivity.'[108] Modernisation became much more of a byword, to be accompanied by the accelerated growth of promising small- and medium-sized enterprises.[109]

With respect to textiles and clothing, the new Plan saw restructuring and modernisation as twin imperatives.[110] This sounded rather more like the profession's own agenda as expressed in the report of the textile sectoral committee involved in the preparation of the Plan: the report had gone so far as to claim that restructuring was excessively limited to large firms and to spell out four axes of 'Modernisation'.[111]

There was then a change in the orientation of industrial policy. The Textile Division, clearly reinforcing its position *vis-à-vis* the Ministry of Finance while at the same time responding to pressure from its own constituency, managed in difficult negotiations to gain the use of CIRIT funds for securing the financing of 'exceptional investment programmes'. The definition of 'exceptional' turned out, however, to be relatively lax – any amount of investment which exceeded the (traditionally low) average of the textile branch in question. Further-more, the professional associations gained the right officially to intervene in the CIRIT selection process by appending their opinion to each proposal. This new 'modernisation' programme was implemented in July 1971. The professional associations had manifestly succeeded in once again imposing their own adjustment agenda of managed com-petition on the Division, which had originally set out to order from above. The role of the professional associations seemed as entrenched as ever as they sought to limit competition by winding down old firms (*assainissement*) and helping others modernise whether they possessed the slightest of competitive advantage or not. This enabled them to maintain the balance among textile interests, and they had comman-deered the CIRIT process to this end. Furthermore, the celebrated clash between large and small capital which was emphasised by some,[112] and which might have been expected, did not take place.

(c) Summary: State, Industry, and Capture

Although there is considerable variation in the associational systems of the industrialised countries, *the French case serves as an illustration of policy capture common across a number of high-wage textile producers. The French case is doubly significant because it took place in the context of what was typically regarded as a strong state with a weak civil society*.[113] In the CIRIT case, which provides insight into the nature of state–industry relations in the French textile sector, the various departments of the state administration vigorously defended their own notions of adjustment policy. However, the sectoral services of the Ministry of Industry revealed themselves to be dependent for their influence within the Administration on their legitimacy in the eyes of their client sector.

The Textile Division thus functioned in two directions, and was in fact as much an intermediary between the industry and elite state policy-makers as it was an organ of the state itself, *representing a fusion of state and market agents in a single pattern of governance*. The sectoral agency could take little initiative without the active coopera-tion of the sector for which it was responsible, and particularistic interests in fact gained representation through capture of the state bureaucracy.[114] The much-vaunted separation between state and market could not be observed, and they combined to form a system of governance in the sector.

This ambiguous relationship of dependency-responsibility *vis-à-vis* an industrial sector is best understood in relation to information and the development of expertise. In order to prepare initiatives, the sectoral divisions depended on their industrial constituencies for information and expertise and for the articulation and expression of problems and grievances as they occurred. This expertise and sensitivity to the industrial world became the trump card for the sectoral divisions of the Ministry of Industry when they sought to take initiatives which necessarily involved bargaining with other departments over shared or disputed jurisdictions, especially with the Trésor.

Very compartmentalised from each other, these bureaucratic agencies functioned in a closed circuit with the employers' organisations of their respective industrial sectors, organisations which to some extent they considered *extensions of themselves* in the industrial world. The employers' organisations veritably transformed information in accordance with the balance of forces within their ranks, an equilibrium which these organisations vigorously sought to maintain despite all sorts of state and economic pressures pushing the other way.[115] The state had little chance to impose its own priorities, especially in so far as the state also relied on the professional associations to legitimate initiatives taken in the industrial domain.

Policy-makers were apparently aware of this difficulty. In the National Assembly, during the discussion of the Ministry of Industry's proposed budget for 1974, committee reports expressed suspicion about the use of the 'Crédits d'Action de Politique Industrielle' (CAPIs) which constituted the principal instrument of sectoral intervention outside specialised sectoral programmes.[116] The professional associations acted as a 'veritable screen'[117] between firms and the organs of the state.

From the point of view of the Textile Division, this situation also undermined the credibility of the sectoral service in its machinations with the Trésor. The Trésor was responsible, in the last analysis, for any intervention in the industrial domain which involved a financial outlay and was the self-proclaimed guardian of the 'general' against 'particular' interests in the disbursement of assistance to industry and the economy.[118] The victory of Industry over Finance in the CIRIT initiative was therefore an exception to the general rule, but presumably confirmed the suspicions of the Ministry of Finance, as the employers' organisation commandeered the process in a sophisticated display of policy piracy.

Compared with other industrial sectors, aid to the textile and clothing sector remained strictly limited despite the demonstrable political influence of the sector. What accounts for this paradox? In essence, the employers' organisations had successfully fought for this state of affairs, using the dependent Textiles Division of the Ministry of Industry as a 'Trojan Horse' in the market to undermine the state's restructuring agenda. They were unwilling to accept higher levels of state aid if that meant losing control of the restructuring process. If the sector was low among state industrial policy priorities, this did not signify that the state itself was uninterested in textiles: 'One must not lose sight of this characteristic of the textile employers, who prefer themselves to take in hand – requesting *ad hoc* the means from the authorities – the direction of redeployment.'[119]

Like earlier policy initiatives, CIRIT left the process of restructuring in the hands of the employers themselves. Private interests thus translated, through capture, into public policy. These private interests controlled the terms of competition across the textile and clothing sector, at least in the domestic market. Despite the availability of technological solutions to their competitive weaknesses, technology did not mean change.[120]

However, it must be recognised that state policy towards the industry was not confined to sector-specific interventions. Trade policy was a prime example – policy prerogatives were shared between the EU and its member states. Trade policy was, then, much more difficult to manage but would become increasingly important in terms of producer control of the structure of the market.

Of course the steady transnationalisation of the sector was eventually likely to undermine the state–industry game. The severe economic crisis associated with the oil shock exposed this problem dramatically. The problem was exacerbated by the simultaneous introduction of the Kennedy Round tariff reductions and the ongoing process of European market integration. An uncompetitive sector was at the end of the rope as domestic policy initiatives were less and less able to have an impact on the structure of the market and the terms of competition. The tensions of the 1974 crisis reopened distributional conflict across the sector. When questions of international trade were raised particularistic interests of the textile and clothing sector came to represent the 'national' interest in the global textile and clothing trade regime.

The capture of the trade regime will be analysed in the next chapter. Meanwhile, this chapter turns briefly to *associational patterns among textile interests in Italy. The contrast with the French case was dramatic. A similar historical pattern of close cooperation, yet on a background of a contrasting industrial culture within the Italian textile and clothing associations, fostered market-led adjustment through a dynamic strategy of flexible specialisation. The Italian industry was able to replace the French sector as the premier producer of fashion articles in Europe.*

FLEXIBLE SPECIALISATION AND ASSOCIATIONAL SYSTEMS IN THE ITALIAN TEXTILE AND CLOTHING INDUSTRY

In Italy, a distinct industrial culture (as manifest in the practices of Italian producers) and associational system developed in the 1970s and 1980s. This yielded a correspondingly different pattern of state–industry relations and a far more successful outcome in terms of adjustment to intensifying competitive pressures. There were of course some similarities: Italian textile and clothing employers associations were very tied to their locality and region, and they were protectionist like their French counterparts on the whole. However, they placed market-led adjustment at the top of their agenda, with relatively little reliance on specific state interventions or state resources.[121] What state assistance there was became harnessed to the adjustment strategy of the professional associations.

Many analysts have addressed the question of specialisation, segmentation, and the division of labour. An important puzzle consists in determining the proper degree of specialisation for firms to engage in, relative to the resulting cost structures in the context of the potential markets (final demand) for their products. Specialisation implies problems of coordination when it comes to integrating diverse production processes with the dynamic structure of final demand. Each firm in a particular pattern of specialisation requires information about the nature of final demand as well as information on intermediary inputs from other specialised firms. In a complex production stream such as the textile and clothing, the result is either networks of firms working together with greater or lesser degrees of collective coordination (often these networks operate across state borders), or the integration of this process into a large corporate entity (vertical integration). Either way, the specialised knowledge which yields cost advantages in the production process must be rendered relevant to the dynamics of final demand.

As was demonstrated in Chapters 1 and 2, large integrated firms were not necessarily successful competitors in the textile and clothing sectors. Firms in the sector were often pushed towards a strategy of specialisation, but then remained exposed to the imperfections of the market as a coordinating mechanism when it came to adapting to rapidly changing patterns of final demand. This was magnified by the perfidy of the 'textile cycle'. Specialisation therefore poses a problem of information with regard to both production processes and the market for eventual outputs. At some stage, the process of production which has been fragmented through specialisation, based on techno-logical and organisational expertise in relation to production pro-cesses, must be reintegrated so as to produce products in line with consumer preferences. This specialisation based on the cognitive capa-city of firms, 'is therefore accompanied by the development of new modes of co-ordination...'[122]

This implies that the geographical proximity of a network of firms in a fast moving market may be a considerable advantage, and the development of 'industrial districts' of small and medium firms con-stitutes the necessary underlying condition.[123] As was argued in the Introduction to this book, *the international division of labour in the textile and clothing sector did not depend on traditional notions of comparative advantage, but on the specific competitive advantages of firms in their institutional and organisation context.*[124]

The mechanisms of cooperation which emerged among small and medium Italian textile and clothing firms replicated the sorts of coordinating mechanisms normally associated with large integrated corporations, but did not suffer from bureaucratic rigidities or the problems of overcapitalisation associated with large corporations in the industry. The role played by the employers associations and their close relations with local authorities and the state was crucial to creating the conditions for sharing expertise and market information cooperatively. In contrast to the situation in the French textile and clothing sector, the dense local networks of the Italian employers' organisations did not lead to ossification, but to dynamism and adaptation to global markets.

The Italian industry was (and remains) particularly fragmented in terms of corporate structure when compared to other advanced industrialised countries (even more so than the French industry). Nonetheless, these small and medium firms are heavily concentrated into industrial districts in the north of the country: parts of Veneto, Lombardy, Tuscany, and Piedmont.[125] While there was relatively little in the way of direct state support for the industry, local initiatives to promote the adjustment and competitiveness of the industry have been many and varied. These have been carried out by a number of different local institutions, but local employers associations were invariably central to the process. Firms tended to be completely 'immersed' in their local environment, including the associational system and the specific set of market interdependencies peculiar to the locality.[126] In this sense, there are cultural, political, as well as organisational dimensions to Italian textile and clothing industrial districts. These districts constitute a series of institutionalised interdependencies of labour, business organisations, firms-as-members, and local government. Employers' organisations, while central in terms of inter-firm cooperation, are clearly not the only players.[127] These districts constitute sub-systems of socio-economic governance in the broadest sense, organising local responses to the pressures of the global market.

Structural change in the global context of the Italian textile and clothing sector, in particular intensified cross-border competition (transnationalisation) within the EU and with LDC producers, was one of the factors which led to important changes in the industrial culture and associational system in Italy, from the 1970s onwards. The second pressure was that of state intervention in the sector. The early years of the 1970s were bad ones for the industry as it adjusted to the new EU Common Market and low-wage competition. The state sponsored a sectoral aid programme enacted by legislation in 1971, which was extended beyond its original 1975 horizon. In 1978 another more limited programme was implemented.

The first of these programmes concentrated on restructuring, rationalisation, and modernisation and favouring the more capital-intensive sectors. The second had more to do with maintaining the employment base and encouraging production in the disadvantaged south of the country, and therefore probably benefited the labour-intensive clothing industry most.[128] The most important point, however, is that the intervention of the state provided an incentive for a reorganisation of the associational system in the sector. The interests of the industrialists and other players in the district-state–market complex, would be facilitated by the emergence of a single inter-locuteur which could bargain with the state on the terms of sectoral assistance and could articulate the industry's point of view at the EU level as well.[129] The aim was to encourage a market structure which favoured the maintenance and indeed development of the domestic sector, from upstream to downstream activities, and refuted the 'changing international division of labour' thesis which of course implied the sector's inevitable decline.

The result was a new association, Federtessile, which grouped together the most important national level subsectoral professional associations in the country, from spinning and weaving processes to clothing manufacture, and from the cotton industry to the silk producers. By 1978 (with state aid all but over) the association had come up with a plan to develop the Italian industry into the premier sector in the European Union.

As in the French case the professional association sought to limit the direct intervention of the state into the affairs of individual firms, but in other respects the contrast between the practices of the French and Italian associations and firms could not be more clear. The aim of the association was not to preserve an untenable status quo among interests in the sector, but to promote the development of the industry and to *'refuser la fatalité'*, to use a phrase which was popular among the French professional associations but seldom lived up to there. Federtessile worked hard to make sure that the state's priorities were those of the professional associations, including trade protection but also a dynamic export strategy and constant investment in modernisation.[130] In this case 'capture' had positive implications and resulted in a radical restructuring of production and the EU market.

Although the strategy was developed at the peak level, Federtessile was a long way from constituting a centralised associational system. The peak association *was* able to develop a national strategy and the *élan* to go with it, but much of the coordinating work went on at the local level and Federtessile policy-making was not free of controversy when it came to conflicts of interest between, for instance, capital intensive and labour intensive subsectors of the industry. Local forms of coordination were therefore fundamental to, indeed the *sine qua non* of, the success of Federtessile's textile development plan. There was a coexistence of cooperation and competition, as district-level processes helped to mediate the price structure of inputs and other market relationships.[131] Taken together, the national and district level became an innovative and integrated set of institutions for governing market and production relationships in global competition, and the economic success demonstrated that low-wage competition could be confronted.

Members of local associations could build on local market interdependencies which were in turn facilitated by the geographical concentration of firms into districts: 'the costs of transportation, information etc. among firms [were] very low and the external economies quite high.'[132] The local associations were particularly effective in providing 'new' services to their members: (a) promotional activities for the products of industrial districts (which helps upstream and downstream producers alike), especially in export markets; (b) negotiation of advantageous prices from suppliers external to the district, especially raw materials; (c) organising contractual relationships among interdependent firms in the district, thus providing an integrative rationale to the behaviour of the many small firms involved.[133] This is in addition to the provision of sophisticated computerised market information systems and the requisite assistance with information technology to facilitate just-in-time flexibility in the production process.

Two examples can illustrate the point.[134] The first is the Como silk district of northern Lombardy.[135] This district accounted for some 10 per cent of all Italian textile fabrics exported in 1985, and is synonymous with the quality of fabric required for high fashion throughout Europe. The Como silk district's industrial success has placed Italy in lead position in the European silk industry and a keen competitor with Asian (Japanese, Chinese) production. The production stream in the district is dominated by small producers of both intermediary and finished goods, and these firms are tightly knit in a pattern of market and socio-cultural interdependencies. Producers at all stages of the production stream press their partners to specialise and modernise so as to maximise the district's productive efficiency as a whole.

The associational structure of the district involved sector-specific organisations, which went so far as to act as a consortium for raw silk imports and foreign trade promotion. There are also inter-sectoral 'territorial' associations representing industrialists across the district, which are in turn divided into sectoral councils. Given the importance of silk production to the overall prosperity of the district, these associations coordinated the provision of such collective goods as an expensive water pollution clean-up and organised secure water supplies for the industry.

The major competitive challenge to the district came from the introduction in about 1980 of a new form of synthetic silk from Japanese manufacturers, an imitation which even experts have difficulty distinguishing from the real product. Between 1981 and 1985, 52 firms went to the wall.[136] Local employers' organisations sponsored the *Tessile di Como* which successfully rationalised contractual relations among producers, created a marketing information system to monitor shifting patterns of demand, promoted research and development, and even created a collective trademark for the district's producers of finished goods. Local government, the employers' organisations, and local banks provided the finance, all under the guidance of the district's inter-industry organisations.

A second case concerns the textile and clothing manufacturers of the Veneto.[137] Rising labour costs in northern Italy (among the highest in Europe) were having an intensified impact on the Veneto clothing industry by the early 1990s. Particularly in the Vicenza district,[138] small and medium firms had come to dominate high-quality, brand-name textile and clothing production in a complex web of contractual relationships with the major fashion houses and large textile firms and with each other. This pattern of governance was instrumental in the extraordinary international success of the Italian fashion industry. Despite the collective commitment of firms to the district, a culture of entrepreneurial individualism dominated the years of rapid growth in production in the late 1970s and the 1980s.

More recently, competitive pressures led the industrialists to contemplate increasing the degree of overseas subcontracting in the clothing industry. If this were to be carried out in an uncoordinated way, there was a considerable risk that the set of market interdependencies would break down and that entire segments of the production stream would migrate overseas (as occurred in Germany, Holland, and was occurring in France). Nonetheless, if some degree of outward processing were not pursued, then the district's industry faced a dramatic contraction, with the collapse of downstream clothing production rebounding upstream to the fabric and yarn producers.

This situation and risk sparked a collective response to the problem in the 1990s. The district clothing federation has been highly conscious of the need to plan the adjustment of the industry so as to preserve the knowledge base of entrepreneurs, the skills of the workforce, and to prevent entire segments of the production stream from disappearing overseas. Thus the employers' organisation has developed a strong sense of solidarity, encouraging the retention of high value-added production in Italy, planning the dislocation of more casual and less exclusive/lower quality clothing through outward processing, all the while maintaining a strategy based on quality and exclusive brand-names.[139]

The success of the Italian textile and clothing industry is therefore embedded in the competitive practices of firms as developed through

the integration of the employers' organisations with political authorities at national and particularly district level. Sophisticated systems
were developed to govern local production and market structures in
a context of rising global market competition. By simultaneously
capturing national and local policy processes, the professional associations controlled the terms of state assistance and of course international trade policy (see Chapter 4). At the local level they developed
forms of market coordination, technological diffusion, and a pattern
of market interdependencies built on specialisation, flexible production strategies responding to volatile consumer preferences, and subcontracting relationships. The result was an almost ideal-typical case
of 'flexible specialisation'[140] in marked contrast to the French or the
UK textile and clothing sectors.

The analysis certainly affirms that the associational structure and
the integration of state and market actors has made up for market
imperfections in a fragmented production stream. In fact, however,
one must move conceptually beyond economists' notions of market
imperfection to a notion of 'market structuration' and governance
through political interaction: the associational systems which articulated the perceived self-interest of producers were a crucial variable in
the process of structuring the market and the ongoing global competitiveness of Italian producers. Markets were fundamentally shaped by
the political interaction of organised social forces and the pattern of
their integration into the institutions of political authority.

CONCLUSION

This chapter has demonstrated the importance of understanding the
ways in which the interests of socio-economic groups are articulated
within a particular pattern of political institutions. Across the
advanced industrial economies, textile and clothing interests were capable of mobilising politically to defend their perceived socio-economic
interests within the body of the state's institutions. Each national set of
state–industry relations differed in important ways from the others,
but effective capture of at least limited elements of the policy agenda
occurred across the cases analysed.

The emphasis here has been on the domestic state, but it is clear that
the issues around which these associational groups were mobilised
were very much transnational in nature, given that the system of
production and market structure to which producers were obliged to

adjust (or fail) was effectively transnationalised. This is yet further confirmation of the point made in the Introduction concerning the conceptualisation levels of analysis in the international trade regime and wider international system. The traditional conceptualisation of the global system as separate domestic and international levels is effectively an irrelevant concept when measured against the strategies pursued by the socio-economic actors themselves. While associational and policy-making mechanisms may remain essentially national in scope, conflict over the structure of the market and other distributional questions fails to respect in any way the discreet categories of traditional (domestic versus international) analysis. This point will become even more evident in the next chapter where the analysis of the political economy of capture is extended to consideration of the institutions of the trade regime.

This chapter also casts light on the conceptual issue of structure versus agency in the global political economy. Associational systems were crucial to understanding how firms, as agents in their respective organisational or institutional context, effectively structured competition by contesting the nature of the market and its distributional consequences. This conflict took place simultaneously within the institutions of governance of several advanced industrial states in a context of increasingly global market and production structures, and textile and clothing groups squared off against other agglomerations of socio-economic interests.

As will be demonstrated in the next chapter, these simultaneous conflicts of interest came to a head in the politics of the trade regime, but the dynamics of associational systems can also hold the key to a failed or a successful outcome in terms of the competitive practices of firms. This is because associational systems and policy processes constitute the organisational context of industrial culture. Some associational groups (particularly France and the UK) used their political resources in such a way as, at the end of the day, to worsen their status as economic liabilities to their respective national economies. Others (Italy in particular) commandeered the policy process to produce a radical industrial success story, accelerating adjustment to the intensified competition borne of increasing transnationalistion.

Finally, and most importantly, this chapter demonstrates more than any other in this work that the formal institutions of political authority and the socio-economic insitutions of the market are fused together in an integrated pattern of governance. This chapter showed explicitly how the particularistic interests of private market actors were inserted into the policy-making processes of the state and were locked in distributional struggle with other socio-economic actors (who were often located in other political systems) to affect the structure of the market. Market actors appropriated the mantle of political authority for particularistic ends, however much this was portrayed as the public interest. In the light of this evidence it is difficult to argue that states and markets are anything but mutually interdependent.[141] Market structure was far from being the spontaneous order of the economics textbooks; it was the result of the conscious articulation of policy preferences in tandem with the corresponding competitive practices of firms. The next chapter goes on to extend the analysis to the international trade regime and the rise of protectionism under the guise of the MFA.

Notes

1. There are typically two notions of 'capture' in the literature. In some cases associated with the public choice literature, regulatory capture is used to illustrate the somewhat dogmatic point that regulatory regimes are initiated to serve the regulated. A second notion of capture, and the one employed here, denotes cases where a particular set of interests in the political economy acquire excessive influence over the official bodies, supposed guardians of the 'public interest', to which they are in theory subject. In these cases, the institutions of state and the definition of the public interest is effectively appropriated by private interests in limited regulatory domains, but this situation is far from inevitable. See William W. Bratton and Joseph A. McCahery, 'Regulatory Competition, Regulatory Capture, and Corporate Self-regulation', *North Carolina Law Review*, vol. 73/5, June 1995, pp. 1903–25.

2. For a more conceptual discussion of patterns of interest intermediation in relation to the textile and clothing sector, see Geoffrey R.D. Underhill, 'Neo-Corporatist Theory and the Politics of Industrial Decline', *European Journal of Political Research*, vol. 16, 1988, pp. 489–511.

3. Andrew Martin, 'Political Constraints on Economic Strategies in Advanced Industrial States', *Comparative Political Studies*, vol. 10, no. 3, October 1977, p. 333.

4. One also might argue that most 'consumers' have ambiguous interests in the sense that a large proportion of them might also be producers through their employment, and therefore worried about the issue of industrial job losses in general.

5. Martin Wolf, Hans H. Glismann, Joseph Selzman and Dean Spinanger, *Costs of Protecting Jobs in Textiles and Clothing* (London: Trade Policy Research Centre, 1984), p. 32.

6. See discussion in Richard Friman, *Patchwork Protectionism: Textile Trade Policy in the United States, Japan, and West Germany* (Ithaca: Cornell University Press, 1990), pp. 65–71; David A. Lynch, *National and International Sources of American Foreign Economic Policy: The North American Free Trade Agreement*, unpublished PhD thesis, University of California at Santa Barbara, 1995, esp. ch. 5.

7. Friman, op. cit., p. 70.

8. Lane Steven Hurewitz, *Textiles*, a volume in the series *The GATT Uruguay Round: A Negotiating History*, ed. Terence P. Stewart (Deventer/Boston: Kluwer Law and Taxation, 1993), p. 68, note 366.

9. One should note that, particularly in the clothing sector, employment levels continue to decline sharply, reducing the influence of the workforce, as voters, to a considerable extent.

10. Interview with Mr W. Tagliani, Second Secretary (Responsible for Textiles), Office of the US Trade Representative, Geneva, 29 May 1996.

11. Interview with Mr Robert Shepherd, now retired, formerly MFA and Uruguay Round textile negotiator (1980–94), Office of the US Trade Representative Office, Geneva, and Chair (1976–9) of the Committee for the Implementation of Textile Agreements (CITA), 30 May 1996.

12. Tagliani interview.

13. Shepherd interview.

14. Tagliani interview.

15. Interviews with Shepherd and Tagliani; the Democratic Party has its share of similar supporters.

16. See William R. Cline, *The Future of World Trade in Textiles and Apparel* (Washington, DC: Institute for International Economics, 1990), pp. 208–30; Hurewitz, op. cit., pp. 68–72.

17. Shepherd interview.

18. Tagliani interview.

19. Shepherd interview.

20. Ibid.

21. Ibid.

22. See Lord Hailsham, 'Elective Dictatorship', *The Listener*, 21 October 1976, pp. 496–500.

23. Caroline Miles, 'Protection in the British Textile Industry', in W.M. Corden and G. Fels (eds), *Public Assistance to Industry: Protection and Subsidies in Britain and Germany* (London: Macmillan, 1976), pp. 184–214.

24. See Janet Walsh, 'The Performance of UK Textiles and Clothing: Recent Controversies and Evidence', *International Review of Applied Economics*, 5/3, 1991, pp. 297–303.

25. Ibid., p. 302.

26. See the example of Courtaulds, in Arthur Knight, *Private Enterprise and Public Intervention: The Courtaulds Experience* (London: Allen & Unwin, 1974).

27. See ibid., ch. 5.

28. Miles, 'Protection in the British Textile Industry', op. cit., pp. 189–90.

29. J.P. Hayes, *Making Trade Policy in the European Community* (London: Macmillan/Trade Policy Research Centre, 1993), p. 109.

30.   See for example William Lazonick, 'The Cotton Industry', in B. Elbaum and W. Lazonick (eds), *The Decline of the British Economy* (Oxford: Clarendon Press, 1986), pp. 18–50, and Janet Walsh, *Structural Change and Industrial Decline: The Case of British Textiles*, unpublished PhD thesis, University of Warwick, 1989, esp. pp. 155–84.

31.   Including employment subsidies, half of which went to preserve jobs in the textile and clothing industry; Organisation for Economic Cooperation and Development, *Textile and Clothing Industries: Structural Problems and Policies in OECD Countries* (Paris, 1983), pp. 111–12, 117 hereafter OECD Report.

32.   The (confederated) peak association representing employers in the UK.

33.   Hayes, *Making Trade Policy*, op. cit., p. 110.

34.   Ibid., pp. 117–19.

35.   See France, Conseil Economique et Social, 'Le Devenir des industries du textile et de l'habillement', report published in *Journal Officiel* (Avis et rapports du Conseil Economique et Social), 25 February 1982, p. 221, based on UNEDIC figures; hereafter referred to as 'CES Report'.

36.   See Monique Thouvenin, 'Aperçu sur l'industrie du coton et des fibres alliées dans le massif vosgien et sa périphérie', *Revue géographique de l'est*, vol. xix, no. 3–4, July–December, pp. 215–36, on product specialisation in Alsace and the Lorraine. The Vosges tended to become increasingly specialised in cotton spinning and weaving, thus increasing their vulnerability to the main thrust of low-cost competition, with Alsace moving towards the higher value added activities of dyeing and printing/enhancement and away from cotton manufacture.

37.   Several examples can be cited from the local and regional press, but one which particularly stands out was the closure in autumn 1976 by Rhône-Poulenc Textiles of their Péage-de-Roussillon factory in the rural Midi.

38.   Thouvenin, op. cit., p. 217.

39.   The crisis elicited, for example, the 'Plan Vosges' in 1978, a state and local government effort to draw other industries to the region and improve local infrastructures to that end (see Daniel Bruhnes and Samia Ismail, 'Le Point sur le textile et l'habillement', *Les Dossiers de l'économie Lorraine*, no. 58, May 1980, p. 32). One can also gauge the political impact of the problem by the intensity of parliamentary questioning and debate by Vosges deputies in the National Assembly. During the crisis, both Philippe Séguin, prominent in the RPR, and Christian Pierret of the Socialists, both became effective spokesmen for textile interests. Both were members of the commission of enquiry into the problems of the textile industry (See the National Assembly Report), the former as *Rapporteur*, and Pierret was a constant critic of government policy at the time. See for example the debate on the 1981 budget for the Ministry of Industry in the *Journal Officiel* (édition débats parlementaires), no. 79, 14 November 1980, p. 3843.

40.   See France, INSEE, *Roanne: bassin d'emploi dominé par le textile*, Paris: INSEE, 1979.

41.   Rhône-Poulenc's textile division employed 27,000 in 1967, and only 15,000 by 1977 (*J'Informe*, 5 October 1977).

42. See for example *L'Humanité*, 19 August 1978, and the questioning of Industry Minister Giraud by deputies Séguin and Pierret in the National Assembly Report, vol. II-2, 'Auditions', pp. 105–6.

43. *Les Echos,* 21 July 1977.

44. Yves Mény and Vincent Wright, *La Crise de la sidérurgie, Européenne 1974–1984* (Paris: Presses Universitaires de France, 1985), p. 39.

45. See CES Report, p. 221.

46. Such as in the case of Montefibre, Schlumpf, or the Boussac-Willot affair.

47. Much has already been cited on the furore surrounding the Boussac case. For evidence of parliamentary discontent, see for example the debate over the 1979 budget of the Ministry of Industry in *Journal Officiel* (édition débats parlementaires), nos. 83 and 84, 20–21 October 1978, pp. 6454–5, where redundancies and firm employment strategies were a major issue.

48. This became increasingly clear throughout the 1981 election campaign, which put the Left in power and in which industrial crisis was a major issue.

49. *Chômage partiel* – workers were placed on reduced hours with subsidised compensation payments as a means of avoiding genuine lay-offs.

50. A look at France, Projet de loi portant règlement définitif du budget de ... (year), annexe, *Rapport au parlement sur les fonds publics attribués à titre d'aides aux entreprises industrielles* (years 1973–82), will verify this.

51. For a general historical account of the emergence of the French *patronat*, see Jean Lambert, *Le Patron* (Brussels: Bloud and Gay, 1969), where there is considerable reference to the textile families of the Nord and Est of France. See also Suzananne Berger, 'The Traditional Sector in France and Italy', in Berger (ed.), *Dualism and Discontinuity in Industrial Societies* (Cambridge University Press, 1980) on developments in the post-war era.

52. See below: section on the historical development of state–industry relations in the sector.

53. See David S. Landes, 'French Business and the Businessman', in Edward Meade Earle (ed.), *Modern France: Problems of the Third and Fourth Republics* (Princeton University Press, 1951), p. 336. These practices have also been discussed above in relation to corporate structures and sectoral performance (the role of traditional firms) in Chapter 2.

54. Marcel Boussac, for instance, was reluctant to engage in restructuring which would result in large-scale redundancies in the small Vosges communities in which his factories were located and toward which he felt a paternal responsibility. These attitudes had their origins in the last century. With respect to the paternalism of the textile families of the Nord, see P. Pierrard, *Histoire du Nord* (Paris: Hachette 1978, pp. 359–60), or Lambert, *Le Patron*, op. cit., pp. 95–7; p. 128. The social-Catholic movement, beginning in the 1870s, was perhaps a more systematic attempt by the French *patronat* to define their paternalistic role in society (see ibid., pp. 125–35).

55. See Berger, 'The Traditional Sector', op. cit., pp. 104–9; p. 144.
56. Henry W. Ehrmann, *Organised Business in France* (Princeton University Press, 1957), pp. 247–50.
57. Ibid., p. 316.
58. See for example *L'Aurore*, 31 December 1976, on the government's measures to help the textile industry.
59. Mény and Wright, *La Crise*, op. cit., p. 41.
60. Benoît Boussemart, *Industrie de main d'oeuvre et division internationale du travail: l'avenir de l'industrie textile de la région Nord-Pas-de-Calais*, 3 vols, unpublished thesis, Doctorat ès en Sciences Economiques, Université de Paris X (Nanterre), December 1984, p. 611, note 113.
61. Ehrmann, *Organised Business*, op. cit., p. 39.
62. CES report, p. 223.
63. Erhard Friedberg, *L'Etat et l'industrie en France: rapport d'enquête* (Paris: CNRS, Groupe Sociologie des Organisations, mimeo 1976), pp. 119–21.
64. Ibid., p. 117.
65. Ibid., p. 125.
66. One is reminded that the large firms were relatively recent creations, with the exceptions of Prouvost and Boussac.
67. Friedberg, *L'Etat et l'industrie* p. 142. The role of the professional associations in structuring the process of concentration in the sector has already been mentioned above in ch. 2.
68. CES Report, p. 223. In the late 1980s, the UIH changed its name to Union Française des Industries de l'Habillement (UFIH).
69. Comité pour la Coordination des Industries Textiles de la Communauté Economique Européenne. As will become clear in Chapter 4, the French UIT played a key role in the internal politics of COMITEXTIL.
70. Chris Farrands, 'Textile Diplomacy: The Making and Implementation of European Textile Policy 1974–1978', *Journal of Common Market Studies*, vol. xviii, no. 1, September 1979, p. 38. The EU associations were effectively dominated by the French federations.
71. Interview with Mr Heinz Berzau, Observatoire Européen du Textile et de l'Habillement, Brussels, 30 April 1996.
72. René Mouriaux (*Les Syndicats dans la société française*, Paris: Presses de la Fondation Nationale des Sciences Politiques, 1983), refers to the traditional weakness of the French labour movement, which represented a minority of workers (pp. 66–70), lacked unity (p. 214), and was rife with inter-union rivalries that were a disservice to the movement itself.
73. Mény and Wright, *La Crise*, op. cit., p. 39.
74. Ehrmann, *Organised Business*, op. cit., p. 467.
75. However, there were many accusations that textile firms neglected their responsibilities in this regard.
76. The notable exception was the solid consensus in favour of trade protection.
77. The UIT had even resigned from the pre-war central employers' organisation, the Confédération Générale de la Production Française, in protest over the Matignon agreements during the Front Populaire government. See Ehrmann, *Organised Business*, op. cit., p. 15.

78. Neither textiles nor clothing were among the priority sectors of the five-year economic development plans in the post-war period.
79. The following discussion relies on Robert Jim Berrier, *The Politics of Industrial Survival*, unpublished PhD thesis, Massachusetts Institute of Technology, 1978, pp. 30–40.
80. As labour costs were the major factor in clothing industry competition, protection was often considered adequate to ensure survival. Relative to textiles, clothing also had a more fluid and fragmented structure, coupled with reduced political resources, which meant that few other demands were successfully translated into policy. The crisis which erupted in 1974 was, furthermore, not initially as acute for the French clothing sector as it was for textiles. As has been argued, France did consistently better in downstream (clothing) activities than most of her industrialised competitors, at least up until the second oil shock in 1979–80.
81. Philip M. Williams, *Crisis and Compromise: Politics in the Fourth Republic* (London: Longman, 1972), p. 384.
82. Lynn Krieger Mytelka, 'The French Textile Industry – Crisis and Adjustment', in Harold K. Jacobson and Dusan Sidjanski (eds), *The Emerging International Economic Order: Dynamic Processes, Constraints, and Opportunities* (Beverly Hills: Sage, 1982), p. 135.
83. Berrier, *The Politics of Industrial Survival*, op. cit., p. 142.
84. Ibid.
85. Mytelka, 'The French Textile Industry', op. cit., p. 136.
86. The FDES was a state lending agency which drew on funds from the *Caisse des Dépôts et des Consignations*, an extension of the state deposit bank system.
87. Mytelka, 'The French Textile Industry', op. cit., p. 137.
88. OECD Report, p. 106.
89. Ibid., p. 161.
90. Berrier, *The Politics of Industrial Survival*, op. cit., p. 152; Williams, in *Crisis and Compromise*, op. cit., chs 25 and 26 on 'Interests and Causes' and 'Pressure Politics' respectively, gives an account of how entrenched interests could resist pressures for change under the Fourth Republic.
91. It is interesting to note, however, that the government, doubtless in response to the pressures exerted, took upon itself the task of gaining time for the textile and clothing firms by delaying until 1966 the intra-EU tariff reductions in relevant product categories.
92. Fifth Plan (1966–70), cited in Mytelka, 'The French Textile Industry', op. cit., p. 141, and France, Plan, *VIᵉ Plan de développement économique et social* (Paris: Imprimerie des Journaux Officiels, 1971), p. 52; hereafter referred to as 'Sixth Plan'.
93. Berrier, *The Politics of Industrial Survival*, op. cit., pp. 154–5.
94. Friedberg, *L'Etat et l'industrie*, op. cit., p. 158. However, as will be seen, contact between the bureaucracies and the professional associations was on a continuum and was not limited to periodic approaches in periods of crisis.
95. Friedberg, *L'Etat et l'industrie*, op. cit., p. 91.

96.   Ibid., pp. 160–1; the following account of the CIRIT initiative relies heavily on the excellent research on state–industry relations by Friedberg, which uses the textile sector as one of its detailed case studies.
97.   Friedberg, *L'Etat et l'industrie*, op. cit., p. 162.
98.   In fact 40 per cent of the proceeds of the tax eventually went to the ITF: cf. Arrêté du 29 mars 1966, 'Modalités d'attribution, de répartition, et d'utilisation du produit de la taxe parafiscale créé par le décret no. 65–1163 du 24 déc. 1965', *Journal Officiel* (édition lois et décrets), no. 78, 2 April 1966, p. 2672.
99.   Friedberg, *L'Etat et l'industrie*, op. cit., pp. 163–6.
100. Article 6 of Arrêté du 21 avril 1966, 'Modalités de répartition... de la taxe parafiscale créé par le décret no. 65–113 du 24 déc. 1965', *Journal Officiel* (édition lois et décrets), no. 102, 3 May 1966, p. 3535.
101. A relatively modest level of official in the hierarchy.
102. Friedberg, *L'Etat et l'industrie*, op. cit., p. 168.
103. It was created by administrative decree: Arrêté du 21 avril 1966, op. cit., pp. 3535–6.
104. Friedberg, *L'Etat et l'industrie*, op. cit., p. 177.
105. Ibid., p. 168, footnote 1; p. 178.
106. Ibid., pp. 178–80.
107. Ibid., pp. 141–3.
108. Sixth Plan, op. cit., p. 52.
109. Ibid., pp. 51–2.
110. Ibid., annexe on sectoral programmes, p. 215.
111. France, Préparation du VIᵉ Plan, Comité Industrie Textile, *Rapport du comité industrie textile* (Paris: La Documentation Française, 1971), pp. 38–9. Note: the opinions of the sectoral committee report were not necessarily those of the Plan. The Committee tended to be dominated by the employers and their organisations. The president was an industrialist and President of the knitting industry federation. Of the remaining members, thirteen were industrialists or professional association officials, seven represented various ministries, and four were trade union representatives (annexe 9 of the report).
112. For instance Mytelka, 'The French Textile Industry', op. cit.
113. See the strong-state–weak-state argument formulated by Peter J. Katzenstein (ed.), *Between Power and Plenty* (Madison, Wisconsin: Wisconsin University Press, 1978). Atkinson and Coleman pointed to some of the weaknesses of this argument, arguing that it was difficult to generalise based on macro-level analysis and that the sectoral level revealed a mixed picture of state–industry relations within any one national system; Michael Atkinson and W.D. Coleman, 'Strong States and Weak States: Sectoral Policy Networks in Advanced Capitalist Economies', *British Journal of Political Science*, vol. 19, no. 1, January 1989, pp. 47–67.
114. Ezra N. Suleiman, in *Politics, Power, and Bureaucracy in France – the Administrative Elite* (Princeton University Press, 1974), ch. xii, particularly pp. 319–36, argues that traditional portrayals of the French administration as representing the 'General Interest' as opposed to individual groups are at variance with empirical studies. On p. 323 he

points to the particular tendency of French interest groups to gain representation through the state bureaucracy.

115. Friedberg, *L'Etat et l'industrie*, op. cit., pp. 50–2.
116. France, Assemblée Nationale, 5ᵉ Législature, 1ʳᵉ Séssion Ordinaire de 1973–1974, *Avis présenté au nom de la Commission de la Production et des Echanges sur le Projet de Loi de Finances pour 1974*, tome v, 'Développement Industrielle', no. 686, 10 October 1973, p. 22.
117. *Commission de la Production et des Echanges*, op. cit., 1974, p. 20, citing the example of the Comité Centrale de la Laine, the woollen industry federation.
118. Friedberg, op. cit., p. 38; pp. 75–6.
119. Benoît Boussemart and Jean-Claude Rabier, *Le Dossier Agache-Willot: un capitalisme à contre-courant* (Paris: Presses de la Fondation Nationale des Sciences Politiques, 1983), p. 156; citation from footnote 6.
120. See Geoffrey R.D. Underhill, 'When Technology Doesn't Mean Change: Industrial Adjustment and Textile Production in France', in Michael Talalay, Chris Farrands and Roger Tooze (eds), *Technology, Culture, and Competitiveness in the World Political Economy* (London: Routledge, 1997), pp. 139–50.
121. State intervention in the sector tended to be either general measures such as support for employment levels in industry or regional subsidies, or related to 'lifesaving' for firms in crisis. The textile and clothing sector was never regarded by the state as one of strategic importance. See Pierre Dubois and Giusto Barisi, *Le Défi technologique dans l'industrie de l'habillement: les stratégies des entrepreneurs français et italiens* (Paris: CNRS, Groupe Sociologie du Travail, 1982), pp. 45–8.
122. P. Moati and E.M. Mouhoud, 'Information et organisation de la production: vers une division cognitive du travail', *Economie appliquée*, vol. XLVI, no. 1, 1994, p. 63.
123. Ibid., p. 63; see their discussion of the role of knowledge and information in flexible specialisation in ibid., especially pp. 56–68.
124. Ibid., p. 66.
125. Giorgio Barba Navaretti and Giorgio Perosino, 'Redeployment of Production, Trade Protection, and Firms' Global Strategies: The Case of Italy', in G.B. Navaretti, R. Faini, and Aubrey Silbertson (eds), *Beyond the Multifibre Arrangement: Third World Competition and Restructuring Europe's Textile Industry* (Paris: OECD, 1995), p. 170. See also F. Pyke, G. Becattini and W. Sengenberger (eds), *Industrial Districts and Inter-Firm Co-operation in Italy* (Geneva: International Institute for Labour Studies, 1990). These large areas should really be disaggregated into smaller localities, such as the Modena knitwear district (see Mark H. Lazerson, 'Subcontracting in the Modena Knitwear', in Pyke, *et al.*, *Industrial Districts*, op. cit.), or the Como silk production district (see J.P. Lopez Novo, 'Community, Market, Association and the Small Firm: The Case of an Italian Industrial District', paper presented to the annual sessions of the European Consortium for Political Research, Workshop on Meso-Corporatism, Amsterdam, 10–15 April 1987).
126. Dubois and Barisi, *Le Défi technologique*, op. cit., pp. 254–5.

127. See Michael J. Piore, 'Work, Labour, and Action: Work Experience in a System of Flexible Production', in Pyke *et al.*, *Industrial Districts*, op. cit.

128. For details of state intervention in the sector, see Antonio Mutti, Nicolo Addario, and Paolo Segatti, 'The Organisation of Business Interests: The Case of the Italian Textile and Clothing Industry', European University Institute Working Papers no. 86/205, EUI, Department of Political and Social Sciences: Badia Fiesolana, 1986, pp. 14–17; also Dubois and Barisi, *Le Défi technologique*, op. cit., pp. 45–8.

129. Mutti *et al.*, 'The Organisation of Business Interests', p. 19.

130. These points are well developed in ibid., pp. 27–9.

131. See Lazerson, op. cit., and Carlo Trigilia, 'Work and Politics in the Third Italy's Industrial Districts', both in Pyke *et al.*, op. cit., pp. 108–33 and 160–84.

132. OECD Report, op. cit., p. 138.

133. Mutti *et al.*, 'The Organisation of Business Interests', op. cit., p. 40.

134. There are in fact many such examples to choose from; see Fabio Sforzi, 'The Quantitative Importance of Marshallian Industrial Districts in the Italian Economy', in Pyke *et al.*, op. cit., pp. 75–107.

135. The following case relies on research by Lopez Novo, op. cit.

136. Lopez Novo, 'Community, Market Association', op. cit., pp. 20–1.

137. Pascale Mattei, 'L'Exemple du Veneto: l'industrie italienne cherche à s'adapter à la crise', *Journal du textile*, 6 April 1992.

138. See Mutti *et al.*, 'The Organisation of Business Interests', op. cit., p. 71.

139. Mattei, 'L'Exemple du Veneto', op. cit.

140. See M. Piore and C. Sabel, *The Second Industrial Divide* (New York: Free Press, 1984).

141. See Theda Skocpol and Ellen Kay Trimberger, 'Revolutions and the World-Historical Development of Capitalism', in Barbara Hockey Kaplan (ed.), *Social Change in the Capitalist World Economy* (London: Sage 1978), p. 132.

4 Capturing the Global Trade Regime

The first two chapters in this book analysed the material under-pinnings of the political economy of international trade in the textile and clothing sector. In particular, the chapters assessed the impact of liberalisation and intensified competition on the domestic sectors of key OECD countries. Chapter 3 demonstrated the corresponding role of associational groups in these same countries, demonstrating their substantial grip on the policy-making process of market structuration. This fourth chapter will look at how these associational groups extended their capture[1] of the policy process into the international domain. The purpose of this chapter is, then, to demonstrate the ways in which private policy preferences were aggregated into a transnational coalition of interests, including the relevant segments of state admin-istrations, supporting an exceptional and protectionist trade regime in the textile and clothing sector. As import competition intensified across the global economy, domestic adjustment policies across the OECD economies diminished in terms of their utility in controlling the adjustment process. The result was that increasing attention was paid to developing a firmly protectionist trade regime. *A transnational policy process emerged in symbiosis with the transnational structure of production and the market in response to the pressures of globalisation.*

State regulatory and policy processes are permeated by the private interests which constitute the market.[2] In the textile and clothing case, this was as true of international trade policy and the structure of the global economy as of the domestic economy.[3] The rules of interna-tional trade underpin the access of producers from the various parts of the global economy to each others' home jurisdictions. The rules of international trade, combined with the rules concerning the interna-tional circulation of money and the mobility of capital for investment, likewise determine the pattern of international production and investment, in the context of the competitive practices and positions of firms. Thus *the politics of trade manifest a clear link between the polit-ical dynamics of the trade regime and the market game of competitive advantage as played by firms.* The two are an integrated unity. Just as private market interests are fully integrated into the institutions of states and the international trade regime, firms in turn rely on political authorities, states for the most part but also international institutions, to give official expression and legal force to the outcome of bargaining across levels of analysis in the global economy. Furthermore, private interests become intimately involved in the implementation and mon- itoring of trade agreements, often goading governments to take action despite their better instincts by bringing trade disputes before the recognised official bodies.

State and international regulatory and policy processes are, then, at the heart of operationalising markets as broader systems of govern- ance in the international political economy. States and their competing domestic interests share the global economic space in a situation of interdependence, and use their respective sovereign jurisdictions and the competitive advantages of their firms as bargaining tools. This bargaining process, with the rules which result, develops the structures of the international market via the practices of firms and constitutes the transnational economic underpinnings of distributional conflict and, ultimately, world order. Domestic industrial adjustment and international distributional conflicts are played out across the insti- tutional layers of the global system.

As the market becomes increasingly transnationalised (through outward investment, foreign sourcing, and networks of intra-industry and intra-firm trade, as well as through the traditional import and export of finished goods), state policies too may become similarly transnationalised.[4] Via the regulatory processes of international trade policy-making and the institutions of the international trade regime of which the World Trade Organisation forms the core, competing pri- vate particularisms become transformed and legitimated as public or even 'national' interests within the global economic order. This applies to trade and production as much as to monetary, financial, environmental policy or social standards. Where there is policy failure, the non-decisions of the powerful in the integrated state/market system of governance tend to predominate in an ongoing pattern of conflict of interest. Where agreement is possible, however partial, a more cooperative set of rules may emerge.

The private interests which were able to dominate or at least shape the decisions taken have at that stage successfully institutionalised their preferences (or compromises) in the international trade regime. Once achieved, these victories are difficult to dislodge in view of the complexity of bargaining across institutional layers in the global sys- tem. Coalitions of interest sharing broad policy preferences (or capable of strategic compromise) were able over time to dominate the institutions of political authority in the international trade regime.

If it is through the regulatory processes of the international trade regime that private particularistic interests are converted into public and legitimated purposes and responsibilities, then a crucial variable for understanding the way the international trade regime evolves will be the nature of the private interests themselves and, especially, the ways in which they are organised and articulated within the body of the state with respect to trade policy-making. Sometimes these coalitions of private organised interests are tied to democratic forms of government, a factor which often greatly complicates the policy process; other times they are not. Either way the institutions of the state are neither unitary nor rational nor necessarily even conscious of the way they convert private preference into the evolving structure of the market.

Chapter 3 has demonstrated that in a number of crucial market economies in the international trading system, protectionist interests which had been negatively affected by the restructuring attributable to intensified transnational economic competition (initially induced by post-war trade liberalisation policies) effectively captured the domestic policy agenda. This chapter will show that this capture extended to the international trade policy agenda over several decades. Their policy preferences became institutionalised in the Short-Term (STA) and then Long-Term Arrangement on Cotton Trade (LTA) and more comprehensively in the Multi-Fibre Arrangement and its protocols of renewal from 1974 onwards. Employing protectionism, coalitions of interests representing economic liabilities were able to forestall partially the adjustment process and to constitute a political blockage to the otherwise relatively liberal trade policies of high-wage countries with regard to manufactured goods. These groups were unable on the whole to appropriate adequate state financial resources by way of subsidies to support their weak competitive position. Transnationalisation of trade and production weakened the effectiveness of these essentially domestic instruments of policy anyway, and the rules of the EU internal market and the GATT were in principle to circumscribe the use of subsidies in general. As a consequence they turned to so-called 'voluntary' import quotas as a political compromise. This enabled them to resist for some time the imperatives of market-led adjustment and demonstrates how, through trade policy, the politics of industrial adjustment in an open economy crosses the institutional layers (or levels of analysis) of the global system of governance. Firms-as-agents, through their associational groups and their institutionalised ties to state policy-makers, made use of their political resources to structure the market in accordance with their distributional preferences. This was to the disadvantage of important competing interests in the global economy such as consumers, retail importers, and LDC producers, but in the end the reality of capture was the driving force behind the emerging global market structure in the textile and clothing sector.

This chapter will begin with a brief discussion of the Short-Term and Long-Term Arrangements (STA/LTA) for international trade in cotton products. These agreements were precursors and indeed prototypes for the eventual MFA which emerged in 1974. The chapter will then go on to analyse the establishment of the Multi-Fibre Arrangement under the auspices of GATT. As in the case of the STA and the LTA, the driving force behind this initial (and relatively liberal) MFA was the United States. The chapter will argue that the US trade authorities, in concert with the industry itself and its partners in Congress, were responsible for the successful implementation of this agreement. This success, combined with a dynamic strategy of industrial restructuring on the part of US entrepreneurs and a rapidly falling dollar throughout the 1970s, led to a diminished interest in the MFA on the part of the US textile coalition. At the same time, the relatively weak response of the EU authorities in terms of implementing the MFA and the diversion of low-wage imports from the US reinforced the protectionist sentiment in Europe during the same period.

Of particular importance were the mounting political pressures in France, which served as a bastion and launch-pad for transnational protectionist coalition-building throughout the 1970s. The French industry and government forged transnational alliances within the EU and indeed across the Atlantic which attempted to manage the distribution of gains and losses in the sector through a programme of market structuration based on ever tighter import quotas. Having captured the policies of the French government in the early 1970s, French textile and clothing interests came to dominate the EU's sectoral trade policy agenda, forming effective alliances with the French state, other national associations and state policy-makers, and to control the pan-EU associations themselves. The first and second MFA renewals thus saw an enhanced protectionism take root. Nonetheless, the transnationalisation of production eventually penetrated even the French professional associations, and from the early 1980s there were attempts to accommodate the interests of firms engaged in foreign sourcing, particularly outward processing traffic (OPT).

The rise of foreign sourcing and of especially OPT might have presaged a limited relaxation of the MFA, but by the mid 1980s and in the lead-up to the third renewal of the agreement, the rising US dollar had re-ignited the protectionist fervour of the American industry. The fourth MFA of 1986 was, however, to be the last major renewal of the agreement. It will remain for Chapter 5 to explain why the same parties who worked to intensify the control of low-wage imports reversed their policy and agreed to the liberalisation of global trade in the sector.

FROM STA TO MFA

This section will analyse the transformation of the global textile and clothing trade regime in the post-war period. This evolution exhibited contradictory tendencies. On the one hand, there was a significant liberalisation of trade among the advanced economies, and the introduction of preferential treatment to assist the LDCs, many of them textile and clothing exporters. On the other hand, import quotas against LDCs in the domain of textile and clothing products were steadily tightened over time.

In the initial post-war period the United States possessed the most advanced economy with correspondingly high wages in relative terms. As European countries recovered from wartime destruction and intensified their industrial development efforts, and as countries in Asia, in particular Japan, began a process of rapid development, these economies began to constitute an increasing competitive challenge to the dominance of US industry in international trade and in its own domestic markets. Not surprisingly, the more labour-intensive industries such as clothing assembly and traditional textile production were often hit the hardest. This import competition was particularly acute from rapidly industrialising countries such as Japan. Given the power of the textile coalition analysed in Chapter 3, Congress was not slow to translate the pressure into changes in the Administration's trade policies.

In the 1950s the GATT began to have an impact on the trade policies of the advanced economies, particularly with regard to US-European trade. In this context, Japan's application for membership of GATT was an important benchmark because it implied the entry of an economy at a significantly different level of development (although this was to change rapidly) and with much lower wage costs, with foreseeable implications for traditional textile and clothing producers.[5] Although Japan formally joined GATT in 1955, 'this was largely symbolic'[6] and the integration of Japan into the global trade regime remains an ongoing issue in the 1990s, particularly as far as the US is concerned. The US was nonetheless the original sponsor of Japan's accession to GATT, but since the 1930s had feared the threat of Japanese textile and clothing exports into the US market.[7] As is usual with American trade policy matters, a compromise which theoretically preserved the free-trade credentials of the sponsoring country, the US, yet protected the domestic industry in question, was found: 'state policy-makers were, in effect, held hostage by Senate supporters of the industrial alliance.'[8] The Japanese accepted a series of 'voluntary' export restraints across a range of specific textile and clothing products, mostly cotton fibre-based. In 1956 these pioneering GATT Voluntary Export Restraints (VERs) were agreed by Japan and the United States for a five-year period. The agreement was implemented in 1957 and affected some twenty cotton products, but exports from other emerging producers such as Hong Kong soon filled the gap thus created by Japan's 'restraint'.[9] Meanwhile, some fourteen countries had invoked GATT article XXXV against Japan, an article which allowed existing members to exclude new entrants from the benefits of GATT provisions as long as the country invoking the article considered it right and proper; many also applied article XXII balance of payments restrictions.[10]

As the restraint programme did not have the desired result, the textile coalition was again active and spurred the US government to seek allies internationally for a broadening of the protectionist framework. The UK sector was under considerable pressure and clearly saw the introduction of GATT disciplines in the textile and clothing sector as unrealistic.[11] Likewise western European governments scarcely relished the prospects of dismantling the import controls they had retained despite Japanese entry into GATT. This proved to be the fertile ground the United States (erstwhile apostle of free trade) needed to convene an international conference of textile and clothing importing and exporting countries, all of course under the legitimating auspices of the GATT. What was emerging in US trade policy, soon to be supported by other economically advanced countries with substantial textile and clothing industries, was the concept of 'market disruption', a concept not originally in the GATT lexicon and which had to be nurtured and developed so as to serve its function for the emerging trade protection regime in the sector.[12]

The outcome of the conference was the Short-Term Arrangement, in effect from October 1961 to September 1962, authorising bilateral restrictions on imports of some sixty-four categories of cotton textiles and clothing products.[13] US officials aggressively implemented the agreement, even resorting to the unilateral restrictions permitted under exceptional circumstances by the accord. As pressure on the US administration scarcely abated (and the STA was anyway seen as temporary), negotiations continued and resulted in a broadening and extension of the STA into the Long-Term Arrangement (LTA). The agreement sought to bring the rather large number of bilateral restrictions under the comforting and legitimating umbrella of GATT, and also to offer the low-wage producers the prospect of predictable if controlled growth in their export markets in industrialised countries. The quotas on LDC imports would permit at least 5 per cent annual import growth if they were imposed for any more than a year.[14]

The role of the textile coalition in the emergence of the LTA was patent.[15] The Kennedy administration was at the time attempting to launch what came to be known as the Kennedy Round of GATT multilateral trade negotiations, aiming at a substantial liberalisation of trade with a broad sectoral coverage. The administration's key piece of legislation for the Round, the Trade Expansion Act, was effectively the hostage of the textile coalition. It typically took little to spur Congressional leaders representing textile and clothing industry interests into action – the protectionist instincts were deeply ingrained and key southern Senators controlled the vital Congressional Committees. In the end, the American Cotton Manufacturers Institute unanimously approved of supporting the Act in view of the successful conclusion of the LTA.

The OECD remarks that two crucial developments served to undermine, in the eyes of US and other high-wage industrial lobbies, the value of the LTA as an apparent solution to the adjustment problems of the textile and clothing sector.[16] First, the use of man-made fibres increased rapidly, reducing the importance of cotton-based products in international trade. Second, the rapid rise in the demand for clothing in high-wage countries, faster than the corresponding rise in demand for textile production, was taken up by rising *net* imports. In other words, more fibre types were competing with low-wage imports, and domestic producers were failing to take advantage of increases in demand. Whereas until the late 1960s the charge to protectionism had been led by cotton interests, a more broadly based cross-sectoral and transnational coalition was to emerge over time.

Their grip on the trade policy process would prove unshakeable, first in the US and eventually in Europe. In 1971–2 the United States negotiated several bilateral VERs on man-made fibre and woollen products,[17] and on 20 December 1973 the first MFA was signed to be implemented as of 1 January 1974.[18]

THE FIRST MFA AGREEMENT

The MFA agreement and subsequent renewals emerged out of the volatile economic climate of the early 1970s and the ongoing influence of the textile coalition on US trade policy-making. However, over time the strong interest of US textile and clothing interests in ever-tightening protectionist arrangements abated somewhat. US firms eventually found the 1970s relatively favourable to their continued development (see Chapter 1), not least owing to the success of US officials in controlling the growth of imports and to the rapid decline of the dollar in an otherwise difficult economic climate. In contrast, protectionist sentiment increased dramatically in the EU during the same period, parallel to the emergence of new competitive pressures which implied a need for dramatic restructuring efforts in a number of countries.

(a) MFA I and the US Lead

In 1972 the GATT Council had set up a Working Party on Textiles to investigate the issue of trade pressures and their wider socio-economic implications, and to identify multilateral solutions to them. The Working Party transformed itself into a GATT negotiating group involving some fifty countries in all.[19] The negotiation led to the Arrangement Regarding International Trade in Textiles, or MFA, which became the central feature of the exceptional and protectionist trade regime for textile and clothing products. It was nonetheless supplemented by a host of other negotiated and unilateral arrangements to restrict imports from low-wage developing countries and even middle-income countries such as Spain and Portugal. Neither the rhetoric nor the reality of the GATT system prevailed in textiles and clothing over a period of some thirty years, as trade policy-making remained embedded in the distributional politics of industrial adjustment in the sector across a series of key advanced economies. This said, the first MFA was far and away the least restrictive, but it boasted far more comprehensive product coverage relative to the LTA.

From the cotton-based product list of the LTA, the MFA came to cover virtually all textile and clothing products. About the only exceptions to the agreement were 'handloom' or craft-based products, but these had to be certified if the exemption were to apply.[20] This said, product coverage did not depend solely on the text of the Agreement alone. The MFA in fact consisted of two parts: the main text, and bilateral accords.[21] The main text laid down the principles behind the agreement and provided in article 3 for emergency restrictions in the event of market disruption where bilateral accords had not been reached. These were invoked at the outset as importing countries sought to implement article 4, which stipulated the negotiation of the bilateral accords with individual exporting partners.

Thus the agreement could be couched in relatively liberal terms, yet within the constraints set out in the main text the importers could negotiate more or less restrictive bilateral accords, and use their discretion with regard to the implementation of article 3. In this way, article 1.2 stated that

> The basic objective shall be to achieve the expansion of trade, the reduction of barriers to such trade, and the progressive liberalisation of world trade in world textile trade, while at the same time ensuring the orderly and equitable development of this trade and avoidance of disruptive effects in individual markets and on individual lines of production in both importing and exporting countries.

The objectives in this passage seem relatively benign and further paragraphs in article 1 bear this assessment out: the agreement is to promote the 'economic and social well-being of developing countries' while promoting their exports (art. 1.3); it was not to be employed so as to forestall ('interrupt or discourage') the adjustment process in the advanced countries by preventing the operation of comparative advantage in textile trade (art. 1.4); safeguard measures were to be employed so as to promote adjustment (art. 1.5) and the measures were considered both exceptional and temporary. Article 6 prescribed more liberal treatment for new market entrants and small exporters, and other provisions insisted that the restrictions be applied flexibly and equitably, including transfers from one product category to another and carry forward or carry over from one period to another (art. 4; art. 5). Special treatment was to be granted to reimports (outward processing traffic) according to art. 6.6. Furthermore, the actual 'growth threshold' was higher than it had been for the LTA: imports from LDCs were subject to a minimum growth rate (or maximum restriction depending on one's point of view) of 6 per cent per annum (annex B, para. 2). A Textile Surveillance Body would ensure the impartial and equitable implementation of the agreement over its four-year duration.

The real key to the agreement, however, was the detailed bilateral accords. These were negotiated with the relatively vulnerable LDC exporting countries (who were entirely dependent on advanced economy markets), not in the comparative safety of GATT multilateral discussions, but one-on-one. They faced the full raw power over their market outlets which United States and European Union officials represented. These bilateral negotiations determined the precise list of products which would be restricted, and the rate of growth of each product category. Failure to reach a bilateral accord could result in the importing country imposing the tighter emergency restrictions allowed for in article 3. Article XIX and other GATT safeguards remained available to importing countries. The deck was heavily stacked in their favour but the 6 per cent threshold at least remained in place for the duration of MFA I.

(b) Europe Takes the Driver's Seat

The United States was clearly the driving force behind MFA I, motivated by the apparently perpetual need to contain Congressional fervour for even greater levels of control over imports and the desire to seek multilateral legitimacy for an overtly protectionist project.[22] The US was also quick to negotiate and implement bilateral agreements which locked import growth across a wide range of product groups into the 6 per cent threshold.

A number of factors combined to remove the US from the driving seat and to lead to EU initiatives for a much more restrictive MFA by the renewal date at the end of 1977. In the first place, changes in the international monetary regime and the subsequent substantial devaluations in the US dollar provided relief from import competition to combine with the MFA itself. As established in earlier chapters, most of this competition was from advanced country firms anyway, meaning that devaluation had a significant effect on US labour costs relative to the main sources of competition[23] and was not overly counterbalanced by the relative weakness of LDC currencies. Taking 1980 as the base year index level of 100, real exchange rates between the US and the rest of the OECD were at 111.40 in 1973, and declined steadily towards the 1980 level of 100. The equivalent real exchange rate figures for the principal textile and clothing exporting LDCs was 95.3 in 1973, rising to a high of 103.85 in 1976, settling to the base level of 100 in 1980.[24] In other words, real exchange rates with developing countries varied relatively little from the collapse of the fixed exchange rate regime 1971–3 to 1980 (and monetary factors can be relatively discounted), whereas the dollar fell significantly in real terms relative to OECD competitors in the same period. This helped an investment-led recovery in the industry which was briefly interrupted by the 1975–6 recession.

Second, the American administration took a tough line on implementing MFA I. The United States was quick to negotiate rather restrictive bilateral accords and was active in the use of safeguard clauses. The MFA was an effective trade instrument for the USA especially when combined with other factors such as exchange rates which affected global competition in the sector.

Third, and no doubt partially as a consequence of exchange rate fluctuations but also owing to consistent adjustment efforts on the part of US firms, American producers adapted relatively well to external competition. As established in Chapter 1, production rose during this period despite the sluggishness of demand growth, productivity improved, and the industry used its MFA/devaluation breathing space to considerable positive effect. This was helped by the oil crises, which improved the competitiveness of US artificial and synthetic fibres firms (man-made fibres had become crucial inputs to the industry), but there seems little doubt that the industry's efforts at rationalisation and modernisation were primarily responsible.[25] The textile sector of course fared better on the whole than the clothing industry.

Fourth, the EU member states' interest in the MFA was intensified by the poor performance of the Commission in implementing the first MFA, particularly in relation to the negotiation of the bilateral accords. The Commission had proved relatively inexperienced in the negotiation and implementation process. This was not surprising given that the Commission had only recently taken on the responsibility for trade negotiations from member states, given the relative youth of the EU customs union itself. Commission officials were reluctant protectionists anyway, given that the EU was supposedly concerned with encouraging market forces, not constraining them through quotas. In addition, the EU trade policy-making process was a cumbersome one to say the least. Each member state had first to reach a policy consensus among the governmental agencies involved, then they had to reach an EU-wide common position among the member states, and only then could the Commission receive a negotiating mandate. The

Commission then had to make sure in an ongoing fashion that tentatively negotiated deals were actually ratifiable in the Council of Ministers and at the level of the member states themselves. These cumbersome procedures, the lack of experience with and commitment to administering quotas, and slow progress on the bilateral accords, weakened the effectiveness of the MFA for EU producer firms.

There never had been anything approaching unanimity in favour of the MFA among the member states of the EU, but the US initiative had provided an easy set of coat tails on which to ride. However, not only had the EU travelled on US coat tails in this instance, but the Commission proved much less determined and effective at negotiating the all-important bilateral accords from 1974 onwards, certainly much less so than the United States itself.[26] To add to the problem, as some perceived it, the Commission itself was more in favour of free trade and assisting the development prospects of the LDCs than otherwise and was therefore inherently uncomfortable with the MFA in the first place. The result was that there was severe criticism of the Commission by the textile lobbies, and by the governments, of a number of EU member states.[27] The pressure was already mounting to reinforce the protectionist tendencies of the agreement, especially at the level of the bilateral accords, or to turn to unilateral solutions. The problem was compounded by the very effectiveness of US protection, and many LDC exports were diverted towards Europe when US quotas were either entirely filled or safeguard mechanisms had been employed. By way of comparison, American imports rose only 3 per cent in the year 1974–5, whereas in the EU there was a major jump of 41 per cent.[28] This striking difference in the relative success of EU versus American import policy was bound to intensify protectionist sentiment. The US had demonstrated that protection *could* work; all that was needed was for the Commission to *make* it work.

Finally, European textile and clothing firms adjusted poorly to the general economic crisis of the mid 1970s – the impact was severe. While the US industry was to benefit from its investment in modernisation and rationalisation throughout the 1970s, many European industries were not so well situated. They had only recently begun to adjust to intra-EU competition, external tariffs linked to the Kennedy Round were only just being phased in, and the impact of low-wage competition coincided with crucial changes in both the growth rate of demand (stagnation and decline set in) and its composition in terms of consumer preferences (see Chapter 2). The firms in some member states, and the Netherlands and Germany come to mind, had already shed much of their labour-intensive clothing industry through outward processing traffic and other forms of foreign sourcing, but the industries of Britain, France, and Italy remained in the firing line. Serious protection against other OECD or indeed EU competitors was not possible as a result of international trade law, so the spotlight was on the LDC exporters and the MFA. When the impact of the general economic crisis is combined with the relative failure in terms of bilateral accords plus the diversion of erstwhile US imports, many EU member states faced an explosive reaction from their institutionally entrenched textile and clothing lobbies. Against this background, policy had tilted decisively in favour of protection. Capture began to work its way with the EU's trade policy process in textile and clothing.

In order to understand how the EU became the driving force behind the MFA it is necessary to once again examine the policy process from the bottom up – from the level of industrial firms and their associational groups through the institutions of member states and of the EU, to the level of global negotiations themselves in turn. In line with the arguments sustained throughout this book, the next section will examine how competitive pressures led the textile coalition in France, and through capture the French government, to assert control of the EUs sectoral trade policy agenda. The next section looks at the political economy of this transnational policy capture, which led to the renewal and substantial tightening of the terms of the MFA upon its renewal in late 1977.

RENEWING THE MFA: FRANCE, TRANSNATIONAL CAPTURE, AND THE EU ON THE OFFENSIVE

This section will argue, building on the analysis in Chapter 3, that the French textile and clothing professional associations demonstrated a remarkable capacity to dominate not only the policy-making institutions of their own state, but those of the EU trade policy process as well. This was not easily done. The Union des Industries Textiles (UIT) and the Union des Industries de l'Habillement (UIH), together federating the broad mass of textile and clothing professional associations in France, first faced considerable if ultimately unsustained opposition from their own government when it came to defining trade policy in the mid to late 1970s. The governments under the presidency

of Giscard d'Estaing (1974–81) favoured a liberal market-led adjustment policy for French industry and the economy as a whole, and were
relatively uncomfortable with the idea of ongoing protection in one of
the country's most important industrial sectors. A protectionist textile
and clothing trade policy also conflicted strongly with France's
declared policies of helping LDCs with their development problems.
At several junctures the French government attempted to cast doubt
on the MFA as an element of French trade policy. These efforts of
the government eventually proved fruitless as the realities of capture in
the policy process worked their way over time.

Even once the battle was won in France itself, success on the EU
level was far from guaranteed. France faced an array of countries
which regarded freer trade in the sector as in their national interest,
especially the Netherlands, Denmark, and federal West Germany.
Firms in these countries were highly dependent on outward processing
traffic in their clothing industries and tighter protection risked fore-
closing the option of the ever-increasing levels of imports linked to the
foreign sourcing activities of domestic manufacturing firms. Nonetheless, helped by the entry of Great Britain and Ireland into the EU,
and by the success of French professional associations at dominating
the EU-level trade associations (COMITEXTIL and the Association
Européenne des Industries de l'Habillement or AEIH), the French
government eventually proved highly successful at appropriating the
EU's textile and clothing trade policy agenda for itself and its industrial clients. MFA II (1978–81) proved a substantially strengthened
protectionist agreement with far more effective EU implementation
procedures, and for MFA III (1982–5) the accord was tightened yet
again. French textile and clothing interests were able to forge links
with other EU trade associations and, through French government
sponsorship, with other member governments, effectively transnationalising their domestic coalition. Taking advantage of the existing institutions of the MFA and the likelihood of at least tacit US support
for MFA renewal, French interests helped forge a transnational protectionist coalition which remained relatively stable until the early
1990s. One would not wish to deny the protectionist tendencies and
efforts of other EU member state textile and clothing industry associations, but the lead role of the French sector was similar to the role
France came to play in the development of the EU's Common Agricultural Policy and long-running EU opposition to the liberalisation
of international trade in agricultural products in a series of GATT
negotiating rounds.

(a) A Legacy of Complacency: From 'Orderly Development' to Protection

While protectionist sentiment was never absent, it took the onslaught of the oil crisis and ensuing economic downturn to generate a virtually undying commitment to a greatly reinforced MFA on the part of French textile and clothing interests. However, the pre-1974 crisis period was notable for the prevailing complacency about the future of the sector in both state and industry circles. The CIRIT restructuring process (see Chapter 3) was in place and was theoretically encouraging the necessary restructuring, and the industry was riding on a wave of unprecedented expansion of consumer spending. The 1969 devaluation of the franc gave the impression that the industry was both confronting import competition and performing better on export markets. Furthermore, the wave of corporate concentration at the close of the 1960's was judged as positive evidence that the sector had adjusted and was successfully integrated into international and EU markets. The attitude seems to have been one of guarded confidence.

Warnings were not lacking, however. Investment had been falling in real terms throughout the 1960's, though this was less marked in clothing.[29] Jacques de Bandt's 1969 report to the EU Commission had forewarned that further restructuring of the industry would be necessary in view of likely developments in the international division of labour.[30] J-P. Lévy (former Director of the Textile Division at the Ministry of Industry) warned in 1970 that investment was low and that French firms had been unable to respond fully to the opportunities provided by the 1969 devaluation, a situation which resulted in unnecessary imports.

The latent difficulties of the industry were furthermore clear to those who wished to see. Throughout the 1960s, economic journals had discussed the problems presented by changing consumer preferences and the need for an expanded conception of textile and clothing markets.[31] Demand for certain products was outstripping national production,[32] revealing an inability of French firms to adapt to changing market conditions. 'We are not victims of any sorry fate. A textile enterprise can perfectly well be prosperous. It is a simple problem of management,'[33] said André Roudière, chairman of the large wool concern which bore his family name, in 1973.

The preparatory documents for the Sixth Plan (1971–5) and the Plan itself nonetheless manifested the prevailing complacency clearly. Though certain weaknesses (investment, low research expenditure) might compromise the future, 'a relatively modest effort in favour of the sector would have the greatest chances of improving competitiveness'.[34] Concerning the trade balance, it was felt that despite the loss of colonial markets and the rise of imports, the traditional surplus position had been maintained over the previous decade and was larger in 1970 than in 1959, when markets had been fully protected (it is not clear whether or not this figure accounted for inflation). The recent devaluation had boosted exports by some 20 per cent, while imports had diminished slightly[35] The necessary effort in terms of future restructuring (interpreted as corporate concentration) and modernisation were seen as modest. The Minister of Industry publicly expressed the opinion that 'the textile and clothing industries are far from being in decline in France.'[36]

There was, of course, some reason for this optimism, and it lay in the buoyant economic climate of the day. By the end of 1973, production levels in the sector were still ahead of the Sixth Plan quotas; 1971 and 1972 had seen respectively 9 per cent and 7.5 per cent annual growth in the industry.[37] Besides, the industry had already found its scapegoat: it was the 'problem of disorderly competition from countries with economies different from ours', as the Minister of Industrial Development put it.[38] Parliamentarians were already pressing the government about the problem of 'abnormal' competition in textiles from Third World and East Bloc sources and were receiving assurances about the government's 'vigilance' on the matter.[39] More objective analysts of the industry were at the time explicitly aware of the inappropriateness of this complacency in the face of obvious danger signs. Of the textile sectoral committee's report for the Plan, the economic weekly *Les Echos* commented that it was just not serious.[40]

If the textile sector recognised the need for at least modest adaptation, the clothing industry committee was yet more optimistic and complacent about the future. The sector enjoyed a very favourable economic climate with increased consumption spurring industrial growth. It was felt that these favourable developments would continue unabated throughout the period of the Sixth Plan.[41] As if to demonstrate the industry's confidence, in 1972 the Union des Industries de l'Habillement (UIH) put together a plan of action which was assisted and endorsed by the Ministry of Industry. It emphasised competitiveness and the markets of the future, heralding a new spirit. Despite the competition from the Less Developed Countries (LDCs), the industry had adequately met the challenge. The Minister of Industrial Development estimated that the clothing sector had 'proven itself'.[42]

However, the assumption which underpinned this optimism in both industries was that, because the industry *had* adapted, competition which could not be met was almost by definition unfair or 'abnormal', to use the term most commonly employed. It was assumed that adequate safeguards against this 'abnormal' competition would be provided through the LTA, MFA or otherwise. This, then, was the real reason for optimism, and it was made perfectly clear in the reports of the clothing and textile sectoral committees presented to the Plan, to say nothing of general industry opinion.[43] Thus, the industry conveniently declared itself in favour of free trade while putting forward the classic argument for 'temporary' protection.[44] 'Harmonious development' and 'orderly development' of trade became convenient euphemisms for the policies which were to follow in the years of crisis.

It seems clear that in the early 1970s both the extent and the impact of the transnationalisation of trade and production were poorly perceived by the profession, as was the imperative of modernisation.[45] These perceptions, shared by both state and industry, were an inherent part of the stable patterns of state–industry relations, characterised by capture, which were discussed in Chapter 3. They set the scene for a defensive strategy based on trade protection and an unwillingness to make necessary investments and carry out rationalisation. A consensus formed around the issue of protection and safeguards against 'abnormal' competition, and in favour of the 'orderly development' of trade in the sector, which was in theory accomplished by the first MFA.

The concept of 'abnormal competition' logically absolved domestic firms (and to a lesser government policy) from any responsibility for future import surges. Surges would be unfair according to the rules of the game, and therefore required state safeguards. The MFA, originally an essentially American initiative, would do the necessary. The economic conditions under which he agreement was negotiated must, however, be remembered. Consumption and production were still expanding. French exports had undergone a rapid expansion, particularly to the other five countries of the EU, and the trade balance in textile and clothing products was hugely positive. The structure and terms of the MFA assumed, first, that these buoyant economic conditions would continue, and, second, that the machinery necessary for administering the agreement could, and would, be put into place and operate effectively. Both these assumptions turned out to be largely groundless as we know, but for different reasons, and this created constant difficulties.

Optimistic assumptions about macroeconomic conditions under-pinned the economic strategies of most advanced countries at the time. The optimism continued even after the onset of crisis, and France was no exception to the rule. This was clearly demonstrated in the pre-paratory work for the Seventh Plan (1976–80), undertaken in the early crisis years, as well as in the textile industry's own pronouncements on its future. The overall tone of the textile and clothing committee report was little different from the optimistic assertions of the Sixth Plan and its preparatory documents.[46] The crisis was one of the most serious in the industry's history, with clothing production in retreat by some 2 per cent,[47] but it was seen as essentially conjunctural. There remained the attitude that industrial growth was necessary and possible along the lines of the pre-crisis period. The Minister of Industry, Michel d'Ornano, clearly accepted this point of view,[48] and the belief was that the considerable impact of the crisis could be made up over the period of the Seventh Plan.[49] The UIT clearly did not face up to either the profound changes in consumer preferences and demand levels, nor the magnitude of the task of industrial restructuring and modernisation which confronted the industry.[50]

The consensus was sufficiently shared so as to render it plausible, and any grave difficulties which might arise could thereafter be por-trayed as *external* to the industry's own (successful) efforts to face up to transnationalisation. It should not, therefore, be surprising that the onslaught of the crisis accentuated the clamour for the state to come to the aid of the industry. The capture of state authority by the profes-sional associations ensured that this clamour essentially focussed on the control of imports. As latent crisis became manifest in all aspects of the industry, it spawned not a pattern of innovation and adjustment to the new conditions but a renewed emphasis on traditional demands for protection from intensifying international competition. Concern focussed on the GATT Tokyo Round talks and, of course, on the MFA due to expire at the end of 1977.[51] The Seventh Plan sectoral committee report simply assumed that a trade policy compatible with keeping the trade balance in textile and clothing products essentially at 1974 levels would be in place throughout the remainder of the dec-ade.[52]

As imports surged in 1975 and early 1976, it became increasingly clear that the economic assumptions of MFA I were fundamentally compromised and that the EU Commission had proved an ineffectual and reluctant administrator of the agreement when measured against the US authorities. Tighter quotas were called for, as were better safeguard measures in the face of import surges of both quota and non-quota products. Other more radical measures were requested, such as a 'reference price' for certain products below which imports would be banned (a claim of dumping in essence), and a link between import quota growth and the growth of consumption in the importing countries.[53]

If the position of the professional associations was clear, that of the new government of Giscard d'Estaing (which came to office in 1974) was not without a hint of contradiction. The government sought with some difficulty to pursue a more liberal economic adjustment strategy to deal with international competition. This involved improving the competitiveness of industrial firms through exposure to market forces, and even the notion of a redeployment away from so-called declining industrial activities. However, pressure from both the professional associations and parliamentarians in the National Assembly kept protection alive as an option.

It was a test of the strength of textile interests and their ability to shape the policy debate in which they were engaged with the state. They had already captured successfully the policy agenda when it came to restructuring and state financial assistance. The government's resolve would now be tested on trade policy. Caught between its stated policy of liberal market adjustment and the political realities of policy formation in the sector, the government's declarations began to display a certain ambiguity. In 1974, the then newly appointed Minister of Industry, Michel d'Ornano, found himself immersed in the industry's growing problems. Any move towards greater exposure to competitive pressures would lead to the sort of rationalisation which the industry claimed had already been carried out, and would also wrest control of the adjustment agenda away from the industry. Particularly obnoxious to the professional associations and the industry's supporters in the National Assembly was d'Ornano's idea that those sectors with a high level of innovation should be selected for development, and an attempt should be made to anticipate the changes which would take place in the international division of labour, notably the rise of certain LDCs.[54] Given the rise of low-wage production in the developing countries, the relatively weak French textile and clothing industry stood to gain little from such a policy; d'Ornano was signalling that the textile and clothing sector was necessarily in decline.

Clearly the political influence of the textile and clothing sector would be crucial in resisting this market-led adjustment policy. D'Ornano soon contradicted himself, stating his conviction that the sector was 'indispensable to the French economy', insisting however that import restrictions (by now high in his mind) would be of benefit only if firms improved their competitive positions.[55] This reservation indicated the uneasy coexistence of his liberal market ideas with pronouncements of support for a sector in crisis, but even the newly appointed and liberal economist Prime Minister, Raymond Barre, gave his assurances to the industry as he took up the reins of government in 1976, promising to assist the industry by preventing import surges.[56]

Gérard Haesebroeck, a Socialist Party Deputy from the Nord textile regions, attacked the ambiguity of the official position.[57] As the social consequences of crisis came to be felt in textile constituencies during 1975, some of the government's own ostensible supporters also expressed their concern over the future of the textile and clothing industries. They emphasised the problem of 'abnormal competition' the need for 'proper' limitations on imports, and the destructive role of imports from Hong Kong, Korea, Taiwan, Malaysia, and the East Bloc.[58] This political pressure began to have its effect. In the debate on the proposed 1976 budget, d'Ornano had highlighted the imposition of a *visa technique* on imports of certain fibres and woven fabrics and a restriction on the import permits related to imports of cheap intermediary goods outside the MFA quota system.[59] Apparently accepting without irony the 'abnormal imports' thesis as his own, he stated in the National Assembly: 'We are particularly vigilant – I insist on this term – as regards imports which take place under abnormal conditions.'[60]

The year 1976 was particularly hard for the industry with respect to import pressure; the textile balance of trade (clothing not included) slid into deficit for the first time in post-war history, and this was despite other signs indicating general economic recovery from the depths of 1975. Referring specifically to the upcoming MFA negotiations, the Minister of Industry committed the government to a renewal of the accord and a reinforcement and extension of the safeguard clauses in the agreement.[61] France was therefore to press for a hardline approach in negotiations in order to tighten restrictions. By the end of the year, the government was firmly attached to obtaining a much more restrictive trade agreement, and negotiations had begun. It seemed that liberal policies had (at least temporarily) been laid aside and the industry had captured the trade policy agenda. The key factor in the Ministry of Industry's calculations seemed to be the following: though textile consumption in early 1976 was up some 6 per cent on 1973 levels, production in the French industry had fallen by 8 per cent. The trade surplus had shrunk by some 14 per cent as a result. It was claimed that new exports to EU countries had more than compensated for the loss of colonial markets: so, it was concluded, the rise of LDC export capacity was the problem.[62] The Ministry had effectively aligned its thinking with the professional associations, whose refrain of *importations sauvages* was constantly echoed in the National Assembly.[63] Their focus on this issue had clearly paid off, and the government was ready to do battle on behalf of the industry.

(b) Capturing Europe's Trade Policy Agenda

The road to a new MFA was a difficult one. The LDCs of course pushed for the early elimination of the 'temporary' quotas which had taken on various guises since the 1950s. The US administration had been effective in making use of MFA I and was not likely to push overly hard for tighter restrictions at the time it was campaigning for the liberalisation of non-tariff barriers in the GATT Tokyo Round. The Commission was by instinct liberal and inclined to concern itself with the plight of the LDCs, and key member states such as Germany and the Netherlands were opposed to the restrictions, let alone a tighter accord.

In order to claim success, the French government would essentially have to project its own newly adopted trade policy towards the sector into the Commission's negotiating mandate, meanwhile overcoming the more liberal inclinations of some of the other members of the Council. Though changed economic circumstances and a lack of competitiveness lay at the root of the problem, the inefficiency of the EU trade policy machinery and the diversion of imports from the US market had undoubtedly hit the weaker EU producers hard; the Commission had only managed to implement the first bilateral agreements with exporters some two years after MFA I had come into force![64]

The negotiating process first required that a common EU position be defined, and France was determined that it should be its own. To demonstrate that resolve, the junior Industry Minister Antoine Rufenacht unilaterally invoked the GATT article XIX safeguard clause of the GATT for four categories of imports of textile and clothing products which were outside the MFA safeguard clause, and on four additional categories of 'less-sensitive' product groups governed by the Treaty. The restrictions affected a list of low-cost exporting countries and were designed to hold exports at 1976 levels until the new agreement could come into force.[65]

Despite the pressure of imports and of the economic downturn on producers across the EU, the French position was not entirely acceptable in the EU negotiating forum. Calls for a totally new and tougher agreement, with such stipulations as an anti-dumping 'reference price' for various products throughout the Community (as was proposed by the UIH) or a link between import levels and the growth of consumer demand, had to be toned down in the face of opposition from Denmark, the Netherlands, and, most importantly, Germany. These countries had an interest in a relatively open import regime for a simple reason: the labour-intensive segments of their industry, particularly clothing assembly, had been effectively contracted out to offshore low-wage producers through outward processing traffic (OPT). An unduly restrictive MFA might compromise their reliance of this OPT-based strategy imports, particularly for Germany and the Netherlands. In addition, the Commission had its own agenda with respect to aiding the development of the LDCs through preferential and other trading links. In the end, it was agreed that the old accord would simply be renewed, with the new agreement lasting a further four years up to the end of 1981.

This apparent failure of the French government masked an important reality. The addition of the United Kingdom and Ireland to the EU – both had joined in 1974 – helped the French cause (which was anyway backed by Italy). The UK and Italy each controlled as many votes in the Council as France or the Federal Republic, and the threat of ongoing unilateral action by France and possibly others was a distinct reality if the EU itself were not to take robust action. The weak competitive position of the UK industry persisted despite the fact that throughout the late 1970s and the 1980s the UK had the lowest labour costs (social security costs included) of the major EU and indeed OECD producers.[66] This weakness meant that the considerable political resources of the industry were deployed in favour of trade protection. Furthermore, the general impact of the mid 1970s economic crisis was greater in the UK than in almost any other advanced economy, sparking a dramatic rise in unemployment at a time when the ruling Labour Party government was in a minority situation in the Parliament. The UK's increasingly militant trade unions were like a monkey on the back of the government of the day, and many members of the Labour parliamentary party depended on unions to sponsor their election campaigns.

These factors meant that rising unemployment was one of the most salient political issues of the day. Indeed rising unemployment competed with wage demands as a political issue, on a background of and inflation rate which was often over 20 per cent; the two fed each other in a vicious spiral of economic decline and intense distributional conflict. If this picture is placed in the context of a general collapse in capital investment in the UK textile and clothing sector and government policies which had encouraged overmanning in the industry, the one option apparently open to the besieged government was protection. In the end, the UK government proved almost as devoted to protectionism and a reinforced MFA as the French, and was certainly willing to support the French lead in the Council of Ministers. The position of Ireland was little different.

If it had already been agreed that the main text of the MFA would simply be rolled over as of 1 January 1978, one should be reminded that the real substance of the accord lay in its bilateral agreements and the protocols which were eventually to be appended at the time of renewal. Tougher quotas and better safeguards would be sought in the bilateral accords;[67] the Commission would use its enormous market power to pick off the low-cost exporters one by one in bilateral negotiations, threatening unilateral action to the recalcitrant.

The objective of the French government, supported by the UK, Ireland, and Italy for good measure (despite the growing Italian success with exports), was to stabilise the level of growth of all low-wage imports.[68] Products were regrouped according to their 'sensitivity' and each category would henceforth have its own growth rate for imports. Although the six per cent growth rate for imports established by MFA I would apply to the overall basket of products, the growth rate of the most sensitive product groups would be virtually frozen at their 1976 levels, with a looser level of quotas for the other categories. Perhaps most importantly, a new clause, appended to the protocol of renewal, enabled 'jointly-agreed reasonable departures from particular elements in particular cases'.[69] In other words, in consultation with the exporting countries, importers could impose temporary restrictions on product groups not covered by specific quotas in the bilateral accords, or they could tighten existing restrictions, if they considered this necessary.

Furthermore, the Commission (under pressure from member states) was this time resolved to deal with the substantial import pressures coming from low-wage countries not covered by the MFA. Many of these countries had preferential trading arrangements with the EU, and therefore the MFA became complemented by less formal quantitative restrictions negotiated with the ACP nations of the Lomé

Convention, and (more importantly in terms of import competition) the East Bloc plus certain countries of the Mediterranean basin such as Spain, Portugal (aspirant EU members both), and the Maghreb.[70] Thus, with the exception of textile trade among the principal industrialised nations, the totality of textile and clothing trade was under quotas. Largely under French pressure and despite the determined resistance of Germany (the EU's most economically powerful nation), EU textile trade policy had entered an era of protection, as those pressing for a tougher agreement had proved the stronger. The French government felt able to express its 'broad satisfaction' with the new accord.[71]

One further factor was important in this victory for French trade policy. This was the emergence of effective EU-level professional associations with close relations with the Commission, and the powerful influence of the French employers' organisations within them. COMITEXTIL (textile and knitting industries) and the Association Européenne des Industries de l'Habillement (AEIH, apparel manufacture) became more active as a result of both the pressure of imports and the increasing importance of the Commission in negotiating and implementing trade policies which were once the exclusive preserve of the member states.[72] These associations began to penetrate the Commission itself as lobbies, and served to link together the governments, EU level authorities of DG-I (External Relations) and DG-III (Industry), and the industry lobbies of the major textile producer countries in a transnational coalition committed to ongoing trade protectionism in the industry.

Thus the EU-level system of industry associations began to mirror the long-standing situation in the member states themselves – public and private actors became closely intertwined in a situation of ongoing contacts across the broad range of policy issues, particularly the negotiation and day-to-day implementation of trade policy.[73] The focus of attention was the development of a common position on trade negotiations, wherein policy was initially hammered out between the the Commission on the one hand, and Council representatives in the so-called article 113 Committee for trade policy (named after the relevant article of the Treaty of Rome). It is significant that textiles and clothing negotiations were regarded as of sufficient importance by key member states that a separate article 113 textile and clothing subcommittee, which maintained a relatively distinct and autonomous identity from the main committee, was established as the core of the policy-making process in Brussels.[74] Furthermore, the EU level professional associations worked closely with the Commission in monitoring the impact of imports on the industry and the respect of the quota system by the exporting countries, demonstrating how firms and their associations underpin and reinforce state legal processes. Contact with the Commission was ongoing on a virtually daily basis across a range of issues, a situation which the associations use to keep the Commission vigilant on import surveillance and other matters of interest to the industry.

The French professional associations, as national members of the EU-wide associations, emerged as particularly influential participants in the Brussels game, in addition to the pressures they exerted through their own government. 'The COMITEXTIL was very much dominated by the French faction.'[75] In this way the French associations were continuously active on the national and EU level in leading the battle in Brussels for stricter MFA terms as well as a stricter implementation of the terms of the agreement once negotiated. In many ways the French professional associations had to expend little effort to convince their partners from other member-states of the need for reinforced protectionism, partners who were usually more protectionist in orientation than their own governments, but the leadership role was undeniable. Nonetheless, the EU organisations must develop a synthesis of what may be contrasting positions of their individual national associations members, and there have been times when the COMITEXTIL position has differed from the position defended by particular national associations; some national member associations are characteristically more liberal than others, until of course their own vital interests are challenged and protectionist reflexes take over.[76] That said, over time it became increasingly difficult to separate the Brussels textile and clothing trade policy process out from the individual national policy processes; the various actors (personnel, institutions, and associations) were constantly intertwined and from the late 1970s onwards formed an increasingly integrated ensemble in which protectionist sentiments were predominant. Given the ongoing EU commitment to the MFA, *capture had become transnationalised.*

(c) MFA III

In some respects the subsequent renewals of the agreement, which took effect in January 1982 (MFA III) and particularly January 1986 (MFA IV) were less controversial than either the initial accord or the first renewal.[77] The increasingly restrictive MFA had become thoroughly institutionalised in the policies, conceptions, and practices of the principal actors involved in decision-making. Both the EU and the United States authorities seemed to accept that there was little prospect of a major change in trade policy. However, the main text of the MFA had always identified the agreement as temporary, and there was from the late 1970s a general move in the direction of more liberal economic policies throughout the global economy. Even in France there was a renewed attempt to impose a liberal market adjustment policy on the textile and clothing sector, a move which met the same fate as earlier attempts.

A new government under Prime Minister Raymond Barre had been appointed by President Giscard in 1976 with the declared intention of liberalising the French economy. By 1978 the Minister of Industry was André Giraud and he attempted to extend this liberalisation agenda to the domain of trade policy and industrial adjustment. Giraud clearly intended this market-oriented redeployment strategy to apply to the future of the MFA. In a firm display of government will to take control of the adjustment agenda, the Minister let it be known that the MFA would not necessarily be extended or renewed in 1982. He held that it was not desirable that the agreement should be extended indefinitely and that the sector must adapt to technical progress, creativity, and information sharing.[78] A week later, while speaking to knitting industry industrialists at the opening of the Salon International de la Maille (knitting industry international trade fair), he gave no indication that renewal was being considered and exhorted industrialists to help themselves, calling the industry 'defeatist' for relying on protection. Low-cost importers, he said, would be the more convinced if competitiveness were improved rather than protection renewed.[79]

Giraud's refusal to accept the quasi-permanent protection and subsidy of the textile and clothing sector was a clear rejection of the political programme of the professional associations and an open challenge to powerful interests on which the government depended for its electoral success and which were institutionalised in the policy process. Giraud was undoubtedly hoping to exploit the differences between dynamic, transnationalised firms as opposed to the traditional producers. He pointed out, for example, that following the conclusion of an EU trade agreement with China which increased imports of low-cost Chinese textile products, there had been those firms which had wished to resist further imports of cheap unfinished cotton fabrics and those which had pressed to have them *increased* so as to benefit from cheaper inputs for their own finished manufactures.[80]

However, the attempt to exploit potential internal divisions in the sector marked not the victory of his new strategy over traditional industry interests, but its nadir. Shortly after the speech at the Salon de la Maille, Giraud was forced to retract his statement. Pressed in the National Assembly by members of his own coalition, in particular the influential RPR (Gaullist) deputy of the Vosges Philippe Séguin, he supported the principle of renewal, but was vague about the substance.[81] The trade issue was nonetheless soon to take centre stage once again as crisis conditions returned with renewed vigour in 1979–80, the MFA renewal date approached, and the presidential elections of March 1981 drew nearer. Economic interests were rallying to ensure that the market structure, particularly with regard to exposure to global competition, continued to be shaped to their advantage.

Despite the success of MFA II in stemming the tide of the most-sensitive low-wage imports, by 1980 the clothing surplus on the balance of trade no longer compensated for the deficit in textiles, and overall sectoral trade slipped into deficit (a historic occurrence).[82] Domestic market share continued, therefore, to slide. These difficulties were reflected in declining profitability, continuously weakening investment levels, and accelerating unemployment in the sector. In 1980 alone, some 30 000 jobs disappeared, and the situation continued to worsen the following year. Spectacular bankruptcies occurred. The Agache-Willot group (then France's largest textile and clothing concern) began to experience difficulties in 1980, and by 1981 was forced into receivership. The political ramifications, combined with the industry's stranglehold on the policy agenda, played into the professional associations' hands.

The government was anyway becoming increasingly preoccupied with the overall trade balance as a general issue, as the oil price began its second meteoric rise in five years. This made action on the textile front all the more urgent, and possibly more legitimate to government policy-makers. Thus, in early August 1979 France used the 'technical visa' procedure to impose unilateral import restrictions on sweaters and pullovers, including products from EU trading partners.[83] West German industrialists immediately protested that the French were violating the Treaty of Rome, promising to carry the charges before the European Court. The head of the Italian textile employers' federation, Guido Artoni, remarked ironically that the measures would be more damaging to French producers and distributors than to Italy. He noted that up to 60 per cent of imports coming into France from Italy were under contract from French designers, many for re-export, and that, furthermore, the French industry had neither plant which was sophisticated enough, nor the sufficient quality control, to produce certain such articles itself.[84] Eventually, Paris was warned by the Commission, though it protested rather disingenuously that the measures were merely designed to gather better statistics on trade, not to restrict the flow of imports.[85] The affair revealed that, despite liberal rhetoric, the government remained consistently prepared to act to restrict trade, even against fellow EU members or other countries in the OECD. The point was not lost on the Commission as it prepared for MFA renewal. A number of National Assembly deputies continued to argue that MFA quotas were not uniformly (i.e. rigorously) respected across the EU and the government faced all-party opposition over the implementation of the MFA.[86]

Outside the National Assembly, the strongest voice was that of the Union des Industries de l'Habillement, representing a clothing industry perhaps hardest hit of all textile activities by low-wage imports.[87] The UIH added that if its proposed approach caused undue friction with EU trading partners, then recourse should be made to article XIX of the GATT.[88] Each time crisis intervened, trade was the easiest policy issue to raise and the sector's demands and parliamentary support for them had hardened into a doctrinal reflex. Furthermore, the state could be seen to be doing something as long as it reacted to the trade issue, while the professional associations continued to control the adjustment agenda.

The government had of course committed itself to some form of MFA III for 1982. The debate soon turned to the terms of an eventual renewal. The UIT went straight to the point: the diagnosis continued to highlight imports as a problem, so a stricter MFA would be needed.[89] According the the UIT, the import situation had worsened since 1977 and MFA II: manufactured textile imports from 'sensitive' sources were up some 17 per cent per year 1977 to 1979. In the five most-sensitive product categories imports were up 11.7 per cent per year; 6.1 per cent from MFA countries but 18.5 per cent from Mediterranean countries linked to the EU by trade agreements, and 13.5 per cent per year from other 'sensitive' sources. In other words, imports from MFA sources had been controlled relatively well, but the gap had been amply filled by non-MFA countries subject to other forms of 'voluntary' restrictions. Therefore, one of the primary concerns of the UIT was the regulation of imports from these sources. In short, the

UIT was demanding that any trading advantages in textiles accorded to countries with preferential trading links to the Community be compensated by tighter restrictions on other exporting countries, thus restricting imports from all low-wage sources more effectively. The UIT also sought restrictions on imports from some non-EU industrialised economies, and openly requested a bilateral accord to limit imports from the US (a demand demonstrating either purposeful overstatement or extreme political ineptitude).

The UIT next claimed that the experience of past agreements demonstrated a need for two major innovations for the upcoming renewal negotiations. First, they demanded the introduction of a system of global quotas to cover the basket of 'sensitive' product categories from all export sources.[90] Second, the rate of annual growth of imports (i.e. the quotas) was to be linked to the growth of domestic demand for those products. 'Surge clauses' were considered necessary to control unpredictable surges in imports in relevant categories of merchandise, though such clauses were not new. Special attention had also to be paid to quota dodging.

There were some further and rather unexpected innovations in the UIT's demands for MFA III. Despite the overall severity of the protectionist measures the UIT sought, the ongoing transnationalisation of production was affecting the structure of the French industry and, therefore, its perceived interests. For the first time the Union demanded preferential access to import quotas for those French manufacturers which had developed transnational production strategies which therefore relied on foreign sourcing – either OPT (all OPT and reimports were controlled by quotas outside the MFA) or semi-finished intermediary imports for their success. While this development did not herald an open split in the association, it did illustrate the growing ambiguity of the professional associations, which were faced with the expanding OPT activities of some of their most dynamic and profitable members. The strict quota systems demanded by the majority of members could jeopardise the cost-cutting strategies of some firms and their newly won competitiveness. Nonetheless, the UIT had equally to avoid policies which might damage the far more numerous firms with more traditional production strategies.

While the UIT struggled to accommodate the demands of both traditional and transnationalised firms, the UIH was even more vehemently in favour of a tougher MFA. The UIH demanded not only the system of global quotas and the link with domestic demand, but the fixing of new (lower) base rates for quota growth and the creation of 'automatic' surge clauses unlike the existing ones based on consultation with exporters.[91] This was effectively a desire to roll back import penetration levels, and nothing less than the existence of a substantial French clothing industry was considered to be at stake.

However, tensions linked to the transnationalisation of apparel firms were observable even in the ultra-protectionist clothing industry, but not in the UIH itself. In 1980 a reimporters association, the Syndicat National des Fabricants-Importateurs des Industries de l'Habillement, was formed. This initiative was never given the official blessing of the Union des Industries de l'Habillement, and the clothing manufacturers' union refused to adopt a policy of 'canalisation' of imports so as to protect the interests of its less transnationalised (majority) members. The Syndicat thus remained the initiative of a few dynamic firms desiring better access to import licences for foreign sourcing activity, and it was eventually dissolved in 1984. Professional 'solidarity' and the policy agenda had been maintained, highlighting the limits of the transnationalisation which had taken place among French firms.[92] However, this and the UIT example provide evidence of the very real if rather halting changes which were taking place in the coalition of textile and clothing associations,[93] foreshadowing the conflicts of the Uruguay Round.

The growing crisis and associated political pressures in this pre-electoral period eventually attracted a personal intervention by the President of the Republic himself. Before the Chamber of Commerce in Lille (Nord textile region), Giscard d'Estaing emphasised that the government would deliver on trade policy for the sector.[94] There would be better control of the quota system through reinforced surveillance measures and, if necessary, the imposition of import visas on relevant product lines. While the President did emphasise the competition from high-wage industrialised economy producers (a point bound to irritate the UIT and the UIH), the government appeared henceforth committed to defending the producers against low-wage imports. The President would instruct the government to seek the renewal of the MFA in 1981 and thus once more tighten the protectionist noose on the low-wage exporters. There were even measures against industrialised countries. In 1980 alone, France successfully invoked article 115 of the Treaty of Rome (a trade safeguard clause operating only with the agreement of the Commission in Brussels) seventy-five times for textiles alone, more than the *total* (all sectors) for any other EU country.[95]

Despite the President's protectionist commitment and 'Textile Plan' announced in November 1980,[96] nothing was good enough for the professional associations. The UIT president predictably pointed to the insufficiency of measures to control imports in the government's plans, but otherwise declared himself in agreement with the government's analysis. The UIH was more critical, claiming that the measures did not respond to the real problem at all – imports.[97] The UIH in the same breath absolved its member firms from all responsibility for the industry's difficulties.[98] Concerted pressure also came from within the National Assembly, once again largely focusing on the imports issue.[99] The most persistent indeed came from the RPR (Gaullist) deputies, often closely identified with textile interests, who essentially supported the government but revealed an obsessive attachment to the imports issue.[100]

While the government continued to give assurances about imports, the pressure remained unrelenting. Looking ahead to the next MFA, Industry Minister Giraud seemed to accept the industrialists' demand for a link between import quotas and the growth of domestic textile consumption.[101] His new trade policy measures eventually resulted in the Commission authorising France, Italy, and Ireland, under article 115 of the Treaty of Rome, to block certain textile imports transiting from other EU countries, and France was permitted to block certain products from India, the Philippines, Korea, and Taiwan.[102]

In the end Giscard d'Estaing lost the March 1981 elections. His pursuit of liberal trade and adjustment policies had been undermined by the pressures of domestic industrial restructuring which they implied. Popular dismay at rising unemployment levels and industrial decline led to his defeat, undermining the legitimacy of market-led adjustment at least temporarily. The institutionalised political resources of employers' organisations had done much to foster this popular sentiment, at a time when the industry itself was culpable for its failure to invest (see Chapter 2). François Mitterrand swept to power and soon ushered in a large parliamentary majority for the Socialist Party. The new government, under Pierre Mauroy as Prime Minister, was quick to respond to worries about employment levels in the industry. The Socialists clearly wished that the industrial restructuring process, including that taking place in the textile and clothing sector, should no longer translate into job losses.[103] The new government seemed essentially willing to purchase wholesale the professional associations' policy agenda. This resulted in a substantial programme of aid to the industry,[104] but trade policy remained constantly in the forefront as the essential presupposition of other forms of state action in the sector.

The new government was thus more favourably disposed than the previous administration toward restrictive trade agreements and tighter import controls in textiles and clothing, believing itself to be free of any liberal inclinations. The former Barre government had come round to supporting protection because of industry capture of the trade policy process, but this had always been contrary to its preferred policy inclinations and ideological predisposition. While in opposition the Socialist Deputies had pressed for rigid respect of the accords and renewal under stricter terms, and this position was carried into office. The new Socialist Prime Minister clearly had sound domestic support for protectionism which he could ill afford to betray.

At this stage, it is necessary once again to link this domestic level analysis with EU level bargaining processes, the two of which had become irretrievably intertwined. From the beginning, the government had made clear its intention to pursue the hard line in Brussels in order to ensure EU support for its views.[105] The second MFA was to expire at the end of 1981, and given the crisis which had struck the textile sector there could be no question of a simple renewal of the accord.[106] Nonetheless, the acceptance of the French position by Germany and the Netherlands, each with vastly different textile and clothing industries which relied on imports of cheap inputs for their success, would pose problems, and the Commission also appeared to favour a simple renewal. From the outset, the task of the French delegation looked difficult, but the determination of the Mauroy government and the pressure of its domestic constituency was very great. France constantly threatened to use article XIX of the GATT, and had done so under similar circumstances in 1977 and more recently. In fact the new government's trade policies were so resolute as to provide the ironic spectacle of textile *employers* demonstrating in the streets of Lille in support of a *Socialist* Prime Minister's (Mauroy) firm negotiating stance on the MFA in the EU forum.[107]

The demands of the industry were clear enough. To summarise the complex positions of the many professional associations, under a system of 'global ceilings' (quotas to be administered by product category; all exporting countries would be treated as part of a single basket), the industry wanted to combine a reduction in import growth (as regulated by the quotas for sensitive products) with some link between the quotas in the most sensitive categories and the evolution of domestic demand. The industry also sought stricter control of product groups not directly covered by the quotas but still under the MFA safeguard system (to permit the application of restrictions where and when necessary), better fraud control clauses, and terms preventing the transfer of unused quotas from one product group to another or to the following year. Furthermore, it was demanded that a genuine 'minimum price' clause be included in the bilateral accords, not just mentioned in the renegotiated protocol.[108] A more radical demand which presented great political difficulties for any government called for a roll-back of the import penetration level from its then 50 per cent-plus level to 40 per cent.[109] The French government appeared to accept most of these demands, a position which was completely contrary to the Socialists' much-trumpeted concern with helping developing countries to foster domestic industrial development.

In the end the common position agreed in the article 113 textile and clothing committee was along the lines promoted by the French government. The Commission pursued cutbacks in the quotas awarded to dominant suppliers and a link between the growth of domestic demand and the growth of imports. On this latter point the EU was supported by the United States.

The agreement which was to emerge may be considered another French victory on the whole, though France had been backed in the EU by Great Britain, Ireland, Belgium, and Italy,[110] and the US was unlikely to suffer from the EUs protectionist zeal. A 'recession clause', linking a revision of import quotas to the evolution of consumption, was included in the new protocol of renewal.[111] Of course those involved in the renegotiation were well aware that the most important aspect of the agreement would once again be its implementation through the bilateral accords. Therefore, the hard line prevailed in the EU's bilateral negotiations, which were rapidly concluded by the end of 1982. The dominant suppliers' shares (South Korea, Hong Kong, Taiwan, Macao) were cut back, and the growth rate for 'sensitive' quota products was reduced to below 1 per cent. 'Surge clauses' were negotiated to prevent runaway surges in less-sensitive product groups.[112]

The industry therefore appeared to have got what it wanted, despite some points of irritation.[113] But question marks still hung over the future of the industry in France (and elsewhere for that matter). There had so far been a failure to adapt in a way likely to ensure the long-run competitive position of the French industry in global markets. The professional associations were defending a socio-economic *status quo* and associational culture which required that competition remain heavily circumscribed. This demonstrates once again the ways in which markets as institutions of governance are embedded in the socio-economic structures and the institutions of political authority which constitute the state.

There were signs, however, that the strategy might be changing as MFA III came up for renegotiation in 1985. Already the professional associations had become more flexible on the issue of reimports and OPT, as has been noted. However, the UIH (traditionally the most protectionist of the professional associations) began to soften its overall protectionist stance. For the forthcoming MFA IV negotiations in 1985, foreshadowing the eventual elimination of the MFA in the Uruguay Round then in preparation, the UIH altered its position and called for a less extensive agreement, better-targeted on small problem product groups and major export sources.[114] The reasons behind this policy change were most interesting.[115] The UIH claimed that it wished to 'demystify' the import issue and was ready to recognise that the low-wage import phenomenon was really limited to key products and exporters only, as has consistently been argued in this book. More importantly, there was the feeling that MFA IV might be the last, and so demands would have to be realistic in order to get a fourth agreement at all. The experience of the third accord had also convinced the UIH that a perfect system of protection was impossible. The quota machinery was simply too complex and cumbersome to operate, despite an abundance of government will to do so. If protection did not work on all fronts then only the important ones should be covered. This was effectively an admission that 10 years of MFA quotas (longer if one includes the STA/LTA) had been an unsuccessful strategy.

There were other underlying reasons why policy change was slowly germinating in the professional associations, and these provide some of the clearest evidence so far of *the link between changes in industrial structure and shifts in the policy preferences of producer groups*. If the MFA could not contain low-wage competition completely and did nothing to attenuate competition from the advanced countries, then even French clothing firms would have to indulge in some dislocation of production through foreign sourcing, and many were doing so already. Foreign sourcing, especially OPT, in which imports could be directed and controlled by French firms, was on the rise and the consequent reimports contained significant French value-added content. In most cases this enhanced the turnover (though not necessarily the actual level of output) of the firms involved, albeit with costs for the domestic workforce. The need to develop more dynamic French firms in clothing production and to rid domestic manufacturers of the complacent view that French fashion design would sell throughout the world automatically and without effort was as clear as it had been for a decade. Production and marketing would have to be seen as a whole, the UIH admitted at last, as many experts had long insisted. Italian firms had even proven their ability without significant resort to OPT, and had displaced French producers as the leaders in the fashion market. The Italian attitude to the clothing industry was now seen as an example to follow – a more coherent approach to the very real problems faced by manufacturers.[116] Finally, protectionism was seen as a potential problem. First, some EU producers had found that quotas hindered their ability to resort to foreign sourcing strategies. Second, should the Americans act on some of the threats of protection which Congress had been making in relation to the high dollar exchange rates and EU import penetration of US markets, the effect on the EU industry (the largest textile and clothing exporter in the world by far) would be disastrous.

CONCLUSION: THE FOURTH MFA

As it happens, MFA IV (1986) turned out to be a foregone conclusion and was indeed yet stricter in the control of imports than any of its predecessors. This is largely because the United States had seriously re-entered the protectionist game. EU producers were enjoying relatively buoyant market conditions, at least compared to the early 1980s. EU textile and clothing production had risen 10 per cent and 13 per cent respectively in the year 1984–5 immediately preceding the renewal, and as a result the EU even dismantled a number of consistently underused MFA quotas and increased the quotas available to the least developed producers.[117] In contrast, the US industry had faced its sharpest recession in a decade or so, but in rather odd circumstances. From 1982 the US industry had indeed enjoyed the fruits of rising demand in the home market. However, while consumption continued to grow apace in the so-called Reagan boom, production fell dramatically by some 10 per cent in 1984, and imports consequently doubled between 1983 and the end of 1984.[118] The US tightened its import control regime, but this did not stop a succession of textile trade bills from being passed in both the House and the Senate. While legislation such as the Jenkins Bill was vetoed by the President, a real chance existed that the textile coalition, through Congress, would successfully override the veto and the MFA would then be replaced by a unilateral US import regime, completely sapped of multilateral legitimacy in the eyes of the international trading community.[119]

US producers had not completely lost their ability to compete in their home market – far from it. This time the reason for the dramatic growth in import penetration was largely external to the practices of the industrialists themselves. The reason for the import invasion can be largely put down to the US government's monetary and exchange rate policies, which led to the most marked rise in the dollar since floating began in the early 1970s. Cline has amply analysed the effects of the high dollar on the textile and clothing sector,[120] so little more need be said at this stage except that the problem affected the broad range of US manufacturing industry sectors on home and third country markets alike. Although the relocation of clothing manufacture towards Latin America and the Caribbean began in earnest during this period and subsequently accelerated, a factor which undoubtedly increased imports, the high dollar certainly increased the incentives for firms to resort to foreign sourcing strategies in the first place.

The textile and clothing sector was consequently not alone as a sponsor of protectionist legislation in Congress from the mid 1980s onwards. The US government had few options other than to pursue a renewed and reinvigorated MFA despite the administration's hopes for a new GATT round and a dramatic liberalisation of the global trade regime. In the end, the EU and the United States adopted a joint statement laying out their shared objectives for the renewal negotiations,[121] cementing a transatlantic protectionist coalition. The result was, at least in the opinion of the developing country victims of the accord, the strictest MFA since its original signature in 1973. Fibre coverage was extended to prevent low-wage producers from exporting fibres (especially ramie) not covered by the 1981 agreement; safeguard provisions (article 3) were strengthened; the surge clause remained; quotas established in bilateral negotiations were, with some exceptions, as strict as ever.

However, scarcely was the ink dry on MFA IV and the bilateral negotiations under way in earnest than the Uruguay Round was launched in September 1986 at Punte del Este with the stated intention of liberalising the MFA as one of its essential elements.[122] The ever tighter MFA and the solemnly adopted negotiating principles of the new trade round sat uneasily together. That liberalisation was achieved by 1994 is surely difficult to explain in the light of the three decades of ever-increasing protectionism analysed here, but the Uruguay Round and liberalisation of textile and clothing trade is the subject of the next and final chapter of this book.

Whatever the *prima facie* difficulties of explaining the eventual liberalisation of textile and clothing trade in the new Round, the fourth MFA reminds one of the central argument of this book: *that the dynamics of the global trade regime in textile and clothing products, and state policies towards it, were demonstrably interdependent with the changing production structure and pattern of industrial adjustment across the global economic space.* The consistent intensification of competition had just as consistently fed back into the policy preferences identified by producer groups. Trade and industrial adjustment processes existed in a symbiotic relationship, where changing economic structures would eventually yield changes in policy outcome. In the case of France, the balance of forces within the associational groups depended on the avoidance of competition and adjustment. Throughout the industrialised world, the capacity of protectionist textile and clothing interests to capture both domestic and international policy processes, through their relationships with domestic state institutions, facilitated their control and manipulation of the international policy agenda.

In this way, EU and US textile and clothing interests became aggregated into a transnational coalition of interests supporting the increasingly restrictive MFA through its initiation and three subsequent renewals. *These private interests appropriated public institutions for their own market-structuring purposes,* to 'widen the market and narrow the competition,' thus enhancing their profitability.[123] *These private interests in short appropriated the mantle of public legitimacy in aid of their ongoing distributional conflict concerning the structure of the global market.* Although the outcome of the bargaining processes of the international trade regime is often uncertain, the exceptional market size over which the combined EU and United States had jurisdiction ensured that the combined LDCs faced an almost impossible task of resisting the protectionist reflexes of the producer groups which confronted them. The capture of the international trade policy-making process by EU and US interests (albeit supported by other producer countries such as Canada and the Scandinavians) extended from the domestic level to the institutions of the international trade regime, and for them there was little distinction between the politics of domestic industrial adjustment and the politics of international trade. It remains for this book to relate the ongoing changes in global industrial structures, as manifested in the practices of firms involved in the production of textile and clothing products, to the eventual abolition of the MFA at Marrakesh in 1994, which is the subject of the next and final chapter of this book.

Notes

1. For a definition of capture, see Chapter 3, note 1.
2. On role of private interests in regulatory processes, see Leigh Hancher and Michael Moran, 'Organizing Regulatory Space', in Hancher and Moran (eds), *Capitalism, Culture, and Economic Regulation* (Oxford: Clarendon Press, 1989), pp. 272–99.
3. At the level of international policy processes, capture is less likely than at the domestic level because of the enhanced opportunities for mediation of particularistic interests by state officials, and because of the greater complexity of conflicts of interest among the multitude of actors involved. Nonetheless, the direct involvement of industrial lobbies has long marked the GATT process.
4. Robert W. Cox, *Production, Power, and World Order* (New York: Columbia University Press, 1987), pp. 253–65.
5. For a discussion of the accommodation of Japan within GATT, see Gerard and Victoria Curzon, 'The Management of Trade Relations in the GATT', in Andrew Shonfield, G. and V. Curzon, T.K. Warley and George Ray (eds), *Politics and Trade*, volume I of Andrew Shonfield (ed.), *International Economic Relations of the Western World 1959–1971*, pp. 253–83.
6. Ibid., p. 283.
7. William R. Cline, *The Future of World Trade in Textiles and Apparel*, rev. edn (Washington, DC: Institute for International Economics, 1990), p. 146.
8. H. Richard Friman, *Patchwork Protectionism: Textile Trade Policy in the United States, Japan, and West Germany* (Ithaca: Cornell University Press, 1990), p. 95.
9. Robin Anson and Paul Simpson, *World Textile Trade and Production Trends*, Special Report no. 1108 (London: Economist Intelligence Unit, June 1988), p. 108; G.B. Navaretti, R. Faini, and A. Silbertson, 'Overview', in Navaretti, Faini, and Silbertson, *Beyond the Multifibre Arrangement: Third World Competition and Restructuring Europe's Textile Industry* (Paris: OECD, 1995), p. 14.
10. Curzon and Curzon, 'The Management of Trade Relations', op. cit., pp. 254–55.
11. The UK indeed established bilateral restrictions with Hong Kong (its own colony), India, and Pakistan; Anson and Simpson, p. 108.
12. Cline, in *The Future of World Trade*, op. cit., discusses this concept of market disruption (p. 147). He states that the November 1960

GATT Decision on the Avoidance of Market Disruption made 'important changes going beyond the existing Article XIX safeguard mechanism'. Restrictions could be imposed *even if actual injury to domestic industries had not taken place*, permitting discrimination against import surges associated with low import prices not necessarily linked to dumping or subsidies. Discriminatory application of restrictions was, furthermore, permitted. Thus as the cornerstone of protection in the sector it was a powerful device indeed.

13. Friman, *Patchwork Protectionism*, op. cit., p. 107.
14. Anson and Simpson, *World Textile Trade*, op. cit., p. 109.
15. See Friman, *Patchwork Protectionism*, op. cit., pp. 107–10.
16. Organisation for Economic Co-operation and Development, *Textile and Clothing Industries: Structural Problems and Policies in OECD Countries* (Paris, 1983), p. 107; hereafter referred to as 'OECD Report'.
17. Ibid.
18. Navaretti *et al.*, 'Overview', op. cit., p. 14.
19. OECD Report, p. 162.
20. Anson and Simpson, *World Textile Trade*, op. cit., p. 110; a few other natural fibres such as hemp and ramie were excluded because the importing countries did not use them in production.
21. This account of MFA I relies on three sources in addition to the text of the agreement itself: Anson and Simpson, *World Textile Trade*, op. cit., pp. 110–25; Cline, *The Future of World Trade*, op. cit., ch. 6; OECD Report, pp. 106–8, 161–71. Other sources will be cited as needed.
22. Cline, *The Future of World Trade*, op. cit., p. 149.
23. OECD Report, p. 134.
24. Figures from Cline, *The Future of World Trade*, op. cit., p. 61, table 3.1.
25. OECD Report, p. 134.
26. See OECD Report, annex III, p. 164, on the negotiation of bilateral accords by the US and EU. It took over a year for the EU to come up with its first bilateral agreement.
27. See Donald B. Keesing and Martin Wolf, *Textile Quotas against Developing Countries* (London: Trade Policy Research Centre, 1980), pp. 60–4.
28. J. de la Torre and Michel Bachetta, 'The Uncommon Market: European Policies toward the Clothing Industry in the 1970s', *Journal of Common Market Studies*, vol. XIX, no. 2, p. 98.
29. By 1969 investment levels in textiles had not risen relative to 1962, whereas in the USA they had doubled; see France, Plan (6th), *Rapport du Comité Industrie Textile* (Paris: La Documentation Française, 1971); hereafter referred to as 'Textile Committee Report, 6th Plan', p. 14.
30. Jacques de Bandt, *L'Industrie textile de la CEE: analyse et perspectives pour 1975* (Report to the Commission of the EEC, 1969).
31. See, for example, *Les Echos*, 27 November, 1968.
32. *Les Echos*, 17 June 1970.
33. *Le Point*, no. 50, 3 September 1973.
34. Textile Committee Report, 6th Plan, pp. 13–14. Note that these sectoral committee reports were only involved in preparatory work and did not

necessarily reflect the views of the Planning Commission itself. The committees were dominated by industrialists and the employers organisations, with limited representation from trade unions and the Ministry of Industry. They should be regarded as part of the lobbying process available to the industry.

35. Textile Committee Report, 6th Plan, p. 19
36. From the debate over the 1973 budget for Industry, in *Journal Officiel* (édition débats parlementaires), no. 92, 10 November 1972, p. 4933
37. *Les Echos*, 22 December 1973.
38. Budget debate, *Journal Officiel* (édition débats parlementaires), no. 92, p. 4933.
39. Ibid., pp. 4938, 4943.
40. *Les Echos*, 22 March 1971.
41. France, Plan (6th), *Rapport des Comités Industries de l'Habillement, du Cuir, et de la Chaussure* (Paris: La Documentation Française, 1971, hereafter referred to as 'Clothing Industry Report, 6th Plan'), p. 43.
42. *Les Echos*, 14 February 1972.
43. Clothing Industry Report, 6th Plan, p. 18.
44. Textile Committee Report, 6th Plan, p. 14.
45. See Benoît Boussemart, *Industrie de main d'oeuvre et division internationale du travail: l'avenir de l'industrie textile de la région Nord-Pas-de-Calais*, 3 vols, unpublished thesis, Doctorat ès en Sciences Economiques, Université de Paris X (Nanterre), December 1984, p. 610.
46. One is reminded that this committee was dominated by representatives of the employers. Its President was the head of the textile firm Dormeuil, and the few trade union representatives suspended their participation in early 1976. See France, Plan (7th), *Rapport du Groupe Sectoriel d'Analyse et de Prévision Textile-Habillement* (Paris: La Documentation Française, 1976), apps I and II, pp. 75–9; hereafter referred to as 'Textile and Clothing Committee Report, 7th Plan'.
47. Textile and Clothing Committee Report, 7th Plan, p. 18.
48. Ibid., 'Introduction', by Michel d'Ornano, p. 3.
49. Ibid., p. 18.
50. UIT, open letter to Michel d'Ornano from the President of the UIT, in *Memorandum sur l'avenir de l'industrie textile française* (Paris: UIT, mimeo, 8 October 1975).
51. Textile and Clothing Committee Report, 7th Plan, p. 21.
52. Ibid., p. 31.
53. Ibid., pp. 31–2; see also UIT, *Memorandum*, op. cit., pp. 10–13.
54. France, Plan (7th), *Rapport de la Commission Industrie* (Paris: La Documentation Française), 1976, pp. 26–7.
55. *Les Echos*, 29 October 1975.
56. *Les Echos*, 10 November 1976.
57. 'Press Release,' *Agence France Presse* (AFP), 17 December 1976.
58. For example, see the debate on the proposed 1976 budget for the Ministry of Industry, *Journal Officiel* (édition débats parlementaires), no. 100, 7 November 1975: remarks by Pierre Cornet (Ardèche, Républicain Indépendant and therefore Giscard's own party) p. 8022; Jean-Marie Caro (Bas-Rhin, Groupe des Réformateurs, Centristes, et

Démocrates Sociaux and thus a member of the Giscardian coalition) p. 8006; Xavier Hamelin (Nord, RPR Gaullist) p. 8023.

59. Ibid., p. 7997.
60. Ibid., p. 8028.
61. *Journal Officiel* (édition Débats Parlementaires), 17 November 1976, p. 8103.
62. France, Ministère de l'Industrie et de la Recherche, 'L'Industrie textile en France', *Note d'information*, no. 11, January 1977.
63. In fact, a special parliamentary commission of enquiry into *importations sauvages*, which primarily examined the case of the textile industry, had been commissioned. It emerged as the 'Limouzy Report' in 1977: France, Assemblée Nationale, *Rapport fait ... Commission d'Enquête Parlementaire ... les conditions dans lesquelles ont lieu les importations 'sauvages' ...*, no. 3230, 19 November 1977.
64. See Cline, *The Future of World Trade*, op. cit., p. 151; Jose de la Torre, and Michel Bachetta, 'The Uncommon Market: European Policies Towards the Clothing Industry in the 1970s', *Journal of Common Market Studies*, vol. xix no. 2, December 1980, p. 98.
65. *Le Monde*, 21 June 1977; *Le Matin*, 20 June 1977; also Senate Report, p. 142.
66. Janet Walsh, 'The Performance of UK Textiles and Clothing: Recent Controversies and Evidence,' in *International Review of Applied Economics*, vol. 5, no. 3, p. 285.
67. Chris Farrands, 'Textile Diplomacy: The Making and Implementation of European Textile Policy 1974–1978', *Journal of Common Market Studies*, vol. xviii, no. 1, September 1979, pp. 28–9.
68. Unless otherwise indicated, the following account is from Senate Report, pp. 149–152.
69. OECD Report, p. 164.
70. Spain, Portugal, Greece, Turkey, the Maghreb and the East Bloc were also the most popular locations of the OPT operations of many EU firms.
71. Farrands, 'Textile Diplomacy', op. cit., pp. 29–30.
72. Keesing and Wolf, *Textile Quotas*, op. cit., p. 60.
73. Interview evidence, EURATEX (Brussels, 30 April 1996) and confidential sources.
74. Confidential interview sources.
75. Interview with Sanjoy Bagchi, International Textile and Clothing Bureau, Geneva, 28 May 1996.
76. Interview, EURATEX, Brussels, 30 April 1996.
77. This is not to imply that the LDCs were any less opposed to the MFA, merely to draw attention to the ways in which this sectoral protectionism had become entrenched in the advanced economies.
78. *Les Echos*, 7 February 1979.
79. *Le Monde*, 13 February 1979.
80. *Le Monde*, 22 September 1979.
81. *Les Echos*, 23 February 1979.
82. Figures from Boussemart, *Industrie de main d'oeuvre*, op. cit., annex 3, after French Customs statistics.

83. *Le Monde*, 10 August 1979.
84. *Le Monde*, 18 August, 1979.
85. *Le Monde*, 24 August 1979.
86. See *Journal Officiel* (édition débats parlementaires), no. 79, 14 November 1980, pp. 3815, 3843.
87. The UIH, in a White Paper, argued contrary to the government position (and, on most accounts, contrary to trade statistics covering the MFA), that the MFA did not stabilise penetration levels but instead guaranteed a market share to signatories, a phenomenon exacerbated by *détournements de trafic* or quota dodging. See Union des Industries de l'Habillement, 'L'Industrie française de l'habillement: une politique de maîtrise des importations', *Livre blanc de l'habillement* (Paris: UIH, mimeo, 1980), pp. 1–2.
88. Ibid., p. 4.
89. The following discussion of the EU position is taken from: Union des Industries Textiles, *Position de l'industrie textile française sur le renouvellement de l'AMF* (Paris: UIT, mimeo, April 1980).
90. In other words, import ceilings on particular products would not just be established for each importing country individually, but each product category taking all exporting countries together. Once the global quota had been surpassed, *all* imports from *all* sources in that particular category were to cease. This measure was similar to, but should not be confused with, the US 'Global Quotas' proposal in the Uruguay Round, referred to in Chapter 5 below.
91. UIH, 'L'Industrie française de l'habillement, op. cit., p. 8.
92. Mme Bourdeleau, Union des Industries de l'Habillement, interviewed 20 February 1985.
93. This ambivalence towards imports would eventually underpin acquiescence in the abolition of the MFA during the Uruguay Round; see Chapter 5.
94. See extract concerning the textile and clothing industry of France, Président de la République (Valéry Giscard d'Estaing), *Discours du président devant la, Chambre Régionale du Commerce et de l'Industrie de Lille*, 10 October 1980.
95. National Assembly Report, vol. III (annexes), p. 221.
96. See France, Ministère de l'Industrie, 'L'Action du gouvernement en faveur des industries du textile et de l'habillement', *Lettre 101*, no. 141, 18 November 1980.
97. *Les Echos*, 19 December 1980 (for comments of the UIT and UIH respectively).
98. *Les Echos*, 20 January 1981.
99. See the National Assembly debate on the Budget for 1981 (Industry) in *Journal Officiel* (édition débats parlementaires), no. 79, 14 November 1980.
100. See Budget Debate for 1981, op. cit., interventions by Xavier Hamelin, p. 3850; Pierre Weisenhorn, p. 3860; Deputy Aurillac, pp. 3960–1.
101. Interview with André Giraud, *L'Est républicain*, 18 March 1981.
102. *Le Monde*, 23 April 1981.

103. Pierre Joxe (Minister of Industry), Press Release, *Agence France Presse*, 11 June 1981.
104. See France, Ministère de l'Industrie (SERPI), *Programme d'actions pour les industries du textile et de l'habillement* (Paris: Ministère de l'Industrie (Dossiers du SERPI), 26 November 1981).
105. *Le Matin*, 11 July 1981.
106. CES Report, p. 242.
107. *Les Echos*, 4 November 1981.
108. For an account of industry demands, see for example, Union de Industries Textiles, *Le Troisième Accord Multifibre: ce qu'en attend l'industrie textile française* (Paris: UIT pamphlet, March 1981), pp. 3–8. On demands for bilateral accords, see UIT, *Propositions de l'Union des Industries Textiles concernant l'application bilatérale du renouvellement du troisième Accord Multifibres* (Paris: UIT, mimeo, 19 January 1982).
109. UIT, *Le Troisième Accord...*, p. 3.
110. Michael B. Dolan, 'European Restructuring and Import Policies for a Textile Industry in Crisis', *International Organization*, 37–4, 1983, p. 605.
111. Dolan, op. cit., p. 606.
112. Ibid., pp. 608–9. See also Jean-Claude Daumas, 'Le Textile français: déclin ou mutation?', *Profils économiques*, no. 17, 1984–5, p. 78.
113. For example, the EU negotiators used 1982 as the base year for calculating the new quotas, doubtless to assuage pressures from their LDC opponents in the negotiations. The industry would have preferred the much lower 1980 levels. See UIT, *Conditions d'application du troisième Accord Multifibres* (Paris: UIT, circular, 11 April 1983), p. 2.
114. Union des Industries de l'Habillement, *Propositions de l'industrie française de l'habillement pour l'AMF IV*, Conclusion de la Commission Economique (Paris: UIH, mimeo, 15 November 1984). This change in policy was not made public at the time.
115. What follows is taken from the interview with Mme Bourdeleau (see note 92).
116. See Dubois and Barisi, parts 3 and 4. Italian entrepreneurs attempted to adapt to market uncertainties, developing the flexibility of their production lines and linking investment more to long-term considerations than short-term profitability. The result was that the Italian industry responded far better to market shifts than the French sector.
117. Anson and Simpson, *World Textile Trade*, op. cit., p. 120. Several interview sources in Brussels corroborated the point that MFA IV had not been a particularly hard negotiation from the point of view of EU negotiators as conjunctural pressures on EU producers were acceptable and exports were developing well on the whole.
118. Anson and Simpson, *World Textile Trade*, op. cit., p. 119.
119. See Cline, *The Future of World Trade*, op. cit., pp. 208–13.
120. Ibid., ch. 3.
121. The following account relies on Anson and Simpson, *World Textile Trade*, op. cit., pp.119–25. The EU and the US also had negotiating objectives which they pursued individually.

122. 'Ministerial Declaration on the Uruguay Round', 20 September 1986, in *Journal of World Trade Law*, vol. 20, 1986, pp. 583–90.
123. Adam Smith, *An Enquiry into the Nature and Causes of the Wealth of Nations*, ed. Edwin Cannan (New York: Modern Library, 1937), p. 250. For an analysis of the impact of the MFA on profitability, employment, and price in developed country markets, see Fabrizio Guelpa and Marco Ratti, 'Price–Cost Margins in Italian Textiles and Clothing: Structural Determinants and the Impact of Protection', in Navaretti *et al.*, *Beyond the Multifibre Arrangement*, op. cit., pp. 89–101; their findings suggest a particularly large welfare gain for consumers, due to price decreases, should the MFA be successfully dismantled – see p. 95.

5 Dismantling Protectionism: The Political Economy of Liberalisation in the Uruguay Round

By the end of the Uruguay Round, some form or other of exceptional, protectionist trade regime for textile and clothing products had been in place for nearly forty years. This had started with unilateral American restrictions against Japan in the mid 1950s, but had grown into a fully legitimated GATT-based accord restricting imports of textile and clothing products from the world's (often poorest) developing countries to the most advanced industrialised economies. This arrangement was forged from the common interests of producer firms and their associations, integrated into the trade policy processes across a range of influential and wealthy GATT member states. State and market actors together forged the structure of the market for these products in the industrialised countries. These state and market actors, integrated into the global trade policy process, and were largely united in their pursuit of an increasingly restrictive MFA, despite their declaratory posture on the 'temporary' nature of the accord. *By 1986, at the launch of the Uruguay Round, this transnational capture of the global textile and clothing trade regime appeared as entrenched as ever.* Entrenched interests with substantial and institutionalised political resources are difficult to dislodge.

These circumstances provided an inauspicious starting point for the eventual abolition of the MFA, a declared objective of the Uruguay Round. In the past, governments had pursued liberal adjustment objectives with the best of intentions, only to be defeated on their own ground by entrenched particularistic interests (see Chapters 3 and 4). As state policy-makers looked inside the complex machinery of state, they found the distributional conflicts of the market being played out to a rather different agenda, and this capture extended across institutional layers of global governance. Firms were thus actors on two

197

fronts: first, as agents in competition with each other in increasingly global markets. Second, firms, organised through their representative associations, became integrated into the apparatus of state with a view to structuring, to the extent they could, the very terms of competition itself. The transnationalisation of economic space and the intensity of competition in the sector became in themselves a source of protectionist pressures in the political forum of the state. The strategic response in the advanced countries was to pass on the costs of industrial adjustment to the economies of some the most vulnerable states in the global system. The institutionalised socio-political resources of textile and clothing coalitions within the advanced economies proved overwhelming in deciding the outcome of this often desperate distributional conflict, a sectoral conflict taking place on a background of generalised economic crisis.

Yet ultimately the Uruguay Round negotiators succeeded at initiating a historic change in the sectoral trade regime. This chapter aims to explain this paradox of prison inmates, who long ago paid off the prison governor, apparently consigning themselves to the global gladatorial combat of economic competition, which might well constitute imposing a capital sentence upon themselves. The explanatory difficulty is compounded by the fact that there was a virtual absence of voices from within textile coalitions which openly endorsed or called for liberalisation in the Uruguay Round. The sector gave every appearance of tenaciously resisting the dismantlement of the MFA; based on past history, they appeared bound to win.

But the explanation for the eventual agreement to liberalise is once again to be found in the ongoing process of structural economic change in the sector, driven by the strategies of firms-as-agents in competition, and the changing patterns of self-interest which structural change implied. Throughout the MFA period, the main thrust of competitive pressures had been among the OECD economies themselves, and this persistent competitive challenge eventually undermined the domestic strategies of many firms and propelled them towards transnationalisation and adjustment. Despite the MFA, new producers with lower wage costs were still present, and they too altered their strategies to circumvent the quota system. The development of transnational production strategies by high-wage (particularly clothing) manufacturers centred on foreign sourcing activities implied a reassessment of protectionism, which for some even became an obstacle to the reimports which outward processing required. Over time liberalisation became acceptable if not desirable, and the Uruguay Round compromise encapsulates this situation. The accord provides for a ten-year transition period before the final unravelling of the MFA, a period in which the advanced economies maintain an important degree of control over the terms of competition with the LDCs and NICs. Of course it remains to be seen whether the accord will in fact be adhered to at all, but as will be seen 'liberalisation' is perhaps too straightforward a term to describe what actually happened. This chapter will therefore advance the following arguments by way of explaining the liberalisation of textile and clothing trade agreed in the Round.

A combination of factors rendered liberalisation at least an acceptable eventuality. In the first place, the transnationalisation of the industry had been ongoing throughout the period of the MFA, and indeed accelerated in the 1980s. Competitive pressures in OECD markets had not abated because the MFA (and similar quota agreements), as we have seen, was only designed to deal with exports from the low-wage countries, which affected only limited segments of the industry. So OECD producers continued to feel the squeeze of the intensified competition which resulted from the ongoing trade liberalisation among high-wage producers on the one hand, as well as by low-wage producers in the developing world in limited segments of the industry on the other. The pressures of the severe recessions of the early and late 1980s, along with the secular decline in textile and clothing consumption as a proportion of household expenditure (Engel's law) meant that producers would notionally have been forced to adjust their strategies even before low-wage imports were counted.

The ongoing response to this combination of competitive pressures was twofold: the increasing capital and technology intensive nature of yarn and fabric production in the textile industry, and the dislocation of clothing production through foreign sourcing strategies. This latter change was of particular importance: the firms themselves became responsible for an increasing share of low-wage (re)imports from either LDCs, the Eastern European countries, or the Mediterranean producers. Although some countries, particularly Germany and Holland, had undertaken a strategy of dislocation as far back as the 1960s, we have seen that the US, Great Britain, Italy, and France among others were rather more hesitant in this regard.

There was therefore a considerable acceleration of dislocation of production in both Europe and the United States throughout the later 1980s. This was most pronounced in the clothing industry, but vertically integrated textile firms participated as well. The rising tide of imports in the 1980s and 1990s was thus due, to a considerable extent, to the very strategies of firms in the advanced economies themselves. As the changing strategies of firms induced a change in the market structure in clothing production, accelerating the transnationalisation of economic structures, it is not surprising that the policy preferences in favour of protectionism became less pronounced.

The most important feature of outward processing traffic is that *the firms themselves control the terms of trade;*[1] increased imports increase profitability and do not compete with the domestic production of the individual firms involved (but may of course affect domestic competitors who do not resort to such a strategy). In the United States, for example, one finds the paradox at the end of the Round of the clothing manufacturers' organisations scarcely opposed to dismantling the MFA, in contrast to the more virulent opposition of their textile industry brethren.[2] Other countries found themselves permitting major overshooting of import quotas in order to satisfy domestic producers importing or reimporting inputs and/or finished products from low-wage producers.[3] In short, *transnationalisation had become an essential element of firms' strategies in confronting the increase in global competition, and increased imports, albeit controlled by the American and EU producers themselves, was the corollary of this trend.*

Trade policies in high-wage countries eventually adapted in response to industry pressure so as to facilitate this trend. New legal instruments were created, and quotas were often overlooked, thus violating the MFA to the apparent detriment of the selfsame importing countries. Examples of such measures included excluding certain categories of reimports from the quota system and informally and flexibly maintained quotas monitored in relation to the needs of transnational firms and managed in tandem with producer associations. Special trade policy instruments were also introduced or expanded, allowing products which were initially exported for further manufacture or finishing to be reimported, but customs tariffs would only be paid on the value-added performed overseas, not on the overall value of the product.[4] The dramatic increase in OPT traffic in Europe and the US was therefore a *de facto* liberalisation controlled by the firms themselves. Firms became increasingly hypocritical in their opposition to liberalisation, and state policy began to reflect this.

Second, the MFA was perceived by firms, employers' organisations, and state officials alike to be an increasingly inappropriate instrument of trade policy, and to have been of limited success as an instrument of protectionism. While it had often proved successful in limiting or indeed reducing imports of some product categories from specific target groups of countries, the other side of the coin was that it stimulated LDC exports of those products it did not cover. Importing countries attempted to get around this problem by constantly increasing the scope of the accord, but in the longer run this simply gave LDC producers an incentive to change their export mix and to challenge OECD producers in new ways, thereby developing the sophistication and specialisation of LDC producers. Even following the substantial tightening of the accord in 1978 there was a relatively limited effect on *total* imports of textile and clothing products to the advanced economies.[5] The quota system even had the perverse effect of fostering new producer countries of textile and clothing products: as the countries targeted most aggressively by the quotas used up their allowances, countries like Bangladesh, Jamaica, or Sri Lanka were able to use their quota entitlement to foster a domestic industry which would not have survived but for the MFA system itself (often as a result of the FDI activities of firms in quota-bound NICs). These countries now face an uncertain future under liberalisation of the MFA and direct competition with highly competitive giants such as China.

Indeed, even though European and American trade ministries became adept at manipulating the MFA system, developed sophisticated import monitoring capacities to spot runaway import surges, and tightened up the administration of the system over the years, it remained a cumbersome instrument of policy. It was 'voluntary' and required the goodwill of importing and exporting countries alike if it was to be effective; this often meant that it served to close the stable door after the horses had bolted. Exporting countries which found themselves unable to fulfil their quotas developed a robust secondary market in quotas, selling them to countries or firms which had already used up their own. Within the EU, some countries applied the quota system strictly, others (under pressure from their firms which relied on imported inputs) were less rigorous.[6] The ability of states to maintain imports within quota allocations was anyway of limited utility if this was to result in increased imports in non-quota products.

In effect, the MFA, as a state-based instrument of trade policy, was less and less suitable for a global economy characterised by transnational integration of production and trade.[7] Quotas were controlled by the exporting countries and were usually allocated by them to their domestic firms on the basis of past performance. Cheaper, more innovative export producers were therefore excluded from the export markets, and producers in Europe and the USA were denied access to often superior inputs and finished products as a result. At the very least the system needed rationalisation.[8]

Third, the dynamics of the Uruguay Round negotiations themselves were an important, if idiosyncratic, factor in encouraging the eventual outcome of phased liberalisation. The inclusion of the MFA in the Round was a major accomplishment for the developing countries[9] and was important for encouraging them to accept that the talks would cover controversial 'new' issues such as trade in services or intellectual property. It was patently hypocritical for developed countries to maintain an ever-tighter protectionist noose on textile and clothing trade, while singing the praises of liberalisation, even unilateral liberalisation, to the LDCs. This implicit tradeoff was far from sufficient to secure a liberalisation accord,[10] but the status quo would be difficult to maintain. The logic of the negotiations implied some important gesture for the concessions demanded of the LDCs, and the textile and clothing sector was a prime candidate.

The multilateral Round of negotiations of course brought into the open those interests within the high-wage countries which actively lobbied for liberalisation.[11] Negotiators in both the US and the EU were careful to work closely with the textile and clothing industry lobbies so as to legitimate, in their eyes, the eventual decisions taken. One might add that the EU's complex internal negotiating machinery had the effect of dissipating somewhat the pressures from the more protectionist national associations; the fragmentation of interests is more apparent at the EU level than at the level of the nation state.[12] The Commission authorities were able to play relatively liberal associations, such as German and Dutch textile interests which were demanding an ever-increasing share of limited MFA import quotas to cope with the needs and strategies of their firms, against the more traditionally protectionist interests of the Mediterranean countries of the EU.[13] Protectionist textile and clothing coalitions also had to compete with other sectoral employers' associations which saw international trade as an advantage, not a constraint. Furthermore, in view of the relative inefficiency of the MFA as an instrument of trade policy, high-wage producer interests began to look to other ways of coping with imports. These could include the use of anti-dumping clauses, strengthened safeguard procedures (which were included in the Uruguay Round talks), and a more efficient protection of intellectual property measures (TRIPS, or intellectual property issues, were also under discussion in the Round). Perhaps most importantly, access to LDC and NIC markets became important: the eventual success of in particular the EU negotiators at improving access for their domestic producers to hitherto closed markets such as India and other parts of Asia by negotiating lower tariffs on a wide range of the industry's products was integral to legitimating the liberalisation process.[14]

One official recited an anecdote which puts this in perspective: with access to the formerly impenetrable Indian market guaranteed, the UK clothing retailer Marks & Spencer opened a branch in Bombay. The entire stock, consisting largely of UK products, was sold out in the first day of operation and an airfreight operation had to be put in place to cope with demand.[15] The more that domestic companies availed themselves of international market opportunities (particularly but not exclusively OPT[16]), the more the liberalisation of the MFA appeared at least tolerable in the long run. In this complex setting of the overall Round negotiations, a combination of implicit tradeoffs and the dissipation of high-wage producer preferences for protection across a number of fronts was sufficient to result in a phased liberalisation agreement when combined with the shifting structural underpinnings of transnationalisation.

The remainder of this chapter will be structured as follows. It will begin with an analysis of the changing structure of the global market for textile and clothing products, emphasising the enhanced trend towards transnationalisation in both the EU and the United States from the mid 1980s onwards. In this sense, the chapter picks up where Chapters 1 and 2 left off in the mid 1980s. The chapter will then go on to examine the early stages of the Uruguay round negotiations, beginning with the 1986 GATT ministerial declaration launching the Round. From there the chapter will look at the process of building a consensus to abandon the MFA accord respectively in the European Union and the United States. This section will be careful to relate changing structure to shifts in the perceived interests of the textile and clothing constituencies in these key players in the multilateral Round. A final section will draw together these different strands of the analysis to analyse the emergence of the final agreement and the policy-making process which led to it. The aim throughout will be to relate the changing structure of the market to the eventual negotiating outcome. After some forty years of protectionism, the MFA was to be dismantled over ten years, ostensibly leading to a complete liberalisation of trade in the sector. However, the process is as yet far from complete and the pressure of the restructuring process may yet derail attempts to implement the decision.

FIRM STRATEGIES AND CHANGING ECONOMIC STRUC-
TURE: THE ACCELERATING GLOBALISATION OF TEXTILE
AND CLOTHING PRODUCTION IN THE 1980s AND EARLY
1990s

The analysis in earlier chapters clearly established the protectionist credentials of the French and other textile and clothing industry
associations. The French industry and government were leading
organisers of the EU's pursuit of a more vigorous MFA from the
mid 1970s onwards. However, as was mentioned at the end of Chapter 4, even the French clothing industry association, the Union des
Industries de l'Habillement (UIH), was waivering in its long-term commitment to protectionism in 1984.[17] It was recognised that the industry
was changing, along with the negotiating climate in the multilateral
trade regime.[18] This scepticism about protectionism was slow to assert
itself in official pronouncements by professional associations or government when it came to talks on the MFA, but the underlying trends
in global textile and clothing trade and production which sparked this
hesitant reassessment began to accelerate in the mid to late 1980s.

It would be relevant to examine these trends in greater detail. Since
the crisis of the early 1980s, the downstream end of the production
stream has undergone an accelerated restructuring and transnationalisation as firms increasingly turned to foreign sourcing strategies for
the most labour-intensive operations in the complex production process. This has in turn contributed to a dramatic change in the patterns
of trade between the LDCs, as well as other low-wage producer
countries, and the industrialised economies. The strategies of firms
were once again revealed as a crucial agency behind structural changes
in the market. As the strategies of firms changed, the policy preferences and hence the market structuring activities of the textile coalitions, state and market together, were redirected.

The most important single observation which enables one to
understand this acceleration of foreign sourcing, particularly OPT
operations, is that despite all the technological progress in many textile
and clothing production processes, 90 per cent of the total labour costs
in the manufacture of finished clothing are contained in one operation:
sewing. The design and cutting stages of clothing manufacture only
account for 5 per cent of the labour costs involved. It has not been
possible to circumvent the one machine, one worker equation when it
comes to sewing operations.[19] Technological advances in sewing have
helped relatively little, even though faster machines have come on the

market. The problem is that 80 per cent of workers in a clothing factory spend up to 90 per cent of their time positioning and handling the cloth as opposed to actually sewing or performing other manufacturing tasks.[20] The high labour costs in the industrialised economies thus remained a barrier to competitive production of finished articles of clothing,[21] particularly those standardised items with little fashion appeal and relatively low unit value. Firms which could successfully develop networks of subcontractors, either through ownership or contractual links, could remain in clothing production, completing all but final assembly in domestic plants, yet export and reimport the finished product.

The intensification of competition on global markets redoubled this imperative. Unfortunately, statistical analysis of the growth of imports linked to foreign sourcing activity is difficult. National and related international trade statistics are organised by individual product category across the all producers in the sector, not by firm. Thus it is not easy to determine with precision which proportion of imports might be due to domestic firms' reimportation activity linked to OPT. Nonetheless the growing importance of OPT traffic and associated reimports has been recognised by researchers and some convincing analyses are available. Despite considerable variations in the statistical analyses, what is unequivocally established is that there has been a dramatic growth in the phenomenon.

(a) Evolution of the Sector in the 1980s

(i) The European Union

The EU became a key player in the textile trade regime from the early 1970s. The EU industry has evolved in a heterogeneous fashion with some stark contrasts in industry structure and performance among producer countries. Some, like the German and Dutch industries, became transnationalised from the 1960s. Others remained domestically based industries with varying degrees of success on export markets, but structural change has slowly penetrated even the most domestically oriented of sectors. The 1970s and early 1980s (Chapters 1 and 2) were not kind to the European clothing industry on the whole. From the mid 1980s and into the early 1990s fortunes were mixed but on the whole better. The decade, one should be reminded, began with a severe recession across most manufacturing sectors, with textile and clothing output hit particularly hard. The trough was roughly in 1983, leading to a recovery in most countries, depending on the product category concerned and with considerable differences observable in textiles versus clothing.[22] This recovery was underpinned by rising demand in most countries, a rising US dollar up to the middle of the decade, and the implementation of the tougher MFA negotiated in 1981 (MFA III). Variations in this pattern should, however, be noted because they may be expected to prove politically significant. The French textile industry suffered an ongoing if modest decline in production even after 1983. As the French industry and government were traditionally hard liners in MFA negotiations this might be expected to have had an impact on the negotiations. This picture was at least somewhat mitigated by more stable production levels in the French clothing industry. In other key countries, including for once the UK, the picture was rather more positive. Despite the severity of the recession for all concerned, the UK, Italy, Germany, Spain, and the Netherlands, all experienced a considerable recovery in textile production. Their clothing industries fared less well, with production on the whole stagnant, but the exception here was in the UK where, from 1980 levels of 100, production dropped to only 98.3 at the end of the recession (1983), rose to 111.3 by 1987. Nonetheless, the biggest winner of the decade were undoubtedly Portugal, newly admitted to the EU in 1986, for which the textile and clothing sector were particularly significant as well. Portugal's 1986 clothing production level had risen by 32 per cent on 1980 levels despite the recession, and in textile production the rise was 20 per cent.

Thus by the middle to end of the decade the climate in the textile and clothing sector, except perhaps in France, was relatively buoyant as far as production levels were concerned. The goods news was not on all fronts however. Throughout the EU, job losses continued in both the textile and the clothing industry with the exception of Greece and Portugal (textiles and clothing) and Denmark (in textiles). Productivity gains and ongoing restructuring continued to account for the major proportion of these losses.

Import competition was nonetheless intense throughout the period and imports were generally on the rise. This helped to keep prices down no doubt, but placed pressure on EU producers and jobs. However, the situation contrasted sharply when the textile and clothing sectors are compared.[23] In the textile industry the picture was considerably more positive than in the clothing sector, a situation which should not have been unexpected. The EU has long enjoyed a considerable trade surplus in textiles. From 1979 into the early 1980s there was a marked deterioration in the balance, but by 1984 the surplus had returned to its 1974 peak, and set a new record in 1985. This situation was helped considerably by exports to the US as the dollar hit its peak in 1985. The surplus was somewhat reduced from 1987 onwards, and the more so if one makes allowances for the distorting effects of Spanish and Portuguese membership on the figures. The sector continued however to post a trade surplus, in keeping with the increasingly capital-intensive and specialised nature of textile production. The leading export market was the United States by a long way, along with other industrialised economies. A number of developing countries and central/east European increasingly featured as export destinations however, specifically because of the growth of outward processing trade: most of these exports eventually returned as clothing imports. China has grown markedly as a market for EU fibre exports, reflecting Chinese entry on the global textile and clothing trade front in the 1980s. Once again, these exports would return in increasing quantities in the form of imports of finished clothing articles. In terms of imports, high-wage Switzerland, followed by Austria, were paradoxically the largest and second largest sources of EU imports respectively (Austria in fact joined the EU in the early 1990s). Third on the list was Japan; this once again reflects the highly capital-intensive characteristics of contemporary textile production. The US began to regain lost ground once the dollar began to fall in 1985–6.

The trade picture in the *clothing* sector was dramatically different for the EU. The clothing sector deficit had peaked in 1981 and stabilised. Despite some deterioration in 1983, the rise in the American dollar led to a surge in exports to the US market, stabilising an admittedly negative trade balance in the sector. The figures then become confusing, owing to the entry of Spain and Portugal into the EU in 1986. Both were major clothing producers, especially Portugal, and the deficit appears to improve markedly when their industries are taken into account. However, the deficit of the EU10 (in other words excluding the new entrants) in fact almost doubled in 1986. Spain and Portugal's entry into the single market also placed additional competitive pressures on a number of other EU members. Hong Kong and South Korea remained respectively the largest sources of imports, followed by Turkey, what was then Yugoslavia, and China. Competition from MFA and other low-wage producers was much more important in clothing as opposed to textile production.

If this is the overall EU pattern in the 1980s, there were important differences across the member countries. France[24] showed relative strength in clothing as opposed to textile trade. With the exception of Italy, France maintained a surplus in 1987 clothing trade with all her European partners, and overall export growth considerably exceeded imports in the mid to late 1980s. An overall surplus in 1984–5 nonetheless slipped into deficit in 1986 and 1987, probably a result of dollar devaluation, which affected the import prices of most non-EU producers in French markets, but clothing trade remained roughly in balance. In textiles, in contrast, the deficit grew in an ongoing fashion. Stagnant interior demand meant that overall the textile and clothing sector experienced little growth in the mid to late 1980s despite a general economic recovery across the EU. Nonetheless, the situation was far from the desperate days of the early 1980s recession, and a number of firms did particularly well as they adjusted to globalisation.

Germany's industry conformed more to typical expectations for industrialised countries.[25] The German textile industry had a healthy trade surplus in 1986 and 1987, with production rising comfortably. In clothing, the Germany remained a major exporter but was at the same time the world's second largest importer, after the USA. The large deficit in clothing trade meant that textiles and clothing trade had a combined and considerable overall trade deficit. The picture was a complicated one, with a high degree of outward processing and other forms of transnational production (see below). In the later 1980s the fall of the dollar reduced the (dollar-denominated) price of imports from many producers in Asia. In a development which eventually was to become the norm for industrialised countries, the turnover of many firms saw healthy advances in the late 1980s, but *domestic production* did not necessarily increase.

The UK's textile industry demonstrated yet further variation on the general EU pattern, more on the French model.[26] The market for textile and clothing products recovered considerably from the depths of the early 1980s recession, but much of the demand was met by an increase in import penetration. In this situation, the domestic industry experienced modest growth, but growth of any kind was welcome relative to the contraction of the 1970s and early 1980s. Consistent underinvestment in capital-intensive upstream activities has meant that the textile industry benefited relatively little from the recovery in demand. If 1980 is taken as the base year with a production index of 100, then from a recession low of 89.5 in 1982 the index reached 102.7 in 1987. Import penetration and the trade deficit was severe and increased despite improved export performance as the decade moved on. The clothing industry performed on the whole better. Taking the

1980 production index level of 100, the recession low in 1981 was 92.4, and production rose to an index of 110.6 in 1987. Import penetration was already less severe in clothing products, and the trade deficit increased only moderately. Imports and exports grew more or less at the same rate, rising 16.4 per cent each in value terms from 1986 to 1987 alone. The exporters' success in both textile and clothing came particularly on Western European markets, and imports came largely from the USA and low-wage countries, the latter despite the continued reliance on MFA quotas.

Italy will serve as the fourth example of an EU member state.[27] The Italian textile and clothing industry confirmed itself as Europe's largest, and the only industry with an ongoing overall (and indeed substantial) trade surplus. Nonetheless, there was evidence following the middle of the decade that this situation was slowly changing. Growth rates in production were declining, and competition on EU markets intensified. Rising wage costs were eventually to put pressure on the clothing industry's miraculous performance, leading some firms to transnationalise their operations through foreign sourcing. Despite these signs of change it was difficult to argue that the Italian industry approached the end of the decade in anything but a healthy condition.

To summarise the situation in the EU towards the late 1980s, economic conditions for the textile and clothing industry were more positive overall than they had been for more than a decade. The industry continued to undergo rapid restructuring and a commensurate decline in employment levels, but this was attenuated by continued growth in demand and an improvement in export sales. The high-wage countries of the EU on the whole enjoyed ongoing success in capital-intensive textile productions, and some (Italy and the UK) even saw considerable prospects in their labour-intensive clothing industries. Nonetheless, import pressure on clothing production continued, and firms began increasingly to respond through outward processing strategies. After looking at the situation in the United States, the analysis will return to this question of the accelerating transnationalisation of the clothing industry and its impact on the policy preferences of the parties to the Uruguay Round negotiation.

(ii) The United States
The situation in the American textile and clothing industry was somewhat different in comparison to the EU. Despite important improvements in productivity, particularly in the textile industry, US

trade and competitiveness in the industry was considerably distorted by the dramatic rise of the dollar to a high in 1985, and similarly the situation altered rapidly with the return of the dollar exchange rate to lower levels in relation to the primary competitors of the US.[28] If one allows for this exchange rate related distortion, however, then the trend is not all that different.[29] Production levels recovered well from the 1982 trough of the recession: if 1977 is taken as the production index level of 100, there was a considerable fall to 98.1 and then 89.2 in 1981 and 1982 respectively (textiles). Improvement began in 1983 (100.9) and again in 1984 (to 104.2) but 1985 saw yet another drop in production to an index level of 103.2. Once the dollar came down in 1986, recovery was rapid, and by 1988 the production index was at 122.9. The situation in the clothing industry was similar. Once again taking 1977 as the base year production level index of 100, 1982 was the low point at 87.3, 1984 formed a temporary peak at 102.7 with the production index dropping close to the 1977 level at 100.9 in 1985, with a rapid rise to 114.6 in 1988.

Despite this apparent success and regardless of currency fluctuations, demand rose more rapidly than domestic production and the domestic industry lost market share. The trade deficit in the clothing industry grew dramatically throughout the 1980s. Import penetration by EU products was marked in the period of the high dollar, but slowed somewhat following the downward drift of the US currency. Imports from LDCs, many of which pegged their currencies to the dollar and therefore were relatively unaffected by currency fluctuations, rose rapidly and steadily. Between 1983 and 1987 the deficit in clothing trade literally doubled. Performance in the textile industry was similar (although the trade balance had been in surplus in 1981 and therefore started from a stronger competitive position), with the emerging trade deficit more than doubling between 1983 and 1987, increasing from $1.09 billion to $4 billion in these four years.

The American industry was therefore the target of particularly harsh import competition until the middle of the decade, unable to take proper advantage of the considerable improvement in final demand as the recession eased because of the rise in the exchange rate. Even with the fall of the dollar, and the return of fairly promising growth rates in terms of domestic demand, import competition remained tight and the trade deficit increased. This situation was not lost on American producers and the textile coalition, as will become clear in the discussion of the 1986 MFA renewal and the early phase of the Uruguay round negotiations.

(b) The Acceleration of Foreign Sourcing in the Late 1980s

The mid to late 1980s were an important turning point in terms of the structure of the global textile and clothing sector. The economic fortunes and competitiveness of the EU and US industries up to approximately 1988 have been surveyed above. This basic picture however fails to reveal the most important developments. The analysis reveals that the industry recovered somewhat from the recession but remained under considerable pressure of import competition from a variety of sources. An important part of this competition is easily accounted for: it results from the ongoing liberalisation of industrial tariffs and terms of market access among the principal industrialised countries in the global textile and clothing sector. Yet this pressure from high-wage trading partners had been present for some time and there is no particular reason, beyond cyclical economic fluctuations, for this to be seen as an explanation for the continued dramatic rise in imports on industrialised country markets. Yet in every case, imports from low-wage countries also increased despite the ever tighter restrictions implied by the renewal and strengthening of the MFA. What lay behind this surge in imports, most marked in the clothing sector, throughout the 1980s and, as will be seen, continuing into the 1990s?

To answer this question one must move beyond traditional trade statistics measured on a national accounts basis. Territorial units, e.g. states, were becoming an increasingly less relevant basis on which to measure patterns of trade in the industry. The evidence strongly suggests that a significant proportion of the rise in imports was the result of the accelerated dislocation of downstream clothing assembly activities in the sector to low-wage countries: 'In fact, trade in clothing and textiles appears to be much more masterminded by agents in the importing countries,'[30] whether retailers or manufacturers, with an increasing share going to manufacturers themselves. Thus when trade patterns are measured as a function of firms, as opposed to states, the continuous rise in imports make much more sense. Firms managed to maintain or increase their market position, or at the very least survive, through strategies involving the dislocation of production. The dislocation involved initial exports of intermediary goods (which partially explains the improvements in export performance), often finished cloth for clothing manufacture but, increasingly, cut fabrics requiring assembly only. These would then be reimported, sometimes for minor finishing operations but also simply for distribution on local markets or even re-export to third countries.

Most countries developed special legal instruments to aid and abet this process of transnationalisation; state and market evolved together. The United States developed the so-called 'Section 807' provisions in its trade law, wherein import duty would be charged only on the value-added produced overseas, and not on the total value of the product being imported. In this way the firms could benefit in terms of costs from the competitiveness of textile products while avoiding the liability represented by high wage levels in the clothing assembly portion of the manufacturing process. Under current EU regulations, two regimes apply, the first (Fiscal Outward Processing Traffic) being similar to the US system for paying duty only on the portion value added in overseas production of the reimported product. Some products, with prior authorisation and in limited quantities, are duty exempt on reimportation if they consist of fabric produced in the EU. The second involves only countries which have signed preferential (0 per cent duty) trade agreements with the EU, such as Turkey, North Africa and the Central Eastern European Countries (PECOs in EU-speak). In this case reimportation is at 0 per cent duty if the fabric was originally produced in an EU member country.[31]

Under such circumstances, imports into high-wage countries increased while production levels in the clothing industry appeared either to fall or at least failed to keep pace with rising demand. This increase in imports was theoretically constrained by the various quota systems (MFA and otherwise) which had been put in place over the decades (though modified by the existence of a number of preferential trading agreements between the high-wage countries and often adjacent low-wage producers), but the *turnover* of the firms in question might increase significantly through this strategy.[32] While the local industry appeared in decline when measured in terms of production levels, the increasingly transnationalised firms might even be prospering by actively fostering import penetration in important segments of the industry. As long as the element of domestically produced inputs remained high, the upstream (globally competitive) portions of the capital-intensive textile industry were not threatened. Transnationalisation might affect the national trade balance and the level of domestic industrial activity and employment, but it might prove the salvation of domestic firms caught in the intensifying competition on global markets.

Thus the policy preferences of firms will depend on the extent of dislocation, the extent of transnationalisation, of the firms' activities; those firms which have transnationalised effectively control the patterns of imports, and the competitive advantages, which their production strategies imply. Those which remained entirely dependent on local production might face an uncertain future as import competition intensifies, a goodly part of it generated by the reimports of domestic competitors. Those which successfully transnationalise their production facilities might find their competitive positions greatly enhanced. Thus a fragmentation in the interests of the member firms of the professional associations might eventually call into question their certainty as lobbies for protection in a number of countries. Structural change in the sector was the outcome of underlying distributional struggle among firms as agents in competition on global markets, and this was eventually reflected in the trade policy process of the Uruguay Round.

The difficulty is to capture with precision the extent of international sourcing in the countries in question, and the precise effect of this transnationalisation of production strategies on the growth of imports in respective national economies. An OECD study was able to provide data on the proportion of international sourcing of inputs relative to domestic sourcing for textile, clothing and footwear products. The trend was clearly upwards in the major OECD producers, but a breakdown of the individual textile and clothing sectors was not available.[33] Fortunately a number of research institutes specialising in textile and clothing sectors have turned their attention to precisely this question and have attempted to produce at least initial statistical estimations of the extent of dislocation in the industry, and of the proportion of imports which is linked to this process of transnationalisation of production.[34]

(i) The European Union
While countries like Germany and the Netherlands have long resorted to strategies involving overseas subcontracting, for other major producers such as France, the UK, and especially Italy, the dislocation of production is a relatively recent phenomenon. First, however, a few definitional points. 'Outward processing' is often used as a generic term to describe any form of subcontracting followed by reimportation by a country's firms to foreign producers. 'Foreign sourcing' is the more accurate generic term which has been in use in this book. 'Outward processing' (OPT) has a more technical definition, meaning foreign sourcing and reimportation taking place under specific trade policy instruments, in this case under the terms of the EU's Regulation 636/82, the 'value added' import clause which applies only where EU

fabrics are concerned. Imports which result from OPT used in this technical sense are measurable, but do not constitute the total amount of imports linked directly to EU textile and clothing manufacturers. To understand the full significance of imports which result from EU manufacturers, one must look at *all* imports which result from foreign sourcing: overseas plants of EU manufacturers, overseas subcontracting, and other foreign sourcing (for example imports of intermediary goods or finished products to the specifications of the EU firm). The only way to measure all these aspects of foreign sourcing is to look at individual firms and aggregate the data. All these forms of trade, which imply a transnationalisation of production processes and market transactions (economic structure), are controlled by the firm in the industrialised, high-wage country.

The major study on the matter used interviews of 210 firms across the EU for data up to 1988, and a smaller sample of 165 (some went out of business) for data up to 1992.[35] Drawing on this report and an eclectic mix of other sources, a picture emerges in which EU manufacturing firms are playing a major and growing role in the rising import levels and deteriorating trade balance in the clothing industry.

Beginning with Europe overall, it is clear that the proportion of output accounted for by domestic production of manufacturing firms has declined at an accelerating pace; it dropped from 72 per cent in 1983, to 70 per cent in 1988 to only 60 per cent of total output in 1992.[36] To some extent there was a rise in subcontracting to *domestic* firms, a practice which passes the risk on to smaller (often vulnerable) local producers, or home workers. This practice is more widespread in some countries (Italy in particular) than others, and helps to increase the flexibility of the firms in responding to rapid market fluctuations while avoiding the disadvantages of resupply from foreign producers over considerable geographic distance and the delays in delivery time which this implies. Domestic subcontracting constituted 23 per cent of output in 1983, 25 per cent in 1988, and 29 per cent in 1992 across the EU.

The share of output attributable to domestic subcontracting was considerably less, however, than the share constituted by various forms of foreign production – OPT, foreign production by EU subsidiaries, and other foreign sourcing. This proportion rose from 23 per cent of output in 1983, to 30 per cent in 1988, to a remarkable 40 per cent in 1992. OPT (in the technical sense of the term) appeared to account for between 60 per cent and 70 per cent of this total, some 30 per cent of which took place in North Africa, and 65 per cent in the

PECO countries.[37] The proportion may be somewhat lower if more of the smallest firms were to be included in the sample, but interview sources in Brussels, Geneva, and in national governments essentially confirm this aggregate EU picture, depending on the country concerned of course.[38]

It is not easy to translate this figure so as to determine what proportion of *total* imports are initiated by EU producer firms, but one interview subject estimated the share at one third.[39] A second study determined that 29 per cent of total 1990 EU imports were channelled via EU manufacturers or designers,[40] and again the trend has been accelerating upwards. If these figures are more or less on target, it means that some 30 per cent of the imports into the EU are actually fostered by European manufacturers themselves, and the share is rising! Wholesalers, importers, or the sales networks of non-EU firms only control 20 per cent of total imports, and the share of imports controlled directly by producers in developing exporting countries is 'marginal' at best. By 1994, the top ten suppliers of MFA clothing products to the EU were headed by China, with a 10.6 per cent share of the total in value terms, but second in line was Turkey with 10 per cent, followed by Hong Kong (8.9 per cent), then Tunisia (5.8 per cent), Morocco (5.7 per cent), and Poland (5.3 per cent).[41] In other words, of the top six suppliers, four were prime OPT destinations used by EU manufacturers. The further irony is that a proportion of these 'imports' eventually form part of the improved export performance of the firms involved. In the end, EU firms (including large retailers) have styled and branded, or otherwise managed, the importation of most clothing products and the actual value added which accrues to the developing country exporters is relatively low.[42] In this light, the argument over the international trade regime ought really to involve the different factions of the EU textile and clothing industry, as opposed to the developing countries versus the high-wage producers, and as will be seen to a considerable extent it does.

Germany and the Netherlands have traditionally had high proportions of OPT and other foreign-sourced imports in their domestic industries, and the process of dislocation began in the late 1960s. Severe restructuring occurred in the early 1970s,[43] and from that point the clothing industries of these countries were highly dependent on transnational production processes and associated trade patterns. Germany already accounted for nearly half of the EU's clothing imports in the late 1980s,[44] a situation which has changed little, and German clothing imports are sourced in the main from Turkey and the PECO countries.

The proportion of total turnover of German clothing firms attributable to foreign subcontracting or production in 1992 was well over half, at 56 per cent, and this had risen from a level of 37 per cent in 1983 (Table 5.1). German firms were responsible for some 60 per cent of the EU's OPT in the mid 1990s and German firms were actively seeking avenues to increase access to foreign sourcing.[45] In the Netherlands this proportion rose from 61 per cent in 1983, to 66 per cent in 1988, and to a staggering 73 per cent in 1992. This data confirms Germany and the Netherlands as the most transnationalised of the

Table 5.1   Selected EU countries: shares of companies' turnover derived from own production and subcontracting, extra-EU and intra-EU, 1983–92 (% of turnover')

	1983	1988	1992
Germany			
Subcontracting extra-EU	29	39	44
Production extra-EU	8	10	12
Subcontracting EC	3	5	12
Production EC	59	46	32
Total	100	100	100
Netherlands			
Subcontracting extra-EC	40	45	57
Production extra-EC	21	21	16
Subcontracting EC	6	9	8
Production EC	33	25	19
Total	100	100	100
Belgium			
Subcontracting extra-EC	22	21	27
Production extra-EC	5	11	23
Subcontracting EC	20	24	21
Production EC	53	44	29
Total	100	100	100
France			
Subcontracting extra-EC	13	35	31
Production extra-EC	1	7	23
Subcontracting EC	12	10	13
Production EC	74	48	33
Total	100	100	100

Table 5.1   (*contd.*)

	1983	1988	1992
Italy			
Subcontracting extra-EU	2	5	13
Production extra-EC	–	1	8
Subcontracting EC	57	50	50
Production EC	41	44	28
Total	100	100	100
UK			
Subcontracting extra-EC	3	8	15
Production extra-EC	–	–	4
Subcontracting EC	11	8	9
Production EC	86	84	72
Total	100	100	100
EU			
Subcontracting extra-EU	21	23	29
Production extra-EC	7	7	11
Subcontracting EC	23	25	29
Production EC	51	45	31
Total	100	100	100

Source: Michael Scheffer, 'Internationalisation of Production by EC Textile and Clothing Manufacturers', *Textile Outlook International*, no. 51, January 1994, pp. 106–7.

major EU clothing sectors, and certainly those where domestic manufacturing firms are most the most dependent on imports from various forms of overseas production.

The picture is less dramatic for other major clothing producer countries in the EU. France has found itself in a median position, with rapid dislocation towards the Maghreb of the clothing assembly industry from the mid 1980s onwards. Looking at Table 5.1 again, domestic production accounted for 86 per cent of the turnover of firms in 1983, and foreign production a mere 14 per cent. Throughout the 1980s, this domestically based production rapidly shifted overseas, mostly to North Africa and to some extent to the PECOs. By 1992, towards the close of the Uruguay Round talks, 55 per cent of the turnover of French clothing manufacturing firms in Scheffer's sample was produced or sourced overseas, up from 42 per cent in 1988.[46]

French government and professional association officials confirm the extraordinary change in industrial structure in the clothing sector in this period.[47] The leader of the EU protectionist camp was itself fostering many of the very imports it claimed to revile.

The UK was slow among EU producer countries to take the well-beaten path to OPT and other forms of foreign sourcing or production. Even in the 1990s, domestic production and sourcing dominated the industry. Nonetheless, Table 5.1 indicates an upward trend for OPT and other foreign production or sourcing, and by 1992 some 19 per cent of turnover was linked to this phenomenon. The Italian industry, as has been noted in earlier chapters, was by the 1970s the most competitive in Europe and in the strongest position in terms of exports. In view of this it is not surprising that Italian firms relied mostly on domestic production and sourcing. Italian firms had been masters of quick response to fluctuating markets and to the demand for quality, and had relied heavily on domestic subcontracting to achieve this.[48] It therefore comes as a considerable surprise to find the Italian clothing industry more transnationalised than the UK sector, if only just. In 1983, foreign production and sourcing was for the Italian sector entirely marginal, at 2 per cent of the total turnover of firms. By 1988 this had increased to 6 per cent, reaching 21 per cent of turnover by 1992 (Table 5.1).

As the analysis of the Uruguay round negotiating process below will indicate, it is difficult to underestimate the importance of these dramatic developments for the evolution of the global trade regime in the textile and clothing sector. As market and production structures transnationalised, the trade policy preferences of the firms involved would shift also, albeit with a lag. Old protectionist reflexes lingered on at the surface, but the underlying structural changes were to presage an eventual sea change in attitudes, even in the most staunchly protectionist of parties to the negotiation.

(ii) The United States

On the other side of the Atlantic, structural changes in production and trade patterns were also taking place which led to the transnationalisation of the US clothing industry. The developments were not as marked in Europe, and in the absence of comprehensive firm-based studies like Scheffer's precise data is difficult to come by. Nonetheless, there was an undoubted rise in the proportion of US imports attributable to American textile and clothing manufacturers. Having already transferred much of clothing production from the high-wage northeast of the country to the lower-wage southern states, many US firms looked to their hinterland in Mexico and the Caribbean, while others went as far as Asia in the drive to remain competitive on domestic markets.

In 1988, a major study pronounced the US as the least transnationalised of all major textile and clothing producer countries, assuming 'a position of virtual self-sufficiency.'[49] In light of the evidence, however, this appears as somewhat of an overstatement. The notion of self-sufficiency leans more on the role of the US as a major fibre and cotton producer at the upstream end of the production stream than on any assessment of recent developments at the downstream, clothing assembly end. Exports have indeed remained relatively low in textile and clothing relative to the EU, but imports have risen over the last decades as in most high-wage producer countries. As elsewhere, the apparel industry admits of a different pattern with respect to transnationalisation than the textile sector taken on its own. As in the case of their EU counterparts, US clothing manufacturers have resorted to a growing degree to various forms of overseas production and sourcing. Thus American firms have been responsible for an increasing share of the imports, and these imports have served to strengthen the competitive position of the firms resorting to these production strategies.

Thus an important number of US apparel firms have resorted either to outright overseas production, or to OPT under the 'Section 807' provisions of US trade law, the American equivalent to the EU's OPT regulation. The '807' provisions had their origin in the 1970s, and even attracted the support of the textile lobbies (e.g. not just the apparel manufacturers) because these OPT provisions were based solely on US manufacturers' 'made and cut' fabrics. The favoured venues for overseas production and sourcing have of course differed from the Europeans, with US manufacturers choosing either Asian producers or, more typically, regional trade partners such as Mexico and the Caribbean countries.

There were several reasons for this sudden increase in OPT related trade. In the early 1980s it was still at a low level, but beginning to pick up. Then the Reagan administration developed the Caribbean Basin Initiative (CBI) as part of the US strategy in the 'New' Cold War. Part of the accord involved better terms of trade for these relatively poor countries. In the first instance, the CBI excluded textiles and clothing products – quotas and tariffs were maintained in the face of protectionist lobbies from the industry. There were of course some companies (large on the whole) which could see the advantages for themselves of foreign sourcing, and an executive branch decision eventually introduced OPT provisions for the industry. At first the industry was divided in its attitude to these new measures reducing trade protection from low-wage countries. Some textile producers in particular opposed this vehemently. Once it was clear that this element of transnationalisation provided ongoing, perhaps additional, outlets for US manufactured and cut fabric, support grew and became solid.[50] By 1985 the Dominican Republic had become the number two source of OPT imports (Mexico was in first place).[51] Special quotas for the CBI states eventually involved 'guaranteed access levels' for OPT type imports into the US market and considerable liberalisation for reimports of finished clothing made of US fabric.[52]

The move towards OPT and overseas sourcing therefore grew rapidly in the latter half of the 1980s and accelerated again in the 1990s. The first half of the 1990s saw the most rapid expansion of OPT trade, and indeed a major restructuring of the pattern of imports into the United States. Between 1989 and 1993, Mexico and the CBI states doubled their deliveries of imports to the US, and this development was accompanied by considerable increases in US direct investment in the sector in these countries.[53]

The impending conclusion of the NAFTA accord, eventually signed in 1992 provided the further rationale for the acceleration of this trend. Mexico was granted the most favourable OPT trade conditions, and US firms began to shift production rapidly.[54] By 1994, quotas on clothing imports from Mexico had been removed under NAFTA, on the condition that they were composed of US 'made and cut' fabric. OPT finished clothing under section 807 provisions accounted for 71 per cent of US imports from Mexico in 1994.[55] The US state was creating legal instruments at the behest of the industry to facilitate the change in industrial/market structure and the patterns of trade. Furthermore, the success of many firms, and the pressure they placed on their domestic US competitors who had so far declined transnationalisation, had a demonstration effect, and the trend therefore accelerated in Mexico and in the CBI countries as well. Household names in US clothing production began to move their factories, as in the example of Fruit of the Loom which moved major production facilities to Costa Rica and Honduras.[56]

The effects on the overall pattern of imports into the US market were clear. Since 1987 China had been the largest volume source of imports of finished apparel into the American market, and the biggest value supplier from 1992; the other major suppliers were Hong Kong, Taiwan, and Korea.[57] By 1996, however, China had slipped to the number three position in terms of textile and clothing imports combined, and number two in finished clothing. Imports from other Asian suppliers were in retreat after years of growth. These countries could no longer use their MFA quotas to the maximum, such was the growth of imports from the countries involved in OPT trade with American clothing manufacturers. The leading source of imports of finished clothing was Mexico, and these imports were dominated by the OPT activity of American manufacturing firms.[58] The rapid development of this OPT trade corresponded to an equally dramatic drop in employment levels in the dometic US clothing industry, employment losses related to imports but driven almost entirely by the production strategies of firms.[59] Intra-industry and intra-firm trade was on the increase in the region and this was bound to have consequences for US trade policy.

Therefore, while precise figures are difficult to obtain, the evidence is clear. The European phenomenon of transnationalisation of trade and production through intra-industry and intra-firm trade (largely OPT), begun in Germany and the Netherlands, had spread to the US manufacturers. The changing practices of firms-as-agents had resulted in an important transformation, a transnationalisation, of the structures of US production and trade in the textile and clothing sectors of the advanced economies. It remains for this book to demonstrate how this transformation of structure had an impact on the policy preferences of firms, facilitating the eventual liberalisation of the exceptional trade provisions of the MFA in the course of the Uruguay Round agreements signed in 1994 at Marrakesh.

THE 1986 MFA RENEWAL AND THE URUGUAY ROUND LAUNCH

A number of interview sources drew attention to the relationship between market conditions in the textile and clothing sector and the negotiating climate in international trade talks. From the European Union's point of view, the economic climate in the sector was relatively buoyant in 1986 at the dawn of the Uruguay Round. As if to demonstrate the effect this might have on trade negotiations, the EU even eased some of the MFA quotas in bilateral accords when the terms of renewal of MFA IV were negotiated in 1985–6. The picture was not all favourable at the launch of the Uruguay Round, however. The French industry was under pressure and suffering a contraction of production, and there was little tolerance of liberalisation in a country which had proved crucial to EU textile and clothing trade policy in the past. Furthermore, the EU had been joined in 1986 by Spain and Portugal, a development which strengthened considerably the coalition of protectionist members of the Council, led by France and the UK. This was not fertile ground for the abandonment of the MFA and the prospects for liberalisation, despite the 1986 GATT Ministerial Declaration.

US negotiators found themselves in an even tighter corner. The high dollar had put extraordinary pressure on a wide number of textile and clothing manufacturers, and protectionist legislation proposals abounded on Capitol Hill. US negotiators managed to fend off the worst of protectionist moves in the Congress, a number of which were sponsored by the textile coalition. The price was a considerable tightening of the MFA IV protocol of renewal and the bilateral accords negotiated in 1986. In the opening stages of the Round, the global trade regime for textile and clothing was becoming more restrictive, not liberal.

This section will demonstrate how liberalisation of the MFA came to be at least grudgingly accepted by the industry in the US and Europe, though it was not a liberalisation entirely to the satisfaction of LDC opponents of the MFA. Firms acted as fundamental agents of change in two ways. First, structural change in global production and trade came about as a result of the adaptation of firms strategies to a variety of competitive pressures (only some of them from the low-wage producers). The industry, it has been demonstrated, became increasingly transnationalised, particularly in the downstream clothing sector. Second, firms (through their associations) were integrated into the apparatus of the state and controlled crucial political resources in the institutions of the policy process. It was always likely that the changed strategies of firms in the evolving structural setting, and their newly acquired sense of self-interest as agents in both the competitive and the political sense, would eventually translate into a transformation in policy outcome.

The duration of the Uruguay Round negotiation constituted the historical turning point where perceived self-interest caught up with structural change. More flexible and transnational strategies in competition eventually led to alternative policy preferences. Traditional textile coalitions began to fragment, slowly at first, but eventually came to at least acquiesce in the prospect of liberalisation. State agencies which had typically been hostage to protectionist forces helped in the game of persuasion, as they had tried unsuccessfully in the past. The pressures of the LDCs in a complex series of negotiating tradeoffs in the Round were also a contributing factor. However, these potential tradeoffs had presented themselves in various guises before. What weighed most heavily was the eventual indifference to (sometimes mild acceptance of) liberalisation of the MFA over time.

The link between structure and policy manifested itself through the agency of firms and their associations as self-interested actors in the global political economy, wherein state and market were integrated as institutions for the management of distributional conflict embedded in the complex social structures of contemporary capitalism. This section will now proceed to analyse the negotiationg process in the Uruguay round, in particular the evolving positions of the United States and the EU, in relation to the evidence already presented on the changing structure of the global sector in terms of trade and production.

(a) The Dynamics of the Negotiations: The European Union and the United States

It is first worth reminding oneself that the textile and clothing negotiations took place in the wider context of a multilateral trade Round. The negotiating agenda for the Uruguay Round was, furthermore, much expanded in comparison to previous multilateral GATT talks. This time new issues such as TRIPs, TRIMs, and trade in services were added to the agenda, at the same time as old (and painful) leftovers from previous Rounds such as the liberalisation of textiles and agricultural trade returned to haunt negotiators. In this context, the inclusion of textile and clothing sector liberalisation in the talks, through eventual integration of the MFA into regular GATT disciplines, was an important element in persuading the sceptical LDCs to participate fully in the Round. If the textile and clothing talks were to prove unsuccessful, then a conclusion to the Round might prove difficult. The eventual accord on the textile and clothing sector cannot therefore be seen in isolation from the global tradeoffs of the overall Round, but as will become clear they had their own dynamic and the outcome was far from inevitable. In fact the legitimacy of the draft text was in question right up until the closing minutes of the Uruguay Round negotiation. The textile and clothing talks were the last of the Round's negotiating

Groups to conclude on the final night, underscoring the extent of controversy involved and the open-endedness of the outcome.

Second, it is worth pointing out that this section is not intended to be an exhaustive account of the textile negotiations.[60] Its purpose is to demonstrate the broader arguments of the book, particularly concerning the relationship between industry structure and the global trade regime, and the conceptualisation of state and market: the liberalisation process, like the rise of protectionism in the sector before it, was intimately tied to political economy of structural adjustment in the industry. State and market are revealed as an integrated ensemble of institutions for the governance of distributional conflict in the global economy; structural change and political processes proved inseparable. The changes in the global trade regime for textiles and clothing were driven by the underlying distributional conflict among socio-economic agents integrated into the organisational structures constituted by states and markets in the global political economy.

Bearing these points in mind, the section will begin with an analysis of the negotiating position of the United States, followed by an account of the more complex policy processes at work in the EU. The United States proved to be the most intransigent of the industrialised countries when it came to integrating the MFA into GATT and liberalisation of trade in the sector. This is not surprising given the relatively self-contained characteristics of the US industry, with its limited if accelerating transnationalisation. The EU as a whole accepted liberalisation and integration more easily, but not without vociferous and important protests on the part of the industrialists of key member states, especially France.

(i) The United States

The United States delegation entered the Round negotiations with a flurry of protectionist legislation on the floor of both the House and the Senate on Capitol Hill, some of it specifically related to the textile and apparel sector.[61] The textile coalition could clearly assemble a large majority in the Congress in favour of ever tighter protectionist legislation. US officials were constantly on their guard against even minor surges in imports from MFA and other countries. The US for many years had been involved in a rolling series of bilateral negotiations linked to the MFA accord and various protocols of renewal. Some of these bilateral accords lasted barely a year, and US officials were keen to tighten them progressively in the face of constant industry pressure. The only way for the government to stave off the protectionist assault in Congress was to implement the MFA on as strict a basis as the letter allowed, and to take a tough line on any low-wage imports which escaped the MFA net.

This attitude of the United States at the outset of negotiations which were supposedly at last to deliver liberalisation of the MFA appalled the LDCs in Geneva. The negotiating climate was far from healthy in the initial stages of the Round, and a number of interviews revealed that the US industry was as protectionist as ever at the start in 1986. The turning point had in fact come in 1983–4 as the dollar strengthened, US consumption grew rapidly, and imports surged. The Administration, under pressure from the industry and ongoing Congressional threats of protectionist legislation, began to implement the terms of the MFA and to negotiate bilateral accords on a much tougher basis, including a system of 'global ceilings' on whole groups of products as opposed to the original product-by-product basis.[62] US policy appeared unlikely to waver from this tougher line, especially as President Reagan had himself made a personal commitment in writing and later orally to Senators Thurman and Helms, strong supporters of the textile coalition, a commitment which would be difficult to divest.[63] In the preparatory committee for the Uruguay Round, the United States (and the EU for that matter) expressed reservations about its capacity to deliver in the domain of textiles and clothing at all.[64] The result was a 1986 MFA renewal in which the US managed to place quotas on products with fibre types which had not previously been covered, including linen and ramie, and in the case of ramie did not even produce.

These developments appeared in contrast to the eventual GATT ministerial declaration, which theoretically committed the GATT parties to discussions on integrating the textile and clothing sector into the mainstream of the GATT. The declaration was however carefully worded, and under US pressure did not commit the parties to actually *do* anything. The more controversial sections of the declaration had remained in parentheses until the last moment, and some of these provisions were dropped altogether. The final declaration read:

> Negotiations in the area of textiles and clothing shall aim to formulate modalities that would permit the eventual integration of this sector into GATT on the basis of strengthened GATT rules and disciplines, thereby also contributing to the objective of further liberalisation of trade.[65]

The parties were not committed as such to liberalisation, but only to 'aim' to 'formulate modalities' in the expectation that this might lead to liberalisation, and the integration of textiles and clothing into the GATT was subject to 'strengthened GATT rules and disciplines'. There were therefore plenty of escape hatches for negotiators in the US (or the EU for that matter). Liberalisation appeared far from guaranteed, and one might argue it was very much business as usual for the MFA . Of course the LDCs would be much less likely to agree to issues dear to the US, such as the liberalisation of trade in services, if there were no positive outcome on textile and clothing trade, and the US and the EU would have to grapple with this eventuality. However, the US negotiating team was well aware of the strength of protectionist sentiment in Washington, and this was unlikely to abate in the short term as legislative proposals continued to roll onto the floor of the House in particular. Both government and industry were aware of the textile coalition's capacity to block progress on the Uruguay Round. Any eventual agreement would require the coalition's at least tacit blessing. The government would continue to pursue roughly incompatible goals, the tougher MFA and the Round negotiations on integration and eventual liberalisation, for a while longer. The tougher MFA IV had been in many respects the first step in bringing the industry on side.[66]

The first year of the talks was largely devoted to information gathering on trade in the sector, but it is interesting to note that the US did not submit any actual proposals, and nor did the Americans do so in 1988.[67] The shadow cast by the successive proposed textile bills in Congress (1985, 1986, 1987–8, 1990) was long. The mid term review, which began at Montreal in late 1988 and continued on in Geneva until early April 1989, contained a commitment accepted by all parties including the United States that substantive negotiations should take place beginning April 1989, but so far no such substantive negotiations had taken place some three years into a Round then scheduled to complete a little over a year later in 1990.[68]

The only important matters on which there was agreement were: 1. that the 'modalities' for integrating the sector into GATT would indeed involve a phasing out of the MFA; 2. that these modalities would only be acceptable in a context of strengthened GATT rules and disciplines (this latter point was on the insistence of the developed countries and had been strongly resisted by the International Textile and Clothing Bureau or ITCB, which presented a united negotiating front for the LDCs). Agreement on how this was to be done was not forthcoming at the time, and of course without specific modalities, there could be no integration or liberalisation at all. The United States was still not committed to specific measures of any kind in the negotiations, and this position was helped by the fact that the EU delegation 'refused any reasonable language' at the Montreal and Geneva review processes.[69] Any move on addressing the question of specific 'modalities' remained consistently linked to the strengthening of GATT rules and disciplines, a process which was in fact the preoccupation of a separate negotiating group.[70]

The negotiations were nonetheless proceeding slowly toward the idea of a phased elimination of the MFA in stages, increasing the quota growth rates until they were eliminated altogether. The LDCs, under an ITCB proposal (specifically tabled by the Indonesian delegation), initially wanted to do this subsector by subsector in the industry: they proposed first to deal with the spinning sector, then woven products, followed by made-ups and knitwear, and finally finished clothing.[71] The developed countries saw immediate problems with this approach: how would they explain to the spinning sector that they were to take the plunge first? There was an immediate reaction from the sectors implicated in the proposal. Developed countries saw that they would have to *control* the way in which product categories were removed from the quota system if any agreement was ever to be legitimate. Some time limit would have to apply, though how long was a matter of very serious contention, and quotas would have to be dismantled on the basis of MFA product categories, based on the relative sensitivity of the products concerned in the eyes of the developed country importers.

While this slow process of conceptualising (though not yet accepting) 'modalities' was underway in 1989 and in 1990 and the overall textile negotiations were finally on some sort of track, the United States came out with its first serious proposal of the negotiations, one which nearly threw a spanner in the works of the delicate bargaining process. This was the 'Global Quotas' proposal, and it requires some background explanation. The global quotas proposal was very strongly backed by the US textile industry in particular, and the 'textile coalition' in general. The highly protectionist Textile and Apparel Trade Bill of 1987, and the similar Textile, Apparel, and Footwear Trade Act of 1990, were both based on the global quotas idea.[72] Both acts also attempted to tie directly the growth of imports into the US market to the growth in domestic consumption: imports would not grow faster than the US market itself. The 1987 bill had passed both houses of Congress by close to a two-thirds majority in the House and some 60 per cent in the Senate in 1988. President Bush vetoed the bill, and although it failed to gain the necessary two-thirds majority vote for a veto override, it came within some twenty votes of this in the House. This clearly demonstrated that the textile coalition, in the middle of the Uruguay Round, could muster a substantial majority in the Congress in favour of restrictive trade legislation, and this would have to be taken into account in any attempt to phase out the MFA.

Therefore the American administration sought to build its first proposal in the textile negotiations on the global quotas idea.[73] The basic idea of the proposal, presented on 5 February 1990 and which caught the negotiating group by surprise,[74] is that all US imports, from MFA and non-MFA sources and thus including the European Union, Japan, and other developed countries, would steadily be integrated into a single, 'global' quota.[75] The proposal would certainly have removed much of the *discriminatory* character of the MFA system, because all exporting countries (LDCs and advanced economies alike) would progressively have found themselves competing within the same quota basket. The system would begin with an overall quota or ceiling for US imports being established for each product, and each exporting country would have a specific allocation of the whole. During a transition period lasting from 1 January 1992 (assuming completion of the Round) to 31 December 2001 (10 years), countries with quotas based on product categories under the MFA would steadily shift a proportion (10 per cent per year) into a global basket, thereby steadily competing head-to-head for their market share of imports into the US. By the end of the ten-year transition period all products from all exporters would be included in the global basket, and in the global basket each product would have an annual growth rate (based on the import sensitivity of the product) throughout the transition period. The viability of this proposal would, in the eyes of the US delegation, be contingent on the negotiation of strengthened GATT rules and disciplines in the overall Round. The US proposal contained an alternative to global quotas, the so-called 'Tariff Rate' quota system, but this does not appear to have been pursued as vigorously as the global quotas system. The global quotas proposal was then supplemented and clarified in proposals from the US of 5 March 1990, and 14 May. In the latter submission, the American delegation affirmed that at the end of the ten-year transition period all special rules for textile and clothing trade would disappear, representing the end of the MFA or any replacement arrangement such as global quotas.

The American industry largely supported the global quotas idea (itself a modification of the industry's own legislative programme in Congress) as the best of the options being discussed in the textile negotiating group. Consultation with the US industry was constant and ongoing in this regard. The industry however always expressed a preference for a fifteen-year transition period, and this remained their position until the very end of the Round.[76] However, US industry backing was never likely to prove sufficient to make the proposal acceptable in the textile and clothing negotiating group. The EU objected strenuously, because EU exports to the US would have been placed under quantitative restrictions for the first time and in competition with the exports of the LDCs. The global quotas idea therefore created a significant if temporary split between the US and the EU in the negotiations. Many of the smaller LDC producers likewise would have lost the niches which MFA quotas represented, competing directly with the EU and giants such as China or India. It would have put enormous pressure on uncompetitive producer firms everywhere, while transferring the burden of adjustment away from the US industry for the duration of the transition period at least. In short, 'this trick was just too crude to succeed.'[77] The proposals had anyway come at a bad time, when the negotiations were finally beginning to get serious.[78]

Despite the controversy and eventual failure of the global quotas proposal, the US had at last begun to play a substantive role in the negotiations, and the American textile and clothing lobbies were slowly undergoing a metamorphosis in their policy position. This metamorphosis ran more or less parallel to the structural changes taking place in the industry, especially the expansion of foreign sourcing. As the development of foreign sourcing accelerated, the clothing industry lobby in particular began to soften its position and to accept that liberalisation was an eventuality which could not be avoided forever. The Industry had made significant strides in developing just-in-time production methods in the late 1980s (partly a response to the demands of retailers for rapid turnaround of orders), which helped considerably in competition with Asian exporting countries. Rapid restocking of retail outlets could only take place with the co-operation of local producers in the US market. Furthermore, the likelihood of a NAFTA had increased, and the strategies of firms began rapidly to adjust to this eventuality, achieved by 1992. Foreign sourcing and changes in US '807' trade provisions were very much part of the picture. Lastly, the negotiation took place in the context of an implicit

tradeoff: integration of the MFA into the GATT and any corresponding liberalisation of developed country markets was to be set
against enhanced GATT safeguards and disciplines across the board,
and improved market access for high-wage producers in LDC and
NIC markets. Slowly, therefore, the idea of liberalisation came to be
acceptable, reluctantly, to the industry. The legitimacy of the emerging
policy was underpinned by structural changes in production and trade
patterns, and by the tradeoffs involved in the negotiation such as
market access and enhanced safeguards/rule making provisions for the
GATT as a whole, including provisions on the safeguard of intellectual
property.[79]

Once the psychological barrier which prevented open discussion of
liberalisation began to be breached – the end of the MFA became
thinkable – it also became clear that there was not a lot to give up in
the first place. As has been stressed above, the MFA was less and less
relevant to global trade and production in the textile and clothing
sector. It had become an obstacle to many firms which could not
obtain the inputs they required because of quotas, and as the internal
policies of firms changed the insistence on protection of the MFA was
increasingly hypocritical. Major US retailers had long lobbied for
complete freedom of sourcing, but this was increasingly in the interest
of a growing number of producers as well.[80] The quota system had
begun to work against the interests of firms in a rapidly changing
environment. The state-centric trading system of the MFA was proving inappropriate.[81]

Anyway, as the US delegation was keen to impress upon its own
industry among others, the compound growth rates on most MFA
quotas were such that within five to ten years effective protection
would anyway disappear.[82] It would still restrict some specific
exporters, but the level of the quotas was more than likely to exceed
the size of the entire market in the US. Adjustment was underway
regardless, primarily through transnationalisation in the case of the
clothing industry, and if developed country firms could increasingly
control the trade through their own activities and strategies, that was
fine, and a variety of anti-competitive practices would remain perfectly
possible at the firm level. There began to be less and less co-operation
from the apparel industry (the American Apparel Manufacturers
Association) in the control of quota imports, though the textile lobby
continued to be active.[83] If quota growth rates would eventually phase
out the effectiveness of the agreement, the American delegation might
as well push for something in return in the context of the Round!

So there was little to lose, and as the Brussels Ministerial Meeting of December 1990 approached (at which theoretically the Round was to be wrapped up), the US delegation and the industry had accepted the prospect of liberalisation in principle. It was from then on a matter of timing, the famous 'modalities,' and the order in which different product groups were to be liberalised. With the demise of the global quotas proposal, the talks settled on the idea of a phased removal of the MFA's restrictions parallel to an integration of the MFA product groups into the GATT. Having proposed a ten-year transition period under the global quotas proposal, the US now pushed strongly for a fifteen-year transition period. The negotiations were on track for a successful conclusion, but in typical fashion the US delegation, still pursued by the textile industry if considerably less so by the apparel manufacturers, were going to extract what they could in terms of concessions. It is time now to examine the negotiation from the point of view of the other crucial developed country participant, the European Union. The next section does this, and the final section then looks at the last stages of the Round from the advent of the Dunkel draft text to the conclusion.

(ii) The European Union
The European Union was a far less homogeneous political constituency than the United States, itself not renown for the coherence of its policy processes. Complexity and diversity marked the negotiating positions of the EU member states, in line with the contrasting industrial structures of their respective domestic industries. On a number of sensitive questions, the EU employers' organisations proved paralyzed and unable to take a unified stand, deferring to their national members.[84] The EU Commission had the unenviable task of developing a viable negotiating stance out of the conflicting positions in the Council. Eventually it was successful in negotiating a deal which was accepted, grudgingly in a number of cases, by the EU industry and member states. However, as has been pointed out by Peter Sutherland, first secretary-general of the WTO at the end of the Uruguay Round and a former EU Commissioner, 'Without the European Union there would have been no Uruguay Round. Had the member states negotiated individually I cannot believe that in fact global consensus would ever have been achieved.'[85]

The fact that the articulation of interests within the EU was far more fragmented than in any one member state turned out to be an advantage for the Commission, frustrating as the rules of the game might have been at any one time. The Commission negotiators were eventually able to act as brokers among the complex and competing interests, and to induce a result which was quite independent of the positions of any one or group of member states. The EU was capable of facing up to the major tradeoffs of the Round, and playing competing interests (both state and non-state) off against each other, and some serious and sometimes painful horse trading indeed took place.[86] This feature of the Commission's role in the Round was certainly an important element of supranationality involved in the role of the Commission in this case, and it played a game not unfamiliar to those who understand the politics of relatively decentralised federal countries such as Canada or the United States.[87]

It seems generally accepted by those closely involved with the Round that the EU was more willing to accept the prospect of liberalisation from the outset of the textile and clothing talks. In 1986 the EU even loosened some of the MFA restrictions during the renewal negotiations and in the course of drawing up the bilateral accords. The reasons for this were straightforward: a number of member states openly opposed the quota system, and the rapid development of foreign sourcing and OPT meant that a growing number of industrialists had little interest in an ongoing, let alone more restrictive, MFA. The Commission often made much of its more open trade policy in the sector relative to the United States in particular.[88]

However, the EU negotiating stance in the early stages of the Round belied this apparent acceptance of liberalisation. The EU was, at least according to a number of participants in the talks, as intransigent as the US to start with. There are important reasons for this apparent incongruity. In the first place, Spain and Portugal had joined the EU in 1986. These two countries, especially Portugal, were important textile producers, had served as foreign suppliers to EU firms prior to joining, and were looking forward to substantial benefits to their textile and clothing industries as a result of membership. In the case of Portugal, about one third of industrial production and exports were in the textile and clothing sector. Most importantly, the firms in these countries had not even begun to face the question of restructuring and globalisation of markets and production.[89] These countries would be directly and adversely affected by any liberalisation of low-wage imports.[90]

The Spanish and Portuguese delegations added strength to the existing protectionist camp among the member states. Greece, with a relatively backward industry, had little to gain from liberalisation.

While Italy was the most competitive textile and clothing producer in the world (and theoretically a potential free-trader as a result), the markets of developed countries (of which the single European market) were essentially captive as long as the MFA remained in place, so Italy was a key member of the EU protectionist camp. The protectionist credentials of the French industry, well established in professional lobbies both domestically and at the EU level and strongly backed over time by the French government, need little reminder in this book. Belgium had tended to support protection, indicating a split even within the Benelux countries.[91]

Overall, in 1986 the balance within the Council had been upset in favour of the Mediterranean countries. Members in favour of liberalisation were placed in a minority, though a blocking minority in terms of votes on the Council. As one key participant in the EU level negotiations was at pains to point out, it was necessary that France and the southern European countries support each other sufficiently so as to maintain at least a countervailing blocking minority in the negotiations.[92] The entry of new members had rendered this task considerably easier. Only the Netherlands, Denmark, and Germany could be counted on to support liberalisation. The United Kingdom had a liberal trade policy under the Thatcher government, but a protectionist industry, and this tension appears to have reduced the effectiveness of the UK delegation in taking a stand one way or the other in the textile negotiations. One UK official was quoted as admitting that the UK delegation was 'crypto-liberal' when it came to the textile and clothing negotiations in the Round.[93]

The Commission began the negotiation, then, in a contradictory and difficult position. The elimination of the MFA was in principle acceptable, part of a wider tradeoff in the overall Round giving the LDCs some reason to accept the liberalisation of sectors such as services on which they were opposed. However, for an important proportion of the member states, the idea of liberalisation had no legitimacy in their key domestic political constituencies. Only the ongoing process of structural change would, as in the US case, serve slowly to fragment and undermine the vehemence of the array of protectionist forces.

This ambiguity of the EU negotiating position was exposed early on in the talks. In a June 1988 'Communication' (e.g. less than a formal proposal), the EU stated that since February 1986 and the renewal of the MFA, the EU had confirmed its aim of eventual integration of the textile and clothing sector into GATT. However, there were still 'problems' in the EU industry, an over-used euphemism for 'ongoing need for protection'. Progress on textile and clothing matters would depend on parallel progress, to the satisfaction of the EU, on the strengthening of GATT rules and disciplines, on tariff negotiations, on better rules for safeguards, subsidies dumping, TRIPS, and better disciplines for 'balance of payments' and 'infant industry' provisions which were so often employed by developing countries.[94] In other words, the EU was not offerring anything concrete, any more than the US, but at least maintained a declaratory posture in favour of liberalisation. By the mid term review at Montreal (December 1988) and in Geneva through to April 1989, the EU no more served to help the talks along than the United States.[95] The talks were blocked, and no concessions had been made by the developed countries. The LDCs continued to maintain that the balance in the overall Round on which the EU insisted could only be achieved if the textile and clothing negotiations were to succeed from their point of view. After all, the entire textile and clothing sector had been removed from GATT disciplines, and it was up to the developed countries to right this and strengthen GATT Disciplines in the process.

By the time of the mid term review, the EU appeared more or less ready to continue the process of relaxing the MFA quotas, and thus contributing to a limited liberalisation of trade in the sector. However, there was no concrete commitment at this stage, and there was certainly no move to accept an *integration* of textile and clothing products into GATT disciplines. The exceptional trade regime for the sector might become somewhat more liberal, but might also remain outside the GATT. This position was not inconsistent with the needs of an industry undergoing fairly rapid transnationalisation with the countries contiguous to the European market, such as Turkey, the (then crumbling) East Bloc, or the Maghreb. Quotas might continue to be desirable if directed against Asian producers, but for those countries which had become effectively integrated into the EU production structure such as the Maghreb, Turkey, and some of the East Bloc countries, liberalisation was taking place regardless. The EU's trade was already open to these exporters, and often operated on a preferential basis. The crucial point is that the *EU firms controlled the pattern of trade with these countries*, and they had imposed a sort of vertical integration of producers in these countries into the European industry as a whole.[96] What they resisted was a liberalisation of trade with producers where they did not control the terms of trade, particularly East and South Asia.

Yet underneath the surface the EU was effectively committed to liberalisation. The Danish, German, and Dutch governments and their industry associations pursued a liberal policy argument in the special textile trade negotiating committee attached to the Council (the so-called 'Textiles 113 Committee'). The German industry was finding itself short of quotas to cope with the extent of foreign sourcing by domestic firms.[97] Industrialists in other countries began to discover that their access to OPT quotas was insufficient. There was full knowledge, even from the most protectionist camps, that the MFA was ineffectual in containing imports.[98] It was also increasingly accepted that the rising levels of imports were in no small measure the result of European producers themselves, as was established earlier in this chapter. This was long known to be the case in Germany, but this phenomenon as we have seen was also taking place in France and even Italy but was as always limited to exporting countries which industries EU producers controlled. The textile and clothing sectors were anyway not the only industries whose interests were to be promoted in the Round, and agriculture was for most EU members a far more important line of defence. But why were these underlying realities not reflected in the EU's initial negotiating stance?

Industry in the more protectionist countries appears to have adopted a posture of outward expressions of hostility toward liberalisation. Any open acceptance of liberalisation would have to await the results of the negotiations.[99] The French industrialists exhibited their hostility with street demonstrations at the outset of the Round, something they were to repeat in its closing moments. They and others in the protectionist alliance mounted a vigorous campaign throughout the negotiations aimed at saving the MFA. Given that they were developing more open trading relationships with producers with whom they had foreign sourcing arrangements, there was little incentive to open markets to Asian producers as well.

What was required in order to persuade the EU industries, particularly those which had long advocated protectionism and had pinned their colours to the MFA mast, was a serious tradeoff: the end of the MFA, with an appropriate transition period, in exchange for greatly enhanced access to third country markets, better GATT safeguards, and an aggressive pursuit of reciprocity along the lines of American trade policy.[100] Liberalisation was not going to occur at any price, job losses and delocalisation continued, and the political climate therefore remained tense. Over time however, the Commission and national governments proved anxious to respond to the industry, and to work out their strategy in close, in fact daily, consultation with the employers organisations at both national and EU levels.[101] This attitude of the authorities helped a great deal to legitimate the process of negotiating away the MFA, though at the time the relationship was seldom easy.[102]

The Commission's negotiating stance did begin to reflect the changing structural position of the industry following the mid term review. *Le Monde* reported on the outcome of the review, noting the approval coming from EU industrialists, 'numerous in the corridors of Geneva', for the Commission's stance which had made the elimination of the MFA entirely conditional on satisfactory observance of GATT rules and disciplines by exporters and respect for the rules of competition.[103] Some months later the *Financial Times* ran a major article, of considerable symbolic value in the context, on the growing internationalisation of the European and indeed US textile and clothing sectors, particularly the overseas involvement of the larger companies.[104] It was time for a shift in the (so far negative) EU negotiating stance, and this development came in July 1989.

The new EU proposal was the first by major developed country protagonists to begin formulating modalities for elimination of the MFA, both liberalisation and integration of the agreement into GATT,[105] though it would still take a great deal of time and effort until final agreement seemed within reach. Industrial lobbies grumbled all the way, overplaying their hand as much as possible so as to keep governments 'honest' in their eyes. Nonetheless the proposal was a significant step and eventually formed the basis of compromise in the talks.

Briefly, the EU paper, which took the MFA quota system as a starting point, proposed a step-by-step elimination of quotas accompanied by a verification process and ongoing safeguards during the transition period. The timing of the transition period was not stipulated, and it was recognised that this would be controversial, but at the least transition should not start until the end of the Round itself, or on expiry of the MFA in 1991. Crucially, a link was established between negotiation of the transition arrangements for eliminating the MFA and progress in several other negotiating groups in the Round. The underlying point made by the EU was that better access to markets, and the strict observance of GATT disciplines in the sector, had to apply to all bar the least developed countries. That meant that the LDCs which were the target of the MFA had to bind tariffs at lower levels, remove non-tariff restrictions, improve foreign exchange restrictions, and ensure fair competition through the TRIPS, subsidies, anti-dumping etc. negotiations. This parallelism between negotiating groups in the Round was strongly resisted by the ITCB, representing the MFA producers.[106]

A consensus began to develop in the talks around the idea of using the MFA quota system as a starting point for phase-out of the restrictions. Different product groups would be integrated into GATT over a transition period. It seemed unlikely that the LDCs would shake either the EU or the US from implicitly linking the textile talks with progress in other negotiating groups; the logic of the Round dictated that it should be thus. What was then at stake was twofold: the question of *length of the transition period*, and the question of which products in what order, or *product coverage*.[107]

This emerging consensus was greatly disturbed by the US 'Global Quotas' proposal which intervened in February 1990 (see above, this chapter), but ultimately formed the basis for the ATC. For some time the EU was preoccupied with opposing the US idea of Global Quotas, and also with insisting on the need for parallelism and adequate safeguards during the transition period, but the cat was out of the bag. No firm commitments had been made, but an important concession in principle was on the table. This concession became firmer with the EU's extensive and more concrete proposal of June 1990.[108] The signs of a workable tradeoff between LDCs and the EU were evident: the EU would abandon the MFA over time, contingent on the strengthening of other GATT disciplines, but the EU would also gain significant concessions from LDCs in terms of market access.[109] The target was Asia in particular; given that many of the PECO and Mediterranean exporters involved in OPT and foreign sourcing for the EU had little incentive to restrict access for European products to their markets.[110]

By this time even the most recalcitrant of professional associations knew they had an interest in getting out of the MFA circus of constant monitoring and renegotiation;[111] it had become an increasingly ineffectual 'rampart' against low-wage imports.[112] Quota use from Asian countries was in decline by the early 1990s anyway as foreign sourcing activity in the Mediterranean and other European countries accelerated and reinforced its hold on the market, and given the compound growth rates on quota based products, the total of allowable imports under MFA restrictions was at the time beginning to outstrip the entire EU market.[113] If the industry could achieve a clear and predictable transition period and access to the markets of the newly industrialising economies, this would be better than an MFA which had long since ceased to function effectively. As the MFA was worth less and less, it became increasingly of interest to *get something for it*, a conclusion which was being reached in US circles as well.

As the talks began to gel around the idea of step-by-step phasing out of the MFA, the negotiating parties began to think seriously about which products and when. At this stage another and dramatic factor in the negotiating position of the EU must be introduced: the fall of the Berlin Wall. During 1989, political movement in several of the immediately adjacent East Bloc countries, with the tacit approval of the then Soviet administration in Moscow, succeeded in toppling the national Communist regimes from power. The impact on the European Union was direct and almost immediate. First and foremost this of course resulted in the absorption of the German Democratic Republic into Federal Germany: one of the most important 'low-wage' exporters and OPT clients became suddenly part of the EU. German textile and clothing industrialists had already invested heavily in the former East Germany, and with the expectation that wage levels would rise there following unification and integration of the two former antagonists, German foreign direct investment was looking for a new and cheaper European home, and others were looking for new venues for foreign sourcing arrangements.

The former East Bloc came to the EU in other ways. It was obvious from the outset that these errant Soviet Bloc countries sought the benefits of integration into the global market economy, and were well aware that there would be significant costs as well. They would seek membership of GATT and other global institutions with a role in the governance of the market economy. Integration with the market economy would nevertheless happen primarily on a regional basis. It was clear that the EU would be the main trading partner of most of these countries, particularly the so-called 'Visigrad' countries (Poland, Hungary and the Czech Republic) and would have special responsibilities for helping to create conditions of economic and political stability during the transition period. Furthermore, it soon became clear that EU membership was on the cards for at least the Visigrad three early in the next millennium.

The upshot of the situation was a further acceleration of the transnationalisation process in the EU textile and clothing industry. The collapse of the East Bloc had the same galvanising effect on foreign sourcing activities of European firms as NAFTA was to have in the US. Even Italian producers were in on the action this time in a concerted attempt to maintain control of downstream production activities, though traditionally the Italian industry had not employed such foreign sourcing strategies in the past.[114] The move towards dislocation and the commensurate rise in imports had taken another turn. The more that intra-firm and intra-industry trade developed in the sector, the more there was an interest in a successful tradeoff leading to an end of quotas.

Splits began to appear in the EU camp, even among the protectionists. On several occasions, an embarrassed French delegation had to explain to the Portugese why import quotas from Morrocco and Tunisia had been grossly exceeded, to the detriment of Portuguese exports within Europe. Eventually Portugal was bought off with 400 million ECUs of financial compensation. COMITEXTIL, the EU's umbrella textile employers' federation, and its equivalent in the clothing sector, the AEIH, experienced a split in their own ranks with the establishment of ELTAC (European Largest Textile and Clothing Companies). Though few involved in the employers' organisations wished to speak directly about this in the aftermath, it seems that ELTAC was formed in order to pursue rapidly a conclusion to the Uruguay Round textile negotiations by accepting the phase-out of the MFA in return for enhanced market access provisions from both the LDCs and the US.[115] There were also strong lobbies mounted by European consumers associations and in particular by representatives of wholesale importers and large-scale distribution firms. Many of these pressures were orchestrated by the Foreign Trade Association (FTA) based in Bonn and active in Brussels, sometimes teaming up with the ITCB which represented the LDCs in the Round.[116]

Although the MFA was nominally still in place and there was a steady chorus of voices which continued to call for its continuing existence and strict observance, its days were clearly numbered. It was increasingly difficult for the Commission to gain compliance from member states on implementing the quota system.[117] Even when the Commission wanted to protect it was finding its hands tied in a number of ways, and actual quota use continued to decline.

(iii) Toward the Final Act: The Agreement on Textiles and Clothing
The sudden prospect of integrating the eastern and central European countries into the EU was an important turning point, cementing political will and structural change at one and the same time. The EU (privately at least) settled on a ten-year transition period (initially proposed by the US under the global quotas paper) using MFA

product restrictions as the starting point. Following the defeat of the 1990 Textile Bill in Congress, a similar climate accepting an eventual end to quotas was also developing in the United States. The European and American industries continued to maintain an outward posture of hostility towards the idea of an accord to dismantle the MFA, and indeed began to coordinate their strategies in the Round.[118] Privately, this transnational coalition was preparing for a deal. By November 1990 the European, American, and Canadian textile and clothing associations had published a common communiqué backing the emergent EU negotiating position, but pushing for the longer transition period of fifteen as opposed to ten years.[119]

Although the Brussels Ministerial meeting of December 1990 (theoretically to wrap up the entire Round) was a fiasco by all admissions, sometime during the course of 1991 the time appeared right for an eventual deal, and the 'modalities' leading to elimination of the MFA and a liberalisation of trade were slowly developed.[120] In this more positive climate, the MFA was renewed without alteration in mid 1991 for one more year (up until 31 December 1992) pending an outcome to the Round, and there was relatively little controversy on the matter. This provided a further breathing space for the negotiators to work out their remaining differences and deal with the complexities which confronted them. Furthermore, the prospect of an eventual end to the quotas spurred on the process of transnationalisation and restructuring in the American and European industries. The advance of globalisation, which the MFA had managed to constrain but not to prevent, was accepted and mentalities were changing in the developed countries. There would be a price, of course, in terms of improved access to developing country markets and better protection of intellectual property.[121] The negotiations eventually resulted in the textile sections of the Draft Final Act of December 1991, which came to be known asthe 'Dunkel Text' after its author, the GATT Chairman of the overall negotiations. It is worth looking at how agreement came about.

Crucial to the eventual accord were important concessions which were wrested from the LDCs on the product groups for integration and on the timing. Product coverage came to be the most difficult issue in the negotiations, because anything *not* on the list would have to be liberalised as soon as the Round concluded, with no transition period.[122] If the product groups covered by the MFA were the starting point for eliminating discriminatory quotas, there was a large number of quota restraints imposed by both the Americans and the Europeans, as well as Canada, Japan, and other developed countries, which were *outside* the MFA itself. It was eventually agreed that all products under restriction, MFA or non-MFA, would be included in the transition arrangements. This move expanded the list enormously, and was a significant development for two reasons. First, it broadened the negotiations to include all discriminatory arrangements in global textile and clothing trade, including by implication those imposed by developing countries. Second and more importantly, the list was thereby packed with products which were either of little significance to the importing developed countries, or which very few of them had ever restricted in the first place.

This meant that *de facto* the developed importers would enjoy much greater flexibility during the transition period if they were able to maintain freedom of choice over which quotas were to be removed and when. A large percentage of the list could theoretically be liberalised without affecting much in the way of the actual restraints. The importing countries were thus successful at choosing the products they wished to integrate and when,[123] and it is not clear that the developing countries realised the importance of this concession at the time.[124] The talks were finally down to detailed wrangling over numbers, a game the textile negotiators were good at following nearly twenty years of the MFA, but most matters were now agreed in principle.

This nascent agreement was inserted in the Dunkel text of 20 December 1991.[125] The text, although still a draft and containing a number of elements on which there was disagreement, was based on a tentative transition period of ten years (one of the matters on which there was ongoing disagreement) with 1990 taken as the base year for calculations.[126] There would be a three stage process of integrating product groups covered by quotas into GATT.[127] Assuming that the Round finished in 1992, as was then hoped but did not in fact occur, the transition would begin 1 January 1993. Before that date some 4 per cent of restraints would have to be lifted, and at Stage I a further 12 per cent of 1990 imports would have restrictions removed. This would be followed by 17 per cent at Stage II (January 1996) and 18 per cent by Stage III (January 2000). This meant that at the end of the transition period over 50 per cent of restrained imports remained to be liberalised, the so-called 'cliff'.

Two matters should be noted here. First, each developed country could choose which products they wished to integrate at the various stages of the agreement. That meant they could choose from among a list of *all products under some form of restraint anywhere in the textile and clothing trading system*, whether imported by that country or not or indeed whether a threat to the domestic industry or not. *It was fully possible to 'liberalise' imported products a country did not even produce or trade and had never restrained or intended to restrain, depending on how the list was manipulated.* Under these circumstances, it could well be that before Stage III (year 2000) there would be no meaningful liberalisation at all. Importing countries could start by removing quotas from only those products which were not a serious threat to their domestic industries. Given the numbers, it was not until the 'cliff' that the more sensitive product groups would have their quotas removed. Second, the LDCs remained sceptical that the developed countries would actually confront the cliff:[128] would they not play their usual game, plead for more time, and impose some new 'temporary' restraint agreement? However, in addition to the removal of quotas during the transition period, quota growth rates would also be increased progressively. These increases would be biased in favour of the least developed countries and the smaller exporting countries. Finally, the agreement included safeguard provisions in force during the transition period, the establishment of a Textile Monitoring Body to oversee implementation of the agreement, and other clauses dealing with fraud and circumvention of trade rules. The EU and the US maintained their insistence on a link with market access achievements in other negotiating groups, as well as progress on TRIPS and the strengthening of GATT rules and disciplines.

At least the framework of a workable agreement was in place, warts and all. All that remained was to establish final agreement on disputed numbers and, most importantly, on the time period for transition. The Dunkel draft had stipulated a ten-year transition period, a position accepted by the EU (though not by the industry associations of a number of its member states), but not by the Americans at this stage. The industry lobbies on both sides of the Atlantic, and indeed the US delegation, were united in still holding out for a fifteen-year transition period.

At this stage the reader should be reminded of the negotiating climate of the overall Uruguay Round throughout 1991–2. The atmosphere was far from positive as the EU and the United States were deadlocked on the question of agriculture. Not until the Blair House agreement on agriculture of November 1992 was it at all clear that the Round might be successfully completed at all. In the end the agreement came three years late, on 15 December 1993, to come into force on 1 January 1994.

It must be emphasised that during this drawn out period the employers organisations kept up their vociferous opposition to the emerging deal until the end. US and EU textile and clothing associations banded together in their opposition, publishing counterproposals to those being negotiated by Brussels and Washington. The tenacious French industry was a constant barometer in this regard, and the UIT and UFIH held a high-profile colloquium opposing the emerging GATT deal on 18 December 1992, and sponsored major street demonstrations in Paris on 14 May 1993, attacking Brussels in particular. The European level associations likewise produced their own set of proposals for the negotiations in 1992, insisting in particular on tougher trade sanctions and a fifteen-year transition period.[129] US lobbyists continued their feverish activities on the site of the negotiations in Geneva.

Paradoxically however, this delay in completion of the Round could be turned to the negotiators' advantage in terms of legitimising the final deal in the eyes of the textile lobbies in the EU and the United States. The delay in the overall Round in the first place provided a useful period in which the wrangling over figures on the textile agreement could be brought to an end. In aid of this the MFA was renewed again, unchanged, to cover 1993 and eventually 1994 as well.[130] Given the late termination of the Round as a whole, it should also be noted that the US and EU industries came close to actually achieving their preference of a fifteen-year transition period. Had the talks finished on time, the transition would have begun from 1 January 1991. In the end, the clock began ticking four years later on 1 January 1995.[131] When in early 1993 the US delegation had attempted to introduce a fifteen-year transition period there were by that time few takers and the proposal was quietly dropped.[132]

This did not prevent the controversy from continuing down to the last minutes of the Round itself; the textile negotiations did not finish with a whimper, far from it. *De facto* the industry had their fifteen years, and the deal was done, but US participants in the negotiations later described a scene at the US mission in the small hours of the last night, directly across from GATT headquarters, as lobbyists and congressmen manned their mobile phones and kept up the pressure.[133] The LDCs held out too, with India and Pakistan witholding any serious promise of market access for EU or US firms until the final minutes.[134]

The Textile and Clothing Negotiating Group was the last of the Uruguay Round negotiating groups to come to agreement after seven years of talks, but it did sign the Agreement on Textiles and Clothing (ATC) sections of the Final Act.[135] The ATC was then integrated into the accords establishing the World Trade Organisation signed at Marrakesh in April 1994. It differed little from the Dunkel text draft. In the first year, 16 per cent of products would be removed from quotas rather than 12 per cent, and as already mentioned the starting date was to be 1 January 1995.

The last minute opposition contained a final irony. Throughout the talks many EU and US firms had quietly voiced their preference in favour of liberalisation, no longer having any material interest in the protectionism. In the EU, while clothing industry production and employment levels had been falling steadily, the turnover of firms was on the rise as transnationalisation proved successful. If the US was the most opposed to a deal throughout the talks, in the end the American Apparel Manufacturers Association (AAMA), representative of the US clothing industry, actively lobbied *in favour* of the Uruguay Round Accords in the subsequent Congressional ratification debates. The more recalcitrant textile lobby, the ATMI, took a neutral position and did not attempt to oppose the bill. This was a much more positive outcome than any had imagined. The EU lobbies aquiesced and pursued the negotiations on access to LDC markets for developed country firms, which continued up to Marrakesh, and are ongoing. All pursued a strategy of accelerating transnationalisation of production and market structures, which increased imports linked to foreign sourcing. Globalisation was here to stay, for a good while anyway. At the end the MFA had few real friends in the Round, and few look back today.

Notes

1. This point was made and reinforced by a number of interview subjects active in the textile trade policy process. These included national government officials, officials of private industry associations, EU officials, officials of the WTO, and members of textile research institutes.
2. Interview with Mr William Tagliani, Textile Trade Negotiator, Office of the US Trade Representative, Geneva, 29 May 1996.
3. This point was confirmed by a number of interview sources.
4. In the United States these became known as 'Section 807 imports', referring to the relevant clause in one of the trade bills; in the EU they were referred to as OPT regulations.

5. Bela Balassa, 'Les Tendances actuelles de la spécialisation internationale de la production manufactrière', in Henri Bourguinat (ed.), *Internationalisation et autonomie de décision* (Paris: Economica, 1982), p. 26.
6. French producers often accused the Germans in this regard, prompting their parliamentarians to pose embarrassing questions to the Minister in the National Assembly.
7. This point was made independently by a number of interview sources.
8. Interview with Mr Andrea Meloni, First Counsellor, Italian Mission to the WTO, Geneva, 29 May 1996.
9. Xiaobing Tang, 'Textiles and the Uruguay Round of Multilateral Trade Negotiations', in *Journal of World Trade Law*, vol. 23, no. 3, June 1989, p. 52.
10. Ibid., p. 58.
11. A number of interview sources confirmed that in particular the large-scale clothing distributors and retail groups dependent upon low-cost imports, and consumer groups, lobbied openly in the EU and the US for an end to the MFA. Within the EU for example a body called the Foreign Trade Association organised a vociferous campaign in favour of dismantling the MFA: interview with Heinz Berzau, Observatoire Européen du Textile et de l'Habillement (OETH), Brussels, 30 April 1996.
12. Confidential interview, Brussels 1996.
13. Berzau interview. One should note that the entry of Spain, Portugal, and Greece to the EU in the 1980s greatly strengthened the hand of protectionist forces in the internal EU negotiating process. The achievement of liberalisation in the Uruguay Round is the more remarkable for this, and indicates the extent to which the interests of key countries such as the UK and France had changed in view of the acceleration of OPT.
14. Market access provisions were particularly important to the Europeans as opposed to the US, because the Europeans were major and long-standing exporters. Market access was particularly dear to the Italians within the EU who, as we have seen, were the largest textile and clothing exporters in global markets; Meloni interview.
15. Confidential interviews, Brussels 1996.
16. The United Kingdom negotiators within the EU began with a highly protectionist stance in 1986, and this was despite the very public campaigning of the Thatcher government for free trade inside and outside the EU. When the government observed the success of domestic companies engaging in outward processing, their attitude was observed to soften; confidential interviews, Brussels 1996.
17. Union des Industries de l'Habillement, *Propositions de l'industrie française de l'habillement pour l'AMF IV*, Conclusion de la Commission Economique (Paris: UIH, mimeo, 15 November 1984).
18. Interview with Mme Bourdeleau, Union des Industries Française de l'Habillement, 20 February 1985.
19. GATT Secretariat, *Statistiques concernant les textiles et les vêtements*, Comité des Textiles, Com Tex/33, Rev. 1, 13 June 1984.

20. Robin Anson and Paul Simpson, *World Textile Trade and Production Trends*, Special Report no. 1108 (London: Economist Intelligence Unit, June 1988), p. 34.

21. It was estimated that a Western European textile manufacturer would have to reduce its fabric costs by only 10 per cent to compete with typical East Asian producers, but in clothing manufacture the reduction would have to be of some 30 per cent; see ibid., p. 62.

22. The following account of the EU clothing industry's development and performance is from Anson and Simpson, *World Textile Trade*, op. cit., pp. 177–80.

23. This account of EU imports in textiles and clothing is once again from ibid., pp. 192–201.

24. Ibid., pp. 206–15.

25. Ibid., pp. 215–23.

26. Ibid., pp. 249–60.

27. Ibid., pp. 230–8.

28. See Cline, *The Future of World Trade*, op. cit., ch. 3.

29. Once again the best statistical source on the development of the textile and clothing industry in the mid to later 1980s is the study by Anson and Simpson, *World Textile Trade*, op. cit. pp. 161–7.

30. Michael Scheffer, *The Changing Map of European Textiles: Production and Sourcing Strategies of Textile and Clothing Firms*, Report Commissioned by OETH (Brussels: Observatoire Européen du Textile et de l'Habillement, 1994), p. 11.

31. Ibid., Scheffer, p. xi.

32. The fortunes of individual firms are not necessarily the same as the aggregate fortunes of national sectors. A number of sources point out that falling production levels in a national industry might occur at the same time as the turnover and profitability of firms improved. Because of the dislocation strategies of a number of firms, it was perfectly possible for industry interests to favour the maintenance of the MFA towards China and other Asian producers, but liberalisation towards countries which were destinations for OPT.

33. OECD, *Globalisation of Industrial Activities: A Case Study of the Clothing Industry*, General Distribution OECD/GD(94)107 (Paris: OECD, 1994), p. 20 and Table 18.

34. In particular, the EU Commission sponsored Observatoire Européen du Textile et de l'Habillement (OETH) in Brussels, and the French Centre Textile de Conjoncture et d'Observation Economique (CTCOE) based in Paris.

35. The study by Scheffer, *The Changing Map*, op. cit., pp. 19–22.

36. The following discussion is from ibid., ch. 2 (pp. 23–47), unless otherwise stated.

37. Ibid., p. 57. The lead suppliers in the Maghreb were Morocco and Tunisia, with some 8 per cent each of total EU OPT imports in 1992; Poland was the lead supplier among the PECO countries with 22 per cent of the EU total, followed by the former Yugoslavia with 18 per cent; see *Textile Outlook International*, no. 51, January 1994, p. 103.

38. Sources in the EU Commission confirmed the rapid acceleration of the transnationalisation of production. Officials of the French Ministry of Industry stated that the French clothing industry was 'largely delocalised towards the Maghreb' in the 1980s. WTO officials and members of national delegations in Geneva repeated the story. Different figures were floated as estimates, but the significance of the phenomenon was undeniable to all. The main difficulty with official trade figures is that they tend to underestimate the extent of OPT (Berzau interview) because EU figures on OPT do not include the Mediterranean countries, and other forms of foreign sourcing are not included either. Scheffer's figures, based on a sample of actual firms, would therefore appear to be the most reliable available, and they are correspondingly at the upper end of the estimates which were uncovered in research for this book.

39. Berzau interview; Herr Berzau had previously worked for both the German government and the EU Commission on textile and clothing trade matters.

40. *Textile Outlook International*, no. 51, January 1994, p. 102.

41. *Textile Outlook International*, no. 63, January 1996, p. 104.

42. Scheffer, *The Changing Map*, op. cit., p. 11.

43. Ibid., p. 9.

44. Anson and Simpson, *World Textile Trade*, op. cit., p. 198.

45. Berzau interview.

46. Scheffer, *The Changing Map*, op. cit., p. 28; see also Table 5.1.

47. Officials of the Union Française des Industries de l'Habillement (UFIH, formerly the UIH), of the Union des Industries Textiles (UIT), and officials in both the Ministry of Industry and the the Direction des Relations Economiques Extérieures (trade negotiating officials in the Ministry of Finance) interviewed in March 1996 all remarked on the phenomenon. French officials in Brussels and Geneva, as well as more independent voices, corroborated the story.

48. See Scheffer, *The Changing Map*, op. cit., fig. 2.7, p. 31.

49. Anson and Simpson, *World Textile Trade*, op. cit., p. 161.

50. Interview with Mr Robert Shepherd, now retired, formerly MFA and Uruguay Round textile negotiator (1980–94), Office of the US Trade Representative Office, Geneva, and Chair (1976–9) of the Committee for the Implementation of Textile Agreements (CITA), 30 May 1996.

51. Anson and Simpson, *World Textile Trade*, op. cit., p. 162.

52. *Textile Outlook International*, no. 63, January 1996, p. 86.

53. *Textile Outlook International*, no. 56, November 1994, p. 16.

54. Ibid.

55. *Textile Outlook International*, no. 63, January 1996, p. 84.

56. Tagliani interview.

57. *Textile Outlook International*, no. 56, November 1994, pp. 16–17.

58. Tagliani interview.

59. Ibid.

60. There are two fairly exhaustive accounts of the textile and clothing talks in the Uruguay Round, and these will be relied on extensively, in

addition to interview evidence: (1) Marcelo Raffaelli and Tripti Jenkins, *The Drafting History of the Agreement on Textiles and Clothing* (Geneva: International Textiles and Clothing Bureau, 1995); this account was constructed from the notes of the GATT officials overseeing the textile negotiating group; and (2) Lane Steven Hurewitz, *Textiles*, a volume in the series *The GATT Uruguay Round: A Negotiating History 1986–1992*.

61. See Cline, *The Future of World Trade*, op. cit., esp. ch. 9.
62. Shepherd interview.
63. Shepherd interview.
64. Rafaelli and Jenkins, *The Drafting History*, op. cit., p. 14.
65. Text of the Punta del Este GATT Ministerial Declaration on the Uruguay Round, 20 September 1986, reprinted in Hugo Paemen and Alexandra Bensch, *From GATT to the WTO: The European Community in the Uruguay Round* (Leuven: University Press, 1995), p. 275.
66. Shepherd interview.
67. Hurewitz, *Textiles*, op. cit., p. 27; the US did submit a number of 'Communications' from 1987–9 which put some shape into its negotiating position, but no actual proposals on specific measures to achieve the stated objectives of the negotiation; see Hurewitz, op. cit. p. 41– 43.
68. Rafaelli and Jenkins, *The Drafting History*, op. cit. pp. 18–27.
69. Shepherd interview.
70. As with most matters in the textile negotiations, this provision meant different things to the LDCs and the developed countries respectively. For the LDCs, the whole Uruguay Round was about strengthening GATT disciplines, and integrating the MFA into GATT and attendent measures aimed at liberalisation of trade in the sector were simply part of this wider effort. After all, the VERs in various sectors were modelled on the original Short and Long-Term Arrangements on cotton trade, which became the MFA. For the LDCs, a strengthening of GATT rules would have little meaning without a textile and clothing agreement. For countries like the United States and the EU, 'strengthening GATT rules and disciplines' relative to the textile and clothing negotiations implied a form of tradeoff across negotiating groups in the Round: that the MFA would not be integrated into GATT, and that there would be no consequent liberalisation, unless the negotiating groups specifically devoted to GATT disciplines such as safeguards, GATT articles etc., came to a satisfactory conclusion (interview with Sanjoy Bagchi, International Textile and Clothing Bureau, Geneva, 28 May 1996).
71. Bagchi interview.
72. See Cline, *The Future of World Trade*, op. cit., pp. 224–30 on the 1987 bill; pp. 336–37 on the 1990 bill.
73. The connection between the textile bills and the global quotas proposal in the Round was highlighted by US officials in Geneva. A reasonably detailed account of the US proposals, including a quantitative assessment of its potential economic consequences, is available in Cline, op. cit., pp. 292–97, and pp. 311–23.

74. Quite a number of interview subjects involved in the negotiations, including members of the US delegation itself, admit that the proposals caused a stir.

75. The following account of the US proposals is drawn from Hurewitz, *Textiles*, op. cit., pp. 44–9, and Raffaelli and Jenkins, *The Drafting History*, pp. 42–3.

76. A broad range of interview and written sources substantiated this position.

77. Paemen and Bensch, *From the GATT to the WTO*, op. cit., p. 155. Hugo Paemen was the chief EU Commission trade official in Brussels during the Uruguay Round.

78. Interview with Richard Hughes, Secretary to the GATT Textile Negotiating Group, currently and throughout the Uruguay Round, Geneva, 28 May 1996.

79. Hughes interview.

80. A number of interview sources representing developed and developing countries alike, as well as within the GATT, made this point quite independently.

81. There was overwhelming agreement among EU, US, and LDC interview subjects on this matter.

82. Tagliani interview.

83. Ibid.

84. This was confirmed by a number of interviews with professional association and official sources in the EU.

85. Peter Sutherland, 'Introduction', in Paemen and Bensch, *From the GATT to the WHO*, op. cit., p. 9.

86. Confidential interviews, April 1996.

87. See Michael Smith, 'The European Community: Testing the Boundaries of Foreign Economic Policy', in Richard Stubbs and Geoffrey Underhill (eds), *Political Economy and the Changing Global Order* (London: Macmillan, 1994), pp. 453–68.

88. Whether one accepts their case or not, many officials were adamant that the EU had done a great deal to liberalise textile and clothing trade, given the number of OPT and preferential trade deals with the EU's principal partners in the Mediterranean and Europe.

89. Confidential interviews, Brussels, April 1996.

90. Meloni interview.

91. Confidential interview source, Brussels, April 1996.

92. Ibid.

93. Ibid.

94. Raffaelli and Jenkins, op. cit., pp. 21–2.

95. Refusing (as noted above) 'any reasonable language', according to US officials.

96. My thanks to Patrick Messerlin, Professor of Economics, Institut d'Etudes Politiques de Paris, for making this point about vertical integration during our discussions in Paris, March 1996.

97. Berzau interview.

98. This was admitted by interview subjects representing both the French and Italian industries, textile and clothing sectors, as well as others who observed the talks and negotiating process from close quarters.
99. Interview with M. François-Marie Grau, Director of Economic and International Affairs, Union Française des Industries de l'Habillement, 19 March 1996.
100. Interview with Mr Jean-François Mezaize, Director of Economic Affairs, Union de Industries Textiles, Paris, 21 March 1996; François-Marie Grau (as above); Mr Francesco Marchi, Senior Economist, EURATEX (EU textile and clothing industry federation, replacing COMITEXTIL in January 1996), Brussels, 30 April 1996; Mr Andrea Meloni, as above.
101. This point was emphasised by national and EU officials, and the situation was similar in the case of the United States.
102. The Commission was regarded as the 'Great Satan' by a number of the national employers' organisations (confidential interview sources).
103. *Le Monde*, 11 April 1989.
104. *Financial Times*, 20 September 1989.
105. See GATT document MTN.GNG/NG4/W/24.
106. Raffaelli and Jenkins, *The Drafting History*, op. cit., p. 39.
107. Hughes interview.
108. GATT Document MTN.GNG/NG4/51
109. A range of interview subjects involved in the negotiation process were unanimous in citing this as the EU's position: market access in return for elimination of the MFA. The integration of the MFA into GATT would however take place on terms and a time frame acceptable to the developed countries.
110. It should be remarked that Italy (with its major exporting interests) and to an extent France also wanted market access concessions from the US negotiators, in particular the lowering of certain tariff 'peaks' on textiles and clothing products; Meloni interview.
111. Interview with Mon. Andrieu, Directeur des Affaires Commerciales, Représentation Permanente de la France auprès de la Communauté Européenne, Brussels, 3 May 1996.
112. Mezaize interview.
113. Marchi interview.
114. Meloni interview.
115. Confidential interviews, 1996.
116. These last two points were confirmed by a fair cross-section of interview subjects contacted in the course of this research project.
117. Confidential interviews.
118. *Le Figaro*, 5 July 1990; *Tribune de l'Expansion*, 19 July 1990.
119. *Le Monde*, 15 November 1990.
120. The 1991–2 period was stated by many who participated in the talks, as well as by employers' organisations, to have been the turning point for the textile negotiating group.
121. *Le Monde*, 1/08/1991.
122. Hughes interview.
123. Bagchi interview.

124. Hughes interview.
125. See GATT Document MTN.TNC/W/FA of 20 December 1990, known as the 'Dunkel draft'. The Dunkel draft was a draft final act for the entire Uruguay Round, and the work of Negotiating Group 4 (textiles and clothing) was only part of it.
126. A good base year from the point of view of the importing developed countries.
127. This account of the Dunkel draft draws on *Financial Times*, 21 February 1992, and Raffaelli and Jenkins, *The Drafting History*, op. cit., pp. 77–78.
128. Interview Bagchi (ITCB) and with Hughes (GATT).
129. See *Le Dossier du Commerce International/GATT Uruguay Round: propositions du textile-habillement européen*, published by Association Européenne des Industries de l'Habillement, COMITEXTIL, ELTAC (European Largest Textile and Clothing Companies), and the Comité Syndical Européen du Textile, de l'Habillement, et du Cuir (1992).
130. *Le Monde*, 11 December 1992; *Le Monde*, 27 January 1994.
131. *Le Monde*, 27 January 1994.
132. The US formally pushed for a fifteen-year transition period from early 1993, despite the fact that they had earlier proposd ten years under the global quotas proposal; see Raffaelli and Jenkins, op. cit., p. 84.
133. Shepherd, Tagliani interviews.
134. Hughes interview op. cit.
135. The ATC sections of the Round can be found in General Agreement on Tariffs and Trade, Trade Negotiating Committee, *Final Act...*, op. cit., The Text of the ATC is reproduced in the Appendix.

Conclusion: State and Market in Global Textile Trade

Despite the appearance of a victory for the LDCs, the Agreement on Textiles and Clothing (ATC) as part of the Uruguay Round accords of 1993 was a successful bargain pushed by the developed countries of Europe and the United States. They had used their negotiating power to gain substantial benefits for their industries in exchange for abandoning an accord which no longer worked. Given time the MFA quotas would anyway have outgrown the entire market in the high wage economies. The Uruguay Round might have been the last chance to get what was essentially something for nothing. The transition period which was negotiated is a long one and preparation for it was underway from the early 1990s. The safeguard mechanisms for the transition period are strong, and the developed countries had considerable freedom to choose the product mix and pace of liberalisation and integration into GATT. Structural adjustment to globalisation in the sector was taking place with or without quotas as regional trade agreements (such as NAFTA or the Europe Agreements) intensified competition in OECD markets, and the growing transnationalisation of production forced a rapid restructuring of markets and of the strategies of firms.

At the time of writing the transition period was not yet halfway through. There was still some question in the minds of the LDCs as to whether the agreement would ever be implemented fully, though representatives of the developed countries remain adamant in their determination to stand by the accord. Certainly there is ongoing dissatisfaction in EU and US employers' associations with the extent of the market access provisions negotiated in the Round, and pressure will continue in this direction.[1] It seems nevertheless likely that the liberalisation process was built this time on relatively firm socio-political foundations, while this had not been the situation thirty years prior in the Kennedy Round trade talks. The key point is that while employment and production levels in the clothing sector of most advanced industrial economies is falling, the turnover of the more dynamic EU and US firms is rising thanks to the transnational integration and dislocation of production. Many firms derived substantial benefits from this trend, as they were able to realise lower production costs without passing all of the savings on to the consumer, thus enhancing profitability.

There will be winners and losers in the process, but no longer can one simplistically divide them up according location in high wage versus low-wage economies. The equation is particularly differentiated. Of course, the clothing industries of emerging giants like China and India will do well, especially if their domestic markets expand at the same time as export prospects improve as quotas are removed. This means however that some of the smaller LDC producers, lacking the western market foothold supplied to them by the quota system, will face stiff and perhaps unbeatable competition. They are likely to be casualties of a deal which was supposed to aid the process of development. In the capital-intensive textile sector, the dominance of the advanced countries seems secure, though the Asian industrialising countries will undoubtedly strengthen their position over time.

The clothing industry in high-wage economies appears destined to develop according to strategies of foreign sourcing and emerging transnational networks of firms, including retailers. Even here however there is considerable hope for employment and production in the developed economies. Being close to an ever more volatile and quality conscious fashion market is growing in importance; just-in-time production cannot be operated through imports. Western investment is also moving into Asian markets to take advantage of the new prosperity there.[2] Access to the newly industrialising Asian markets for US and EU firms will prove of growing benefit over time, as exporters and retailers establish a presence which benefits their home industries. Furthermore, Asian producer firms in the more advanced NICs themselves have had to indulge in outward processing and other forms of foreign sourcing as their wage costs have risen in response to social pressures and economic development,[3] in the same way that Japan moved from low-wage clothing and fabric exporter to high-wage delocaliser. The policy discourse in many countries is changing as the material underpinnings of production and the market continue to shift.

So the outlook for firms is mixed. Small poorly managed concerns everywhere will likely crumble under the pressure of global competition. Some small concerns will prove innovative and will adapt to the volatile world of subcontracting and fashion if they have not done so already. Those unable to export and take advantage of market access provisions of liberalisation may face mounting difficulties. However, more than one observer has pointed to a *relocalisation* of textile and clothing industries, along with other labour intensive industries, back to the high wage areas of the OECD through just-in-time production, technological change, and other firm-specific advantages.[4] Though this is likely a limited phenomenon for the clothing industry, the foreign sourcing strategies of high-wage firms still leaves them in the driver's seat in international trade. It is a relationship of power they can maintain, and they no longer need state sponsorship to do it. *The governments of the EU and the US have stopped fixing the market, largely because the firms are now able to do it themselves. The idea that the end of the MFA ushers in an era of free competition of economics textbook myth is a false one.* There is more than one source of competitive advantage for firms in global trade and production, as discussed in the Introduction.

This last point brings the analysis back to the some of the wider arguments raised at the outset of this book. This book has systematically developed the reciprocal and mutually constitutive relationships among economic structure, state policy processes, and the global trade regime. The work began by arguing that while protectionism and liberalisation appear as contrasting policy solutions to economic conditions, they are in fact part of the same phenomenon of structural change in the global economy. The new protectionism was inherent in the politics of the open economy, and the transformations of industrial crisis eventually rendered renewed liberalisation possible. The distributional politics of industrial adjustment processes can yield either policy, depending on the structural position of the material interests involved in the policy process, and on the institutionalised political resources wielded by each. The evidence has strongly supported this contention. The liberalisation of textile and clothing trade among the advanced economies gave rise to competitive pressures which pushed firms as micro-level agents to adapt both their political and their competitive strategies. What was initially fertile ground for the protectionism of the MFA underwent a slow but accelerating transformation, driven both by state policy processes and the behaviour of firms, to the point where liberalisation became if not the favoured at least the acceptable policy option.

In this sense the book argued that there is an intimate relationship between structural change in production and markets and the trade policies pursued by states in international negotiations, mediated by the political and production strategies of the firms and their associations. The politics of domestic industrial adjustment in the open economy was intimately linked to the global game of competition and the trade regime, cutting across the layers of institutions in the global system (levels of analysis). The transnationalisation of economic structures resulting from post-war liberalisation policies set in train a series of distributional conflicts which worked themselves out simultaneously in the political and economic domains, and in this sense state policy processes and market institutions must be seen as integrated ensembles of governance, not as distinct modes of organisation. The institutionalised political resources of textile coalitions proved a potent force for trade protection, but as the material interests of these coalitions fragmented in the face of transnational structural change, there was an eventual end to the MFA. Protection and eventual liberalisation were part of the same process of transformation.

The case has enabled a clear identification of the reciprocal relationship between structure and agency in the changing global political economy, specifically in the trade regime. The causes of change in the trade regime lay buried deep in the socio-economic fabric of the global economy, in distributional conflict mediated by the institutions and policy processes of the state/market ensemble. The motivations and policy preferences of agents in the political economy were understood through an analysis of structure. These agents pursued their perceived self-interest in the context of the institutionalised policy processes of state, through inter-state bargaining and through strategies of competition. The textile coalitions were able to employ these resources in the political economy in order to structure the market in line with their policy preferences. When protection no longer fitted their interests, it withered and was replaced by the open economy despite the ongoing crisis in terms of job losses and lost domestic production. In this analysis it made little sense to separate out as distinct the political and economic aspects of agency in the process of market structuration. To do so introduces an element of abstraction which sharply contrasts with the reality of the case. The firms as agents used their competitive advantages in production and trade, and their political resources, to one and the same end.

The arguments of this book also have implications for the pursuit of liberal policies by states. The dismantling of state supports for industry (including tariff and other external protections) over the past twenty years has struck at the heart of the manner in which governance of the market was successfully accomplished in the post-war period. In many cases, none more so than in the textile and clothing sector, these liberal policies were pursued in ways which undermined the legitimacy of the state in the eyes of key socio-economic constituencies with substantial political resources. It should not have been a surprise that the liberalisation of the Kennedy Round, and of European integration, would generate highly politicised distributional conflict on such a scale, though most economic studies neglect this aspect of liberal policy. Market structures are constantly the object of political controversy as much as their peculiar characteristics structure the terms of economic competition among firms. If liberal policies are to bring the aggregate benefits which economists claim they can, then changes in these market structures must be legitimated on an ongoing basis. If the open economy as a policy is pushed beyond the bounds of the political economy's capacity to bear, resulting in industrial crisis which calls into question the prosperity of key constituencies, then the mechanisms of governance can be undermined and the legitimacy of the democratic state called into question.

The story of the textile and clothing sector has in many ways been the story of rendering market-oriented adjustment to global competition legitimate to the constituent groups involved. While labour could hardly be expected to support liberalisation with enthusiasm, the employers' coalitions eventually acquiesced. Liberal policies must be embedded and legitimated in the socio-political fabric if they are to succeed in the longer run. The economic argument about the benefits of a liberal trading system, even if correct, is in itself insufficient. Caution, patience, and careful preparation of the political groundwork were all crucial to the successful liberalisation of trade through the ATC in the Uruguay Round. In the case of textiles and clothing sectors, it took over a generation to build a hesitant but most likely sustainable coalition for liberal trade and adjustment policies in the advanced countries. One hopes (probably against expectations) that equal tolerance will be on show for the adjustment processes of the LDC emerging market economies as they feel the impact of market opening at a time of rising global inequalities.

Furthermore, the ATC concluded as part of the Round does not represent liberalisation on the lines of the perfect competition of economic textbook folklore. The ATC in many ways simply recognises that the power over the terms of trade which was once exercised through states on behalf of firms in the advanced economies is now exerted through the control which these same firms have developed in global production structures. As the integration of the global textile and clothing industry has proceeded under the leadership of the major multinational firms of the US, Japan, and Europe, this implied an exertion of power through the structure of the market, following a long period of adaptation, as opposed to power wielded through the institutions of state as in the case of the MFA.

States and their policy-makers must seek workable rules and a sustainable governance of distributional conflict as opposed to the dogmatic imposition of economic models of free trade. As Polanyi established so long ago, the free market as such is both utopian and dangerous to pursue as a policy objective. Liberal rules for international trade and production may well bring wider benefits to the global economy and the participating national political economies, but liberalisation requires appropriate socio-political underpinnings first.

Notes

1. This concern was voiced in interviews with EU industry association officials and by trade negotiators from the US and EU respectively who are involved in the MFA transition arrangements.
2. The effects of the Asian financial crisis were unclear at time of writing.
3. For example, Korean firms are involved in foreign sourcing and FDI in the Philippines and Indonesia. Many Asian firms are involved in China.
4. This trend was highlighted in a number of interviews conducted during the research stages of this project; see also by E.M. Mouhoud, *Changement technique et division internationale de travail* (Paris: Economica, 1992); and 'Changement technique, avantages comparatifs et délocalisation/relocalisation des activités industrielles,' in *Revue d'économie politique*, vol. 103/5, September–October 1993, pp. 734–61.

Appendix: Uruguay Round Agreement on Textiles and Clothing*

AGREEMENT ON TEXTILES AND CLOTHING

Recalling that Ministers agreed at Punta del Este that 'negotiations in the area of textiles and clothing shall aim to formulate modalities that would permit the eventual integration of this sector into GATT on the basis of strengthened GATT rules and disciplines, thereby also contributing to the objective of further liberalization of trade';

Recalling also that in the April 1989 Decision of the Trade Negotiations Committee it was agreed that the process of integration should commence following the conclusion of the Uruguay Round and should be progressive in character.

Recalling further that it was agreed that special treatment should be accorded to the least-developed country Members;

Members hereby *agree* as follows:

Article 1

1. This Agreement sets out provisions to be applied by Members during a transition period for the integration of the textiles and clothing sector into the GATT 1994.
2. Members agree to use the provisions of paragraph 18 of article 2 and paragraph 6(b) of article 6 of this Agreement in such a way as to permit meaningful increases in access possibilities for small suppliers and the development of commercially significant trading opportunities for new entrants in the field of textiles and clothing trade.[1]
3. Members shall have due regard to the situation of those Members which have not participated in the Protocols extending the Arrangement Regarding International Trade in Textiles (MFA) since 1986 and, to the extent possible, shall afford them special treatment in applying the provisions of this Agreement.
4. Members agree that the particular interests of the cotton producing exporting Members should, in consultation with them, be reflected in the implementation of the provisions of this Agreement.

---

*annex 1A–5 of GATT Final Act, MTN/FA, 15 December 1993.
[1] To the extent possible, exports from a least-developed country may also benefit from this provision.

5. In order to facilitate the integration of the textiles and clothing sector into the GATT 1994, Members should allow for continuous autonomous industrial adjustment and increased competition in their markets.
6. Unless otherwise provided in this Agreement, its provisions shall not affect the rights and obligations of Members under the provisions of the Agreement Establishing the MTO and the multilateral trade agreements annexed thereto.
7. The textile and clothing products to which this Agreement applies are set out in the Annex to this Agreement (hereafter referred to as the Annex).

Article 2

1. All quantitative restrictions within bilateral agreements maintained under article 4 or notified under article 7 or 8 of the MFA in force on the day before the entry into force of this Agreement, shall, within 60 days following its entry into force, be notified in detail, including the restraint levels, growth rates and flexibility provisions, by the Members maintaining such restrictions, to the Textiles Monitoring Body (herein referred to as the TMB) established under article 8. Members agree that as of the date of entry into force of this Agreement, all such restrictions maintained between GATT 1947 contracting parties, and in place on the day before its entry into force, shall be governed by the provisions of this Agreement.
2. The TMB shall circulate these notifications to all Members for their information. It is open to any Member to bring to the attention of the TMB, within 60 days of the circulation of the notifications, any observations it deems appropriate with regard to such notifications. Such observations shall be circulated to the other Members for their information. The TMB may make recommendations, as appropriate, to the Members concerned.
3. When the twelve-month period of restrictions to be notified under paragraph 1 above does not coincide with the 12-month period immediately preceding the entry into force of this Agreement, the Members concerned should mutually agree on arrangements to bring the period of restrictions into line with the agreement year[2], and to establish notional base levels of such restrictions in order to implement the provisions of this article. Concerned Members agree to enter consultations promptly upon request with a view to reaching such mutual agreement. Any such arrangements shall take into account, *inter alia*, seasonal patterns of shipments in recent years. The results of these consultations shall be notified to the TMB which shall make such recommendations as it deems appropriate to the Members concerned.
4. The restrictions notified under paragraph 1 above shall be deemed to constitute the totality of such restrictions applied by the respective Members on the day before the entry into force of this Agreement. No new restrictions in terms of products or Members shall be introduced except under the provisions of this Agreement or relevant GATT 1994

---

[2] The agreement year is defined to mean a 12-month period beginning from the date of entry into force of this Agreement and at the subsequent 12-month intervals.

provisions.[3] Restrictions not notified within 60 days of the entry into force of this Agreement shall be terminated forthwith.

5. Any unilateral measure taken under article 3 of the MFA prior to the date of entry into force of this Agreement may remain in effect for the duration specified therein, but not exceeding 12 months, if it has been reviewed by the Textiles Surveillance Body (TSB) established under the MFA. Should the TSB not have had the opportunity to review any such unilateral measure, it shall be reviewed by the TMB in accordance with the rules and procedures governing article 3 measures under the MFA. Any measure applied under an MFA article 4 agreement prior to the date of entry into force of this Agreement that is the subject of a dispute which the TSB has not had the opportunity to review shall also be reviewed by the TMB in accordance with the MFA rules and procedures applicable for such a review.

6. On the date of entry into force of this Agreement, each Member shall integrate into GATT 1994 products which, in 1990, accounted for not less than 16 per cent of the total volume of imports in 1990 of the products in the Annex, in terms of HS lines or categories. The products to be integrated shall encompass products from each of the following four groups: tops and yarns, fabrics, made-up textile products, and clothing.

7. Full details of the actions to be taken pursuant to paragraph 6 above shall be notified by the Members concerned according to the following:

- Members maintaining restrictions falling under paragraph 1 above undertake, notwithstanding the date of the entry into force of this Agreement, to notify such details to the GATT Secretariat not later than (1 July 1992).[4] The GATT Secretariat shall promptly circulate these notifications to the other Members for information. These notifications will be made available to the TMB, when established, for the purposes of paragraph 21 below;
- Members which have, pursuant to paragraph 1 of article 6, retained the right to use the provisions of article 6, shall notify such details to the TMB not later than 60 days following the entry into force of this Agreement, or, in the case of those Members covered by paragraph 3 of article 1, not later than at the end of the twelfth month that this Agreement is in effect. The TMB shall circulate these notifications to the other Members for information and review them as provided in paragraph 21 below.

8. The remaining products, i.e. the products not integrated into GATT 1994 under paragraph 6 above, shall be integrated, in terms of HS lines or categories, in three stages, as follows:

---

[3] The relevant GATT 1994 provisions shall not include article XIX in respect of products not yet integrated into GATT 1994, except as specifically provided in the Note to the Annex.

[4] Participants agreed to examine, in the first quarter of 1994, the date and the technical and administrative aspects related to the implementation of this provision.

A. On the first day of the 37th month that this Agreement is in effect, products which, in 1990, accounted for not less than 17 per cent of the total volume of 1990 imports of the products in the Annex. The products to be integrated by the Members shall encompass products from each of the following four groups: tops and yarns, fabrics, made-up textile products, and clothing.

B. On the first day of the 85th month that this Agreement is in effect, products which, in 1990, accounted for not less than 18 per cent of the total volume of 1990 imports of the products in the Annex. The products to be integrated by the Members shall encompass products from each of the following four groups: tops and yarns, fabrics, made-up textile products, and clothing.

C. On the first day of the 121st month that the Agreement Establishing the MTO is in effect, the textiles and clothing sector shall stand integrated into GATT 1994, all restrictions under this Agreement having been eliminated.

9. Members which have notified, pursuant to paragraph 1 of article 6, their intention not to retain the right to use the provisions of article 6 shall, for the purposes of this Agreement, be deemed to have integrated their textiles and clothing products into the GATT 1994. Such Members shall, therefore, be exempted from complying with the provisions of paragraphs 6 to 8 above and 11 below.

10. Nothing in this Agreement shall prevent a Member which has submitted an integration programme pursuant to paragraph 6 or 8 above from integrating products into the GATT 1994 earlier than provided for in such a programme. However, any such integration of products shall take effect at the beginning of an agreement year, and details shall be notified to the TMB at least three months prior thereto for circulation to all Members.

11. The respective programmes of integration, in pursuance of paragraph 8 above, shall be notified in detail to the TMB at least 12 months before their coming into effect and circulated by the TMB to all Members.

12. The base levels of the restrictions on the remaining products, mentioned in paragraph 8 above, shall be the restraint levels referred to in paragraph 1 above.

13. During Stage 1 of this Agreement (from the date of entry into force of this Agreement to the 36th month that it is in effect, inclusive) the level of each restriction under MFA bilateral agreements in force for the 12-month period prior to its entry into force shall be increased annually by not less than the growth rate established for the respective restrictions, increased by 16 per cent.

14. Except where the Council for Trade in Goods or the Dispute Settlement Body decides otherwise under paragraph 12 of article 8, the level of each remaining restriction shall be increased annually during subsequent stages of the Agreement by not less than the following:

(i) for Stage 2 (from the 37th to the 84th month that this Agreement is in effect, inclusive), the growth rate for the respective restrictions during Stage 1, increased by 25 per cent;

(ii) for Stage 3 (from the 85th to the 120th month that this Agreement is in effect, inclusive), the growth rate for the respective restrictions during Stage 2, increased by 27 per cent.

15. Nothing in this Agreement shall prevent a Member from eliminating any restriction maintained pursuant to this article, effective at the beginning of any agreement year during the transition period, provided the exporting Member concerned and the TMB are notified at least three months prior to the elimination coming into effect. The period for prior notification might be shortened to 30 days with the agreement of the restrained Member. The TMB shall circulate such notifications to all Members. In considering the elimination of restrictions as envisaged in this paragraph, the Members concerned shall take into account the treatment of similar exports from other Members.

16. Flexibility provisions, i.e. swing, carryover and carry forward, applicable to all quantitative restrictions in force in accordance with the provisions of this article, shall be the same as those provided for in MFA bilateral agreements for the 12-month period prior to the entry into force of this Agreement. No quantitative limits shall be placed or maintained on the combined use of swing, carryover and carry forward.

17. Administrative arrangements, as deemed necessary in relation to the implementation of any provision of this article, shall be a matter for agreement between the Members concerned. Any such arrangements shall be notified to the TMB.

18. As regards those Members whose exports are subject to restrictions on the day before the entry into force of this Agreement and whose restrictions represent 1.2 per cent or less of the total volume of the restrictions applied by an importing Member as of 31 December 1991 and notified under this article, meaningful improvement in access for their exports shall be provided at the entry into force of this Agreement and for its duration through advancement by one stage of the growth rates set out in paragraphs 13 and 14 above, or through at least equivalent changes as may be mutually agreed with respect to a different mix of base levels, growth and flexibility provisions. Such improvements shall be notified to the TMB.

19. In any case, during the validity of this Agreement, in which a safeguard measure is initiated by a Member under article XIX of the GATT 1994 in respect of a particular product during a period of one year immediately following the integration of that product into GATT 1994 in accordance with the provisions of this article, the provisions of article XIX, as interpreted by the Agreement on Safeguards, will apply save as set out in paragraph 20 below.

20. Where such a measure is applied using non-tariff means, the importing Member concerned shall apply the measure in a manner as set forth in paragraph 2(d) of article XIII of the GATT 1994 at the request of any exporting Member whose exports of such products were subject to restrictions under this Agreement at any time in the one-year period immediately prior to the initiation of the safeguard measure. The concerned exporting Member shall administer such a measure. The applicable level shall not reduce the relevant exports below the level of a recent

representative period, which shall normally be the average of exports from the concerned Member in the last three representative years for which statistics are available. Further, when the safeguard measure is applied for more than one year, the applicable level shall be progressively liberalised at regular intervals during the period of application. In such cases the concerned exporting Member shall not exercise the right of suspending substantially equivalent concessions or other obligations under the GATT 1994 as provided for under paragraph 3(a) of article XIX of the GATT 1994.

21. The TMB shall keep under review the implementation of this article. It shall, at the request of any Member, review any particular matter with reference to the implementation of the provisions of this article. It shall make appropriate recommendations or findings within 30 days to the Member or Members concerned, after inviting the participation of such Members.

Article 3

1. Within 60 days following the entry into force of this Agreement, Members maintaining restrictions[5] on textile and clothing products (other than restrictions maintained under the MFA and covered by the provisions of article 2), whether consistent with GATT 1994 or not, shall (a) notify them in detail to the TMB, or (b) provide to the TMB notifications with respect to them which have been submitted to any other MTO body. The notifications should, wherever applicable, provide information with respect to any GATT 1994 justification for the restrictions, including GATT 1994 provisions on which they are based.

2. All restrictions falling under paragraph 1 above, except those justified under a GATT 1994 provision, shall be either:

   (a) brought into conformity with the GATT 1994 within one year following the entry into force of this Agreement, and be notified to the TMB for its information; or

   (b) phased out progressively according to a programme to be presented to the TMB by the Member maintaining the restrictions not later than six months after the date of entry into force of this Agreement. This programme shall provide for all restrictions to be phased out within a period not exceeding the duration of this Agreement. The TMB may make recommendations to the Member concerned with respect to such a programme.

3. During the validity of this Agreement, Members shall provide to the TMB, for its information, notifications submitted to any other MTO bodies with respect to any new restrictions or changes in existing restrictions on textile and clothing products, taken under any GATT 1994 provision, within 60 days of their coming into effect.

---

[5] Restrictions denote all unilateral quantitative restrictions, bilateral arrangements and other measures having a similar effect.

4. It shall be open to any Member to make reverse notifications to the TMB, for its information, in regard to the GATT 1994 justification, or in regard to any restrictions that may not have been notified under the provisions of this article. Actions with respect to such notifications may be pursued by any Member under relevant GATT 1994 provisions or procedures in the appropriate MTO body.
5. The TMB shall circulate the notifications made pursuant to this article to all Members for their information.

Article 4

1. Restrictions referred to in article 2, and those applied under article 6, shall be administered by the exporting Members. Importing Members shall not be obliged to accept shipments in excess of the restrictions notified under article 2, and of restrictions applied pursuant to article 6.
2. Members agree that the introduction of changes, such as changes in practices, rules, procedures and categorization of textile and clothing products, including those changes relating to the Harmonized System, in the implementation or administration of those restrictions notified or applied under this Agreement should not upset the balance of rights and obligations between the Members concerned under this Agreement; adversely affect the access available to a Member; impede the full utilization of such access; or disrupt trade under this Agreement.
3. If a product which constitutes only part of a restriction is notified for integration pursuant to the provisions of article 2, Members agree that any change in the level of that restriction shall not upset the balance of rights and obligations between the Members concerned under this Agreement.
4. When changes mentioned in paragraphs 2 and 3 above are necessary, however, Members agree that the Member initiating such changes shall inform and, wherever possible, initiate consultations with the affected Member or Members prior to the implementation of such changes, with a view to reaching a mutually acceptable solution regarding appropriate and equitable adjustment. Members further agree that where consultation prior to implementation is not feasible, the Member initiating such changes will, at the request of the affected Member, consult within 60 days if possible, with the Members concerned with a view to reaching a mutually satisfactory solution regarding appropriate and equitable adjustments. If a mutually satisfactory solution is not reached, any Member involved may refer the matter to the TMB for recommendations as provided in article 8. Should the TSB not have had the opportunity to review a dispute concerning such changes introduced prior to the entry into force of this Agreement, it shall be reviewed by the TMB in accordance with the rules and procedures of the MFA applicable for such a review.

Article 5

1. Members agree that circumvention by transshipment, rerouting, false declaration concerning country or place of origin, and falsification of official

documents, frustrates the implementation of this Agreement to integrate the textiles and clothing sector into the GATT 1994. Accordingly, Members should establish the necessary legal provisions and/or administrative procedures to address and take action against such circumvention. Members further agree that, consistent with their domestic laws and procedures, they will cooperate fully to address problems arising from circumvention.

2. Should any Member believe that this Agreement is being circumvented by transshipment, rerouting, false declaration concerning country or place of origin, or falsification of official documents, and that no, or inadequate, measures are being applied to address or to take action against such circumvention, that Member should consult with the Member or Members concerned with a view to seeking a mutually satisfactory solution. Such consultations should be held promptly, and within 30 days when possible. If a mutually satisfactory solution is not reached, the matter may be referred by any Member involved to the TMB for recommendations.

3. Members agree to take necessary action, consistent with their domestic laws and procedures, to prevent, to investigate and, where appropriate, to take legal and/or administrative action against circumvention practices within their territory. Members agree to cooperate fully, consistent with their domestic laws and procedures, in instances of circumvention or alleged circumvention of this Agreement, to establish the relevant facts in the places of import, export and, where applicable, transshipment. It is agreed that such cooperation, consistent with domestic laws and procedures, will include investigation of circumvention practices which increase restrained exports to the Member maintaining such restraints; exchange of documents, correspondence, reports and other relevant information to the extent available; and facilitation of plant visits and contacts, upon request and on a case-by-case basis. Members should endeavour to clarify the circumstances of any such instances of circumvention or alleged circumvention, including the respective roles of the exporters or importers involved.

4. Where, as a result of investigation, there is sufficient evidence that circumvention has occurred (e.g. where evidence is available concerning the country or place of true origin, and the circumstances of such circumvention) Members agree that appropriate action, to the extent necessary to address the problem, should be taken. Such action may include the denial of entry of goods or, where goods have entered, having due regard to the actual circumstances and the involvement of the country or place of true origin, the adjustment of charges to restraint levels to reflect the true country or place of origin. Also, where there is evidence of the involvement of the territories of the Members through which the goods have been transshipped, such action may include the introduction of restraints with respect to such Members. Any such actions, together with their timing and scope, may be taken after consultations held with a view to arriving at a mutually satisfactory solution between the concerned Members and shall be notified to the TMB with full justification. The Members concerned may agree on other remedies in consultation. Any such agreement shall also be notified to the TMB, and the TMB may make such recommendations to the Members concerned as it deems appropriate. If a mutually

satisfactory solution is not reached, any Member concerned may refer the matter to the TMB for prompt review and recommendations.

5. Members note that some cases of circumvention may involve shipments transiting through countries or places with no changes or alterations made to the goods contained in such shipments in the places of transit. They note that it may not be generally practicable for such places of transit to exercise control over such shipments.

6. Members agree that false declaration concerning fibre content, quantities, description or classification of merchandise also frustrates the objective of this Agreement. Where there is evidence that any such false declaration has been made for purposes of circumvention, Members agree that appropriate measures, consistent with domestic laws and procedures, should be taken against the exporters or importers involved. Should any Member believe that this Agreement is being circumvented by such false declaration and that no, or inadequate, administrative measures are being applied to address and/or to take action against such circumvention, that Member should consult promptly with the Member involved with a view to seeking a mutually satisfactory solution. If such a solution is not reached, the matter may be referred by any Member involved to the TMB for recommendations. This provision is not intended to prevent Members from making technical adjustments when inadvertent errors in declarations have been made.

Article 6

1. Members recognise that during the transition period it may be necessary to apply a specific transitional safeguard mechanism (hereinafter referred to as 'transitional safeguard'). The transitional safeguard may be applied by any Member, to products covered by the Annex to this Agreement, except those integrated into the GATT 1994 under the provisions of article 2. Members not maintaining restrictions falling under article 2 shall notify the TMB within 60 days following the entry into force of this Agreement, whether or not they wish to retain the right to use the provisions of this article. Members which have not participated in the Protocols extending the MFA since 1986, shall make such notification within 6 months following the entry into force of this Agreement. The transitional safeguard should be applied as sparingly as possible, consistently with the provisions of this article and the effective implementation of the integration process under this Agreement.

2. Safeguard action may be taken under this article when, on the basis of a determination by a Member[6], it is demonstrated that a particular product is being imported into its territory in such increased quantities as to cause serious damage, or actual threat thereof, to the domestic industry produ-

---

[6] A customs union may apply a safeguard measure as a single unit or on behalf of a member State. When a customs union applies a safeguard measure as a single unit, all the requirements for the determination of serious damage or actual threat thereof under this Agreement shall be based on the conditions existing in the customs union as a whole.

cing like and/or directly competitive products. Serious damage or actual threat thereof must demonstrably be caused by such increased quantities in total imports of that product and not by such other factors as technological changes or changes in consumer preference.

3. In making a determination of serious damage, or actual threat thereof, as referred to in paragraph 2 above, the Member shall examine the effect of those imports on the state of the particular industry, as reflected in changes in such relevant economic variables as output, productivity, utilization of capacity, inventories, market share, exports, wages, employment, domestic prices, profits and investment; none of which, either alone or combined with other factors, can necessarily give decisive guidance.

4. Any measure invoked pursuant to the provisions of this article shall be applied on a Member-by-Member basis. The Member or Members to whom serious damage, or actual threat thereof, referred to in paragraphs 2 and 3 above, is attributed, shall be determined on the basis of a sharp and substantial increase in imports, actual or imminent[7], from such a Member or Members individually, and on the basis of the level of imports as compared with imports from other sources, market share, and import and domestic prices at a comparable stage of commercial transaction; none of these factors, either alone or combined with other factors, can necessarily give decisive guidance. Such safeguard measure shall not be applied to the exports of any Member whose exports of the particular product are already under restraint under this Agreement.

5. The period of validity of a determination of serious damage or actual threat thereof for the purpose of invoking safeguard action shall not exceed 90 days from the date of initial notification as set forth in paragraph 7 below.

6. In the application of the transitional safeguard, particular account shall be taken of the interests of exporting Members as set out below:

   (a) Least-developed country Members shall be accorded treatment significantly more favourable than that provided to the other groups of Members referred to in this paragraph, preferably in all its elements but, at least, on overall terms.

   (b) Members whose total volume of textile and clothing exports is small in comparison with the total volume of exports of other Members and who account for only a small percentage of total imports of that product into the importing Member shall be accorded differential and more favourable treatment in the fixing of the economic terms provided in paragraphs 8, 13 and 14 below. For those suppliers, due

---

When a safeguard measure is applied on behalf of a member State, all the requirements for the determination of serious damage, or actual threat thereof, shall be based on the conditions existing in that member State and the measure shall be limited to that member State.

[7] Such an imminent increase shall be a measurable one and shall not be determined to exist on the basis of allegation, conjecture or mere possibility arising, for example, from the existence of production capacity in the exporting Members.

account will be taken, pursuant to paragraphs 2 and 3 of article 1, of the future possibilities for the development of their trade and the need to allow commercial quantities of imports from them.

(c) With respect to wool products from wool producing developing Members whose economy and textiles and clothing trade are dependent on the wool sector, whose total textile and clothing exports consist almost exclusively of wool products, and whose volume of textiles and clothing trade is comparatively small in the markets of the importing Members, special consideration shall be given to the export needs of such Members when considering quota levels, growth rates and flexibility.

(d) More favourable treatment shall be accorded to reimports by a Member of textile and clothing products which that Member has exported to another Member for processing and subsequent reimportation, as defined by the laws and practices of the importing Member, and subject to satisfactory control and certification procedures, when these products are imported from a Member for which this type of trade represents a significant proportion of its total exports of textiles and clothing.

7. The Member proposing to take safeguard action shall seek consultations with the Member or Members which would be affected by such action. The request for consultations shall be accompanied by specific and relevant factual information, as up-to-date as possible, particularly in regard to: (a) the factors, referred to in paragraph 3 above, on which the Member invoking the action has based its determination of the existence of serious damage or actual threat thereof; and (b) the factors, referred to in paragraph 4 above, on the basis of which it proposes to invoke the safeguard action with respect to the Member or Members concerned. In respect of requests made under this paragraph, the information shall be related, as closely as possible, to identifiable segments of production and to the reference period set out in paragraph 8 below. The Member invoking the action shall also indicate the specific level at which imports of the product in question from the Member or Members concerned are proposed to be restrained; such level shall not be lower than the level referred to in paragraph 8 below. The Member seeking consultations shall, at the same time, communicate to the Chairman of the TMB the request for consultations, including all the relevant factual data outlined in paragraphs 3 and 4 above, together with the proposed restraint level. The Chairman shall inform the members of the TMB of the request for consultations, indicating the requesting Member, the product in question and the Member having received the request. The Member or Members concerned shall respond to this request promptly and the consultations shall be held without delay and normally be completed within 60 days of the date on which the request has been received.

8. If, in the consultations, there is mutual understanding that the situation calls for restraint on the exports of the particular product from the Member or Members concerned, the level of such restraint shall be fixed at a level not lower than the actual level of exports or imports from the Member

concerned during the twelve-month period terminating two months preceding the month in which the request for consultation was made.

9. Details of the agreed restraint measure shall be communicated to the TMB within 60 days from the date of conclusion of the agreement. The TMB shall determine whether the agreement is justified in accordance with the provisions of this article. In order to make its determination, the TMB shall have available to it the factual data provided to the Chairman of the TMB, referred to in paragraph 7 above, as well as any other relevant information provided by the Members concerned. The TMB may make such recommendations as it deems appropriate to the Members concerned.

10. If, however, after the expiry of the period of 60 days from the date on which the request for consultations was received, there has been no agreement between the Members, the Member which proposed to take safeguard action may apply the restraint by date of import or date of export, in accordance with the provisions of this article, within 30 days following the 60 days period for consultations, and at the same time refer the matter to the TMB. It shall be open to either Member to refer the matter to the TMB before the expiry of the period of 60 days. In either case, the TMB shall promptly conduct an examination of the matter including the determination of serious damage, or actual threat thereof, and its causes, and make appropriate recommendations to the Members concerned within 30 days. In order to conduct such examination, the TMB, shall have available to it the factual data provided to the Chairman of the TMB, referred to in paragraph 7 above, as well as any other relevant information provided by the Members concerned.

11. In highly unusual and critical circumstances, where delay would cause damage which would be difficult to repair, action under paragraph 10 above may be taken provisionally on the condition that the request for consultations and notification to the TMB shall be effected within no more than 5 working days after taking the action. In the case that consultations do not produce agreement, the TMB shall be notified at the conclusion of consultations, but in any case no later than 60 days from the date of the implementation of the action. The TMB shall promptly conduct an examination of the matter, and make appropriate recommendations to the Members concerned within 30 days. In the case that consultations do produce agreement, Members shall notify the TMB upon conclusion but, in any case, no later than 90 days from the date of the implementation of the action. The TMB may make such recommendations as it deems appropriate to the Members concerned.

12. Measures invoked pursuant to the provisions of this article may remain in place: (a) for up to three years without extension, or (b) until the product is integrated into GATT 1994, whichever comes first.

13. Should the restraint measure remain in force for a period exceeding one year, the level for subsequent years shall be the level specified for the first year increased by a growth rate of not less than 6 per cent per annum, unless otherwise justified to the TMB. The restraint level for the product concerned may be exceeded in either year of any two subsequent years by carry forward and/or carryover of 10 per cent of which carry forward

shall not represent more than 5 per cent. No quantitative limits shall be placed on the combined use of carryover, carry forward and the provision of paragraph 14 below.

14. When more than one product from another Member is placed under restraint under this article by a Member, the level of restraint agreed, pursuant to the provisions of this article, for each of these products may be exceeded by 7 per cent, provided that the total exports subject to restraint do not exceed the total of the levels for all products so restrained under this article, on the basis of agreed common units. Where the periods of application of restraints of these products do not coincide with each other, this provision shall be applied to any overlapping period on a *pro rata* basis.

15. If a safeguard action is applied under this article to a product for which a restraint was previously in place under the MFA during the 12-month period prior to the entry into force of this Agreement, or pursuant to the provisions of article 2 or 6 of this Agreement, the level of the new restraint shall be the level provided for in paragraph 8 of this article unless the new restraint comes into force within one year of:

   (a) the date of notification referred to in paragraph 15 of article 2 for the elimination of the previous restraint; or
   (b) the date of removal of the previous restraint put in place pursuant to the provisions of this article or of the MFA

   in which case the level shall not be less than the higher of (i) the level of restraint for the last twelve-month period during which the product was under restraint, or (ii) the level of restraint provided for in paragraph 8 of this article.

16. When a Member which is not maintaining a restraint under article 2 decides to apply a restraint pursuant to the provisions of this article, it shall establish appropriate arrangements which: (a) take full account of such factors as established tariff classification and quantitative units based on normal commercial practices in export and import transactions, both as regards fibre composition and in terms of competing for the same segment of its domestic market, and (b) avoid over-categorisation. The request for consultations referred to in paragraph 7 or 11 above shall include full information on such arrangements.

Article 7

1. As part of the integration process and with reference to the specific commitments undertaken by the Members as a result of the Uruguay Round, all Members shall take such actions as may be necessary to abide by GATT 1994 rules and disciplines so as to:

   (i) achieve improved access to markets for textile and clothing products through such measures as tariff reductions and bindings, reduction or elimination of non-tariff barriers, and facilitation of customs, administrative and licensing formalities;

(ii) ensure the application of policies relating to fair and equitable trading conditions as regards textiles and clothing in such areas as dumping and anti-dumping rules and procedures, subsidies and countervailing measures, and protection of intellectual property rights; and

(iii) avoid discrimination against imports in the textiles and clothing sector when taking measures for general trade policy reasons.

Such actions shall be without prejudice to the rights and obligations of Members under GATT 1994.

2. Members shall notify to the TMB the actions referred to in paragraph 1 above which have a bearing on the implementation of this Agreement. To the extent that these have been notified to other MTO committees or bodies, a summary, with reference to the original notification, shall be sufficient to fulfil the requirements under this paragraph. It shall be open to any Member to make reverse notifications to the TMB.

3. Where any Member considers that another Member has not taken the actions referred to in paragraph 1 above, and that the balance of rights and obligations under this Agreement has been upset, that Member may bring the matter before the relevant MTO committees and bodies and inform the TMB. Any subsequent findings or conclusions by the MTO committees and bodies concerned shall form a part of the TMB's comprehensive report.

Article 8

1. In order to supervise the implementation of this Agreement, to examine all measures taken under its provisions and their conformity therewith, and to take the actions specifically required of it in the articles of this Agreement, there shall be established by the Council for Trade in Goods a Textiles Monitoring Body (TMB). The TMB shall consist of a Chairman and 10 members. Its membership shall be balanced and broadly representative of the Members and shall provide for rotation of its members at appropriate intervals. The members shall be appointed by Members designated by the Council for Trade in Goods to serve on the TMB, discharging their function on an *ad personam* basis.

2. The TMB will develop its own working procedures. It is understood, however, that consensus within the TMB does not require the assent or concurrence of members appointed by Members involved in an unresolved issue under review by the Body.

3. The TMB shall be considered as a standing body and shall meet as necessary to carry out the functions required of it under this Agreement. It shall rely on notifications and information supplied by the Members under the relevant articles of this Agreement, supplemented by any additional information or necessary details they may submit or it may decide to seek from them. It may also rely on notifications to and reports from other MTO committees and bodies and from such other sources as it may deem appropriate.

4. Members shall afford to each other adequate opportunity for consultations with respect to any matters affecting the operation of this Agreement.

5. In the absence of any mutually agreed solution in the bilateral consultations provided for in this Agreement, the TMB shall, at the request of either Member, and following a thorough and prompt consideration of the matter, make recommendations to the Members concerned.

6. At the request of any Member, the TMB shall review promptly any particular matter which that Member considers to be detrimental to its interests under this Agreement and where consultations between it and the Member or Members concerned have failed to produce a mutually satisfactory solution. On such matters, the TMB may make such observations as it deems appropriate to the Members concerned and for the purposes of the review provided for in paragraph 11 below.

7. Before formulating its recommendations or observations, the TMB shall invite participation of such Members as may be directly affected by the matter in question.

8. Whenever the TMB is called upon to make recommendations or findings, it shall do so, preferably within a period of 30 days, unless a different time period is specified in this Agreement. All such recommendations or findings shall be communicated to the Members directly concerned. All such recommendations or findings shall also be communicated to the Council for Trade in Goods for its information.

9. The Members shall endeavour to accept in full the recommendations of the TMB, which shall exercise proper surveillance of the implementation of such recommendations.

10. If a Member considers itself unable to conform with the recommendations of the TMB, it shall provide the TMB with the reasons therefore not later than one month after receipt of such recommendations. Following thorough consideration of the reasons given, the TMB shall issue any further recommendations it considers appropriate forthwith. If, after such further recommendations, the matter remains unresolved, either Member may bring the matter before the Dispute Settlement Body and invoke paragraph 2 of article XXIII of GATT 1994 and the relevant provisions of the Understanding on Rules and Procedures Governing the Settlement of Disputes.

11. In order to oversee the implementation of the Agreement, the Council for Trade in Goods shall conduct a major review before the end of each stage of the integration process. To assist in this review, the TMB shall, at least five months before the end of each stage, transmit to the Council for Trade in Goods a comprehensive report on the implementation of this Agreement during the stage under review, in particular in matters with regard to the integration process, the application of the transitional safeguard mechanism, and relating to the application of GATT 1994 rules and disciplines as defined in articles 2, 3, 6 and 7 of this Agreement, respectively. The TMB's comprehensive report may include any recommendation as deemed appropriate by the TMB to the Council for Trade in Goods.

12. In the light of its review the Council for Trade in Goods shall by consensus take such decisions as it deems appropriate to ensure that the

balance of rights and obligations embodied in this Agreement is not being impaired. For the resolution of any disputes that may arise with respect to matters referred to in article 7 of this Agreement, the Dispute Settlement Body may authorize, without prejudice to the final dates set out under article 9 of this Agreement, an adjustment to paragraph 14 of article 2, for the stage subsequent to the review, with respect to any Member found not to be complying with its obligations under this Agreement.

Article 9

1. This Agreement and all restrictions thereunder shall stand terminated on the first day of the 121st month that the Agreement Establishing the MTO is in effect, on which date the textiles and clothing sector shall be fully integrated into the GATT 1994. There shall be no extension of this Agreement.

ANNEX: LIST OF PRODUCTS COVERED BY THIS AGREEMENT

(NB: The complete product list is lengthy and is not included in this Appendix. For the complete list, refer to the Draft Final Act.)

1. This Annex lists textile and clothing products identified by Harmonised Commodity Description and Coding System (HS) codes at the six digit level.
2. Actions under the safeguard provisions in article 6 will be taken on particular textile and clothing products and not on the basis of the HS lines *per se*.

Note:
Actions under the safeguard provisions in article 6 of this Agreement shall not apply to:

1. developing Members' exports of handloom fabrics of the cottage industry, or hand-made cottage industry products made of such handloom fabrics, or traditional folklore handicraft textile and clothing products, provided that such products are properly certified under arrangements established between the Members concerned;
2. historically traded products which were internationally traded in commercially significant quantities prior to 1982, such as bags, sacks, carpet-backing, cordage, luggage, mats, mattings and carpets typically made from fibres such as jute, coir, sisal, abaca, maguey and henequen;
3. products made of pure silk.

For such products, the provisions of article XIX of the GATT 1994, as interpreted by the Agreement on Safeguards, shall be applicable.

Index